ASTRONOMY & SPACE

ASTRONOMY & SPACE

From the Big Bang to the Big Crunch

PHILLIS ENGELBERT

volume 2
HES–P

DETROIT • NEW YORK • TORONTO • LONDON

U·X·L
AN IMPRINT OF GALE

Astronomy & Space:
From the Big Bang to the Big Crunch

by Phillis Engelbert

Staff

Jane Hoehner, *U•X•L Developmental Editor*
Carol DeKane Nagel, *U•X•L Managing Editor*
Thomas L. Romig, *U•X•L Publisher*

Mary Beth Trimper, *Production Director*
Evi Seoud, *Assistant Production Manager*
Shanna Heilveil, *Production Associate*

Cynthia Baldwin, *Product Design Manager*
Barbara J. Yarrow, *Graphic Services Supervisor*
Tracey Rowens, *Cover Designer*
Pamela A.E. Galbreath, *Page Designer*

Susan Salas, *Permissions Associate (Pictures)*

Marco Di Vita, Graphix Group, *Typesetting*

Library of Congress Cataloging-in-Publication Data
Engelbert, Phillis
  Astronomy and space: from the big bang to the big crunch/
  by Phillis Engelbert.
      p. cm.
  Includes bibliographical references and index. Contents: v. 1. A-Her v. 2. Hes-P v. 3 Q-Z
    ISBN 0-7876-0942-0 (set); 0-7876-0943-9 (v.1); 0-7876-0944-7 (v.2); 0-7876-
  0945-5 (v.3); (acid-free paper)
      1. Astronomy—Encyclopedias, Juvenile. 2. Outer space—Encyclopedias, Juvenile.
  3. Astronautics—Encyclopedias, Juvenile. [1. Astronomy—Encyclopedias. 2. Outer space—
  Encyclopedias. 3. Astronautics—Encyclopedias.] I. Engelbert, Phillis.
  qb14.a874   1996
  500.5'03—dc20
                                                        96-12522
                                                            CIP
                                                             AC

☉™ This book is printed on acid-free paper that meets the minimum requirements of American National Standard for Information Sciences—Permanence Paper for Printed Library Materials, ANSI Z39.48-1984.

Printed in the United States of America

10 9 8 7 6 5 4 3

Table of Contents

Table of Contents

Table of Contents

Table of Contents

Table of Contents

Table of Contents

Reader's Guide

Astronomy & Space: From the Big Bang to the Big Crunch provides a comprehensive overview of astronomy and space exploration in three hundred alphabetically arranged entries. The topics included in *Astronomy & Space* can be grouped loosely into the following categories: space objects and phenomena (such as planets, black holes, comets, and solar wind); piloted space missions and scientific satellites; famous astronomers and astronauts; the history of astronomy; observatories; and technological advances in the field. Chronologically, *Astronomy & Space* begins fifteen to twenty billion years ago with the Big Bang, and continues on to recent discoveries such as planets beyond our solar system and the possibility of life on Mars. It extends to the future by describing projects—such as the International Space Station and *Pluto Express*—coming early in the twenty-first century and one possible fate of our universe, the Big Crunch.

The approach taken in *Astronomy & Space* is interdisciplinary and multicultural. The writing is interdisciplinary in that it does not merely address the exploration of the cosmos in a scientific sense, but it also places it in a social and historical context. For example, the entry on rockets includes a discussion of World War II and the entry on the space race addresses the cold war. The set is multicultural in that it features astronomers, observatories, astronomical advances, and space programs from around the world.

Scope and Format

The three hundred entries in *Astronomy & Space* are arranged alphabetically over three volumes. Articles range from one to four pages in length. The writing is nontechnical and is geared to challenge, but not overwhelm, students. More than two hundred photographs and illustrations and numerous sidebars keep the volumes lively and entertaining. Each volume begins with a historical timeline depicting major events in astronomy and space. Boldfaced terms throughout the text can be found in the glossary, while cross-references concluding each entry alert the reader to related entries. A cumulative index in all three volumes provides easy access to the topics discussed throughout *Astronomy & Space.*

Advisors

Thanks are due for the invaluable comments and suggestions provided by:

Teresa F. Bettac
Advanced Science for Kids Teacher, Willis Middle School
Delaware, Ohio

Patricia A. Nielsen
8th Grade Science Teacher/Science Fair Director, Todd County
Middle School
Mission, South Dakota

Jacqueline Ann Plourde
Media Specialist, Madison Junior High
Naperville, Illinois

Jan Toth-Chernin
Media Specialist, Greenhills School
Ann Arbor, Michigan

Dedication and Special Thanks

The author dedicates this work to her husband, William Shea, and her son, Ryan Patrick Shea, for their patience, love, and support. Special thanks to Jan Toth-Chernin for her guidance.

Comments and Suggestions

We welcome your comments on this work as well as your suggestions for topics to be featured in future editions of *Astronomy & Space: From the Big Bang to the Big Crunch.* Please write: Editors, *Astronomy & Space,* U•X•L, 835 Penobscot Bldg., Detroit, Michigan 48226-4094; call toll-free: 1-800-877-4253; or fax: (313) 877-6348.

Timeline

15–20 billion B.C.: "Big bang" marks the beginning of the universe.

10 billion B.C.: Galaxies are formed.

4.5 billion B.C.: The solar system is formed.

4 billion B.C.: Amino acids, the building blocks of life, are formed on Earth.

248 million B.C.: Dinosaurs roam the Earth.

65 million B.C.: Dinosaurs become extinct.

100,000 B.C.: First modern humans inhabit the Earth.

10,000 B.C.: Ice Age ends.

8000 B.C.: Archaic Age begins.

c. 3100 B.C.: Construction begins on Stonehenge.

c. 3000 B.C.: Egyptians create the first 365-day calendar.

c. 1500 B.C.: Chinese astronomers create the first star chart.

1300 B.C.: Chinese astronomers note a nova in the constellation Scorpius.

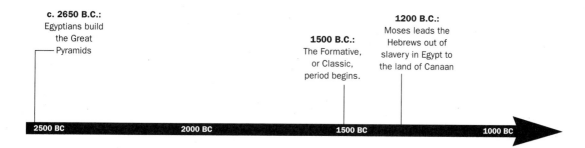

c. 2650 B.C.:
Egyptians build the Great Pyramids

1500 B.C.:
The Formative, or Classic, period begins.

1200 B.C.:
Moses leads the Hebrews out of slavery in Egypt to the land of Canaan

2500 BC   2000 BC   1500 BC   1000 BC

585 B.C.: Greek philosopher Thales correctly predicts a total eclipse of the sun.

c. 330 B.C.: Aristotle writes *De caelo* (*On the Heavens*).

c. 260 B.C.: Greek astronomer Aristarchus proposes that the Earth revolves around the sun.

c. 130 B.C.: Greek astronomer Hipparchus creates a star chart.

46 B.C.: Julius Caesar adds leap year days to the calendar, creating the Julian calendar.

c. A.D. 140: Alexandrian astronomer Ptolemy publishes his Earth-centered theory of the universe.

927: Muslim instrument-maker Nastulus creates the first astrolabe.

1006: Egyptian astrologer Ali ibn Ridwan observes what is considered to be the brightest supernova in history.

1408: Chinese observers note supernova in the constellation Cygnus the Swan, today believed to be a black hole.

1572: Danish astronomer Tycho Brahe observes supernova in the constellation Cassiopeia.

1608: Dutch optometrist Hans Lippershey creates the first telescope.

1609: German astronomer Johannes Kepler publishes his first two laws of planetary motion.

1616: The Catholic Church bans Copernicus' *De Revolutionibus Orbium Coelestium.*

1633: Galileo is placed under house arrest for advocating the sun-centered model of solar system.

1675: Danish astronomer Olaus Roemer measures the speed of light at 76 percent its actual value.

1682: English astronomer Edmond Halley first views the famous comet that is later named after him.

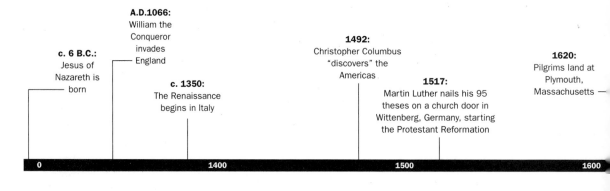

A.D.1066:
William the Conqueror invades England

c. 6 B.C.: Jesus of Nazareth is born

c. 1350: The Renaissance begins in Italy

1492: Christopher Columbus "discovers" the Americas

1517: Martin Luther nails his 95 theses on a church door in Wittenberg, Germany, starting the Protestant Reformation

1620: Pilgrims land at Plymouth, Massachusetts

0   1400   1500   1600

1728: English astronomer James Bradley calculates speed of light to be 185,000 miles per second.

1758: French astronomer Charles Messier begins his catalogue of non-star celestial objects.

1772: German astronomer Johann Elert Bode publishes his law of inter-planetary distances.

1781: German astronomer William Herschel discovers Uranus.

1783: English geologist John Michell suggests the existence of black holes.

1800: William Herschel discovers infrared radiation.

1845: English astronomer John Couch Adams and French astronomer Urbain Leverrier co-discover Neptune.

1847: American astronomer Maria Mitchell makes the first discovery of a comet not visible to the naked eye.

1852: French physicist Jean Bernard Léon Foucault proves that the Earth rotates with his famous pendulum experiment.

1877: American astronomer Asaph Hall discovers moons of Mars.

1877: Italian astronomer Giovanni Schiaparelli describes markings called *canali* on surface of Mars, which is erroneously translated to "canals," fueling speculation of life on Mars.

1889: American astronomer George Hale invents the spectrohelioscope.

1895: German physicist Wilhelm Röntgen discovers X-rays.

1905: Albert Einstein publishes his special theory of relativity.

1912: American astronomer Henrietta Swan Leavitt discovers how to use cepheid variable stars as "astronomical yardsticks."

1914: Einstein publishes his general theory of relativity.

1917: Dutch astronomer Willem de Sitter proposes that the universe is expanding.

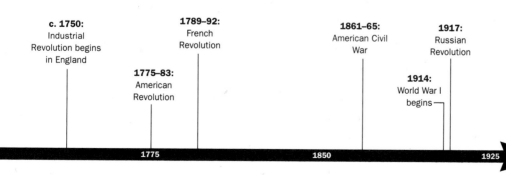

c. 1750: Industrial Revolution begins in England

1775–83: American Revolution

1789–92: French Revolution

1861–65: American Civil War

1914: World War I begins

1917: Russian Revolution

1700   1775   1850   1925

1919: Star observations during a solar eclipse prove Einstein's theory (that gravity bends light) correct.

1923: American astronomer Edwin Hubble discovers that the Andromeda nebula is actually a separate galaxy, establishing the existence of galaxies beyond our own.

1926: American physicist Robert Goddard launches the world's first liquid-propelled rocket.

1929: Hubble pens Hubble's Law, which describes the rate of universal expansion.

1930: American amateur astronomer Clyde Tombaugh discovers Pluto.

1932: American physicist Carl Anderson discovers anti-matter.

1932: American radio engineer Karl Jansky discovers radio waves coming from space.

1939: Ham radio operator Grete Rober builds the first radio telescope in his backyard and maps radio waves coming from throughout the Milky Way.

1943: American astronomer Carl Seyfert discovers bright, violent, spiral galaxies that now bear his name.

1947: The 200-inch Hale Telescope, which for the next thirty years remains the world's largest, becomes operational at Palomar Observatory.

1950: Dutch astronomer Jan Oort suggests comets lie dormant in an "Oort cloud" that surrounds the solar system.

October 4, 1957: Soviets launch *Sputnik 1,* initiating the space race with the United States.

1958: National Aeronautics and Space Administration (NASA) created.

January 31, 1958: *Explorer 1,* the first U.S. satellite, is launched into orbit.

October 4, 1959: Soviet satellite *Luna 3* takes the first photographs of the far side of the moon.

1960: United States launches the *Echo* communications satellite.

1929: Great Depression begins

1936: Spanish Civil War begins

1939–45: World War II

1946: Cold war between the United States and the Soviet Union begins

1950–53: Korean War

1930   1940   1945   1950

April 12, 1961: Soviet pilot Yuri Gagarin orbits Earth aboard *Vostok 1*, becoming the first human in space.

May 5, 1961: Alan Shepard takes a sub-orbital flight aboard *Mercury 3*, becoming the first American in space.

August 27, 1962: *Mariner 2* is launched into orbit, becoming the first interplanetary space probe.

1963: Construction completed on the world's largest radio telescope, at Arecibo Observatory in Puerto Rico.

June 16, 1963: Soviet cosmonaut Valentina Tereshkova rides aboard *Vostok 6*, becoming the first woman in space.

1967: Irish graduate student Jocelyn Bell Burnell discovers pulsars.

1967: Mauna Kea Observatory, which has the world's largest concentration of optical telescopes, opens in Hawaii.

July 20, 1969: American astronauts Neil Armstrong and Buzz Aldrin become the first humans to walk on the moon.

April 13, 1970: Explosion occurs aboard *Apollo 13* when it is over halfway to the moon.

December 15, 1970: Soviet probe *Venera 7* arrives at Venus, making the first-ever successful landing on another planet.

April 19, 1971: Soviet Union launches *Salyut 1*, the world's first space station.

December 2, 1971: Soviet probe *Mars 3* makes first-ever successful landing on Mars.

March 3, 1972: U.S. probe *Pioneer 10* is launched.

December 7, 1972: Launch of *Apollo 17*, the final mission landing humans on the moon.

April 5, 1973: U.S. probe *Pioneer 11* is launched.

May 26, 1973: *Skylab*, the first and only U.S. space station, is launched.

December 4, 1973: U.S. probe *Pioneer 10* flies by Jupiter.

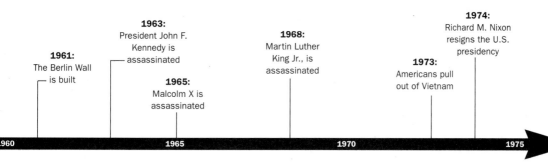

1961: The Berlin Wall is built

1963: President John F. Kennedy is assassinated

1965: Malcolm X is assassinated

1968: Martin Luther King Jr., is assassinated

1973: Americans pull out of Vietnam

1974: Richard M. Nixon resigns the U.S. presidency

1960   1965   1970   1975

1975: European Space Agency founded.

July 15, 1975: *Apollo 18* docks with *Soyuz 19*; Americans and Soviets unite for historic "handshake in space."

August 20, 1977: U.S. probe *Voyager 2* launched.

September 5, 1977: U.S. probe *Voyager 1* is launched.

June 22, 1978: American astronomer James W. Christy discovers Pluto's moon, Charon.

September 1, 1979: *Pioneer 11* becomes the first spacecraft to reach Saturn.

December 6, 1979: American astronomer Alan Guth develops the "inflationary theory" describing the rapid inflation of the universe immediately following the big bang.

1980: The Very Large Array, an interferometer consisting of 27 radio telescopes, becomes operational in Socorro, New Mexico.

April 12, 1981: First launch of a space shuttle: *Columbia.*

June 13, 1983: *Pioneer 10* becomes the first spacecraft to leave the solar system.

June 18, 1983: Sally Ride becomes the first U.S. woman in space, aboard the space shuttle *Challenger.*

August 30, 1983: Guion Bluford becomes the first African American in space, aboard *Challenger.*

November 28, 1983: First Spacelab launched.

January 24, 1986: *Voyager 2* flies by Uranus.

January 28, 1986: Space shuttle *Challenger* explodes just after lift-off, killing all seven crew members.

February 20, 1986: Launch of the Russian space station *Mir,* currently the only space station in operation.

March 13, 1986: First crew arrives at *Mir.*

March 14, 1986: European probe *Giotto* flies in to the nucleus of Halley's comet.

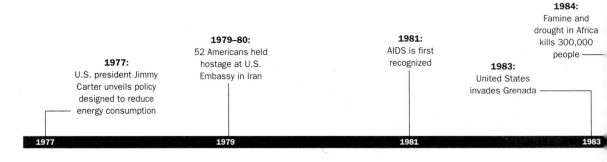

1977: U.S. president Jimmy Carter unveils policy designed to reduce energy consumption

1979–80: 52 Americans held hostage at U.S. Embassy in Iran

1981: AIDS is first recognized

1983: United States invades Grenada

1984: Famine and drought in Africa kills 300,000 people

1977   1979   1981   1983

May 4, 1989: U.S. Venus probe *Magellan* is launched.

August 24, 1989: *Voyager 2* flies past Neptune and heads out of the solar system.

October 18, 1989: U.S. Jupiter probe *Galileo* is launched.

November 18, 1989: NASA launches the *Cosmic Background Explorer.*

April 24, 1990: The Hubble Space Telescope is deployed from the space shuttle *Discovery.*

August 10, 1990: *Magellan* arrives at Venus and begins mapping surface.

April 5, 1991: Compton Gamma Ray Observatory is launched by NASA to produce an all-sky map of cosmic gamma-ray emissions.

September 12, 1992: Mae Jemison becomes first African American woman in space, aboard the space shuttle *Endeavour.*

December 1993: Astronauts aboard *Endeavour* repair the flawed Hubble Space Telescope.

December 7, 1995: *Galileo* reaches Jupiter and drops a mini-probe to the surface.

December 12, 1995: Solar and Heliospheric Observatory is launched to study the sun's internal structure.

January 1996: American astronomers Geoffrey Marcy and Paul Butler discover two new planets orbiting stars in the Big Dipper and Virgo constellations.

January 16, 1996: A team of astronomers led by David Bennett of the Lawrence Livermore National Laboratory announce their discovery that white dwarfs make up at least half of all dark matter.

March 25, 1996: Comet Hyakutake reaches its closest point to Earth in about 20,000 years.

August 7, 1996: Discovery of possible evidence of primitive Martian life, found in a 4.5-billion-year-old meteorite.

September 26, 1996: Astronaut Shannon Lucid returns to Earth after 188 days in space aboard *Mir.*

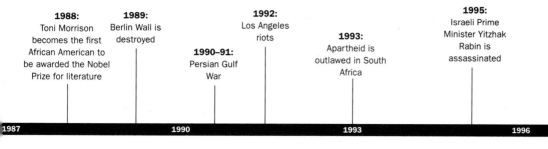

1988: Toni Morrison becomes the first African American to be awarded the Nobel Prize for literature

1989: Berlin Wall is destroyed

1990–91: Persian Gulf War

1992: Los Angeles riots

1993: Apartheid is outlawed in South Africa

1995: Israeli Prime Minister Yitzhak Rabin is assassinated

1987   1990   1993   1996

Words to Know

A

Aberration of light: the apparent movement of stars due to Earth's motion forward into starlight.

Absolute magnitude: a star's brightness at a constant distance from Earth.

Absolute zero: the lowest possible temperature at which matter can exist; equal to -259 degrees Fahrenheit and -273 degrees Celsius.

Absorption lines: dark lines that appear in the **spectrum** of an object, indicating **wavelength**s at which light is absorbed.

Adaptive optics: a system that makes minute adjustments to the shape of a **reflector telescope**'s primary mirror to correct distortions that result from disturbances in the atmosphere.

Aphelion: the point along an orbit of a planet or **comet** that is farthest from the sun.

Apollo objects: the group of **asteroid**s that cross Earth's orbit.

Armillary sphere: an instrument made up of spheres and rings used to observe the stars.

Asteroid: a relatively small, rocky chunk of matter that orbits the sun.

Astrolabe: a primitive star map historically used for timekeeping, navigation, and surveying.

Astrology: the study of the supposed effect of celestial objects on the course of human affairs.

Astrometric binary star: a **binary star** system in which only one star can be seen, but its wobble implies that there is another star in orbit around it.

Astronomical unit: a standard measure of distance to celestial objects, equal to the average distance from Earth to the sun (87 million miles).

Astrophysics: the study of the physical properties and evolution of celestial bodies, particularly concerning the production and use of energy in stars and **galaxies.**

Aurora: a bright, colorful display of light in the night sky, better known as the Northern and Southern lights, that results when charged particles from the sun enter Earth's atmosphere.

B

Big bang theory: the theory that explains the beginning of the universe as a tremendous explosion from a single point that occurred fifteen to twenty billion years ago.

Big crunch theory: the catastrophic prediction that there will come a point, very far in the future, in which matter will reverse direction and crunch back into the single point from which it began.

Binary star: a double star system in which two stars orbit one another around a central point of **gravity.**

Black dwarf: the cooling remnants of a **white dwarf** star that has ceased to glow.

Black hole: the remains of a massive star that has burned out its nuclear fuel and collapsed under tremendous gravitational force into a single point of infinite **mass** and **gravity.**

Blue-shift: the shift of **wavelength**s of an object's light **spectrum** into the blue (shorter wavelength) end of the range of visible light—an indication that the object is approaching the observer.

Bode's Law: the simple yet flawed mathematical formula published by eighteenth-century German astronomer Johann Elert Bode dictating the distances of planets from the sun.

Bolometer: an instrument that can detect **electromagnetic radiation** entering Earth's atmosphere, used in particular to measure **radiation** and **microwave**s from the sun and stars.

Brown dwarf: a small, cool, dark ball of matter that never completes the process of becoming a star.

C

Calendar: any system for organizing time into days, months, and years.

Celestial sphere: the sky, or imaginary sphere, that surrounds Earth and provides a visual surface on which we can plot celestial objects and chart their apparent movement due to Earth's rotation.

Cepheid variable: a pulsating yellow **supergiant** star that can be used to measure distance in space.

Chandrasekhar's limit: the theory that any star with a **mass** greater than one and one-half times that of the sun will be crushed at the end of its lifetime by its own **gravity,** so that it will become either a **neutron star** or a **black hole.** A star below this limit will end up as a **white dwarf** star.

Charged coupling device (CCD): a light-capturing device placed at the end of a telescope that is the modern, computerized version of old photographic plates.

Chromosphere: the glowing layer of gas that makes up the middle atmospheric layer of the sun.

Cold war: the period of tense relations, from 1945–1990, between the former **Soviet Union** (and its Eastern allies) and the United States (and its Western European allies).

Comet: a small body of rocky material, dust, and ice in orbit around the sun.

Command module: the section of the Apollo spacecraft in which astronauts traveled.

Constellation: one of eighty-eight groups of stars in the sky named for mythological beings. Each constellation is bordered by an imaginary line running north-south and east-west across the **celestial sphere,** so that every point in the sky belongs to one constellation or another.

Convection: the process by which heat is transferred from the core of the sun toward the surface via slow-moving gas currents.

Copernican model. *See* **Heliocentric model**

Corona: the outermost atmospheric layer of the sun.

Coronagraph: a modified telescope that uses a black disc to block out most of the sunlight entering its chamber, leaving only the image of the sun's **corona.**

Cosmic dust: solid, microscopic particles found in the **interstellar medium.**

Cosmic rays: invisible, high-energy particles that constantly bombard Earth from all directions. Most are high-speed protons (hydrogen atoms that have lost a electron) although they also include the nuclei of all known elements.

Cosmic string: a giant vibrating strand with tremendous gravitational pull containing trapped **spacetime** from a much earlier period.

Cosmology: the study of the origin, evolution, and structure of the universe.

Cosmonaut: a Russian astronaut.

Cosmos: the universe regarded as an orderly system.

Coudé telescope: a modified **reflector telescope** that has the eyepiece angled so that it keeps the image of an object in view, even as that object moves across the sky.

D

Dark matter: virtually undetectable matter that is thought to account for 90 percent of the **mass** in the universe and acts as the "cosmic glue" that holds together **galaxies** and clusters of galaxies.

Diffraction: deflection of a beam of light.

Dwarf galaxy: an unusually small, faint **galaxy.**

E

Earth's meridian: an imaginary circle on the surface of Earth passing through the North and South poles.

Eclipsing binary star: a **binary star** system in which the orbital plane is nearly edgewise to our line of sight, meaning that each star is eclipsed (partially or totally hidden) by the other as they revolve around a common point of **gravity.**

Electromagnetic radiation: radiation that transmits energy through the interaction of electricity and **magnetism.**

Electromagnetic spectrum: the complete array of **electromagnetic radiation,** including **radio wave**s (at the longest-**wavelength** end), **infrared radiation,** visible light, **ultraviolet radiation, X-ray**s, and **gamma ray**s (at the shortest-wavelength end).

Electroscope: an instrument used to detect electrons.

Elliptical galaxy: the most common type of **galaxy** in the universe; elliptical galaxies vary in shape from circles to narrow, elongated ellipses (ovals) and may be spherical or flat.

Emission lines: bright lines that appear in the **spectrum** of an object, indicating **wavelength**s at which light is emitted.

Epicycle: a small secondary orbit erroneously added to the planetary orbits by pre-Copernican astronomers to account for periods in which the planets appeared to move backwards with respect to Earth.

Equinoxes: the days marking the start of spring and fall and the only two days of the year in which day and night are of equal length.

Event horizon: the surface of a collapsed massive star or **black hole.**

Exosphere: the outer layer of Earth's atmosphere, starting about 250 miles above ground, in which molecules of gas break down into atoms and become ionized (electrically charged) by the sun's rays (also called the "ionosphere").

Extravehicular activity (EVA): an activity performed in space by an astronaut attached to the outside of a spacecraft (also called "space walk").

F

Faculae: bright hydrogen clouds often found near **sunspot**s on the sun's surface.

Flare: a temporary bright spot that explodes on the sun's surface.

G

Galaxy: a huge region of space that contains hundreds of billions of stars, **nebula**e (clouds), gas, dust, empty space, and possibly a **black hole.**

Gamma ray: short-**wavelength,** high-energy **radiation** formed either by the decay of radioactive elements or by nuclear reactions.

Gamma ray astronomy: the study of objects in space by observing the **gamma rays** they emit.

General theory of relativity: the theory in which Albert Einstein demonstrated that **gravity** is the result of curved **spacetime.**

Geocentric model: the flawed theory of the **solar system** placing Earth at the center, with the sun, moon, and planets revolving around it.

Geodesy: the study of Earth's external shape, internal construction, and gravitational field.

Geostationary orbit: a special kind of geosynchronous orbit, in which a satellite travels in the same plane as Earth's equator. A geostationary satellite remains more or less stationary over the same point on Earth.

Geosynchronous orbit: an orbit around Earth that takes twenty-four hours to complete.

Globular cluster: a tight grouping of stars found near the edges of the Milky Way.

Globules: small dark patches of concentrated particles found in the **interstellar medium.**

Granules: Earth-sized cells covering the sun's surface that transfer hot gas from the sun's interior to its outer atmospheric layers.

Gravity: the force of attraction between objects, the strength of which depends on the **mass** of each object and the distance between them.

Gravity assist: a technique used by a spacecraft journeying to distant planets, in which it uses the gravitational field of one planet to propel it toward another, eliminating the need for additional **rocket** motors.

Greenhouse effect: the warming of an environment that occurs when **infrared radiation** enters the atmosphere and becomes trapped inside.

Gyroscope: a navigational instrument consisting of a wheel that spins around a rod through its center. The wheel continues spinning in the same direction, even when the direction of the instrument is changed.

H

Heliocentric model: the theory that the sun is at the center of the **solar system** with the planets revolving around it.

Helioseismology: the study of the sun's interior structure and dynamics, determined by measuring the vibrations of sound waves deep within the sun's core.

Heliosphere: the vast region permeated by charged particles flowing out from the sun that surrounds the sun and extends throughout the **solar system.**

Heliostat: a flat, rotating mirror that collects light at the top of a solar telescope tower.

Heliotrope: an instrument that reflects sunlight over great distances to mark the positions of participants in a land survey.

Hertzsprung-Russell diagram: the graph showing the relationship between the color, brightness, and temperature of stars. It places **absolute magnitude** (or brightness) on the vertical axis and color (or temperature) on the horizontal axis.

Homogeneity: uniformity; the state of being the same everywhere.

Hubble's Law: the distance-to-speed relationship showing that the more distant a **galaxy,** the faster it is receding; it describes the expansion of the universe.

I

Inertia: the property of matter that requires a force to act on it to change its state of motion.

Inflationary theory: the theory that the universe underwent a period of rapid expansion immediately following the **big bang.**

Infrared astronomy: the study of objects in space by the **infrared radiation** they emit.

Infrared radiation: electromagnetic radiation of a **wavelength** shorter than **radio wave**s but longer than visible light that takes the form of heat.

Interferometry: the process of splitting a beam of light (or other form of **electromagnetic radiation**) in two, bouncing it off a series of mirrors, and examining its pattern when it comes back together.

Interstellar medium: the space between the stars, consisting mainly of empty space with a very small concentration of gas atoms and tiny solid particles.

Ionosphere. *See* **Exosphere**

K

Kirkwood gaps: areas separating distinct asteroid belts that lie between the orbits of Mars and Jupiter.

Kuiper belt: the proposed cometary reservoir, located just beyond the edge of the orbit of Pluto, containing an estimated ten million to one billion inactive **comet**s.

L

Latitude: an imaginary line circling Earth, parallel to the equator, that tells one's north-south position on the globe.

Launch vehicle: a **rocket** system used to launch satellites and piloted spacecraft into space.

Light-year: the distance light travels in one year, about 5.9 trillion miles.

Longitude: an imaginary line circling Earth, perpendicular to the equator, that tells one's east-west position on the globe.

Lunar eclipse: the complete or partial blocking of the moon by Earth's shadow that occurs when Earth passes between the sun and moon.

Lunar module: the section of Apollo spacecraft that detached to land on the moon.

M

Magnetic axis: the imaginary line connecting Earth's, and other planet's, magnetic poles.

Magnetic field: the area of a planet affected by magnetic force.

Magnetism: the property of a body to produce an electrical current around itself.

Magnetosphere: the region around a planet occupied by its magnetic field.

Mass: the measure of the total amount of matter in an object.

Mass-luminosity law: the law describing the relationship between a star's **mass** and brightness; the more massive a star, the greater the interior pressure and temperature, and therefore the greater the brightness.

Mesosphere: the middle layer of Earth's atmosphere, existing between 40 and 50 miles above ground.

Meteor: also known as a "shooting star," a meteor is a small particle of dust or a small rock left behind by a **comet**'s tail.

Meteor shower: periods of increased **meteor** activity from a common point in the sky, caused by Earth's passage through the orbit of a **comet** or the debris left behind by a comet.

Meteorite: a large chunk of rock, metal, or rock-and-metal that breaks off an **asteroid** or a **comet** and survives passage through Earth's atmosphere to hit the ground.

Meteoroid: the term that collectively describes all forms of meteoric material, including **meteor**s and **meteorite**s.

Micrometer: a device used to measure minute distances or angles.

Microwave: a subset of **radio wave**s, those with the shortest **wavelength**s (less than three feet across).

Milky Way: our home **galaxy,** which contains the sun and billions of other stars, possibly one or more **black hole**s, star clusters, planets, glowing **nebula**e, dust, and empty space. It is approximately 100,000 light-years in diameter and 2,000 light-years thick.

Molecular cloud: a cool area in the **interstellar medium** in which molecules are formed.

N

Nebula: a cloud of interstellar gas and dust.

Neutrino: a high-energy subatomic particle with no **mass,** or such a small mass as to be undetectable, and no electrical charge.

Neutron star: the extremely dense, compact, neutron-filled remains of a star following a **supernova.**

Nova: a sudden, intense, temporary brightening of a star.

Nuclear fusion: the merging of two hydrogen nuclei into one helium nucleus, accompanied by a tremendous release of energy.

Nutation: the slight shift in the angle of tilt of Earth's axis due to the gravitational tug of the moon as it orbits Earth.

O

Oort cloud: a region of space beyond the **solar system,** about one light-year from the sun, theoretically containing trillions of inactive **comet**s.

Open cluster: a loose grouping of stars found toward the center of the **Milky Way.**

Optical interferometer: a series of two or more optical telescopes that are linked together electronically, with a viewing power far greater than the sum of the individual telescopes.

Ozone layer: the layer of Earth's atmosphere, between 25 and 40 miles above ground, that filters out the sun's harmful rays.

P

Parallax: the observed change of a star's position due to Earth's motion around the sun.

Payload: the passengers, instruments, or equipment carried by a spacecraft.

Penumbra: the lighter region surrounding the dark, central part of the moon's shadow that sweeps across Earth during a **solar eclipse.**

Perihelion: the point along an orbit (of a planet or **comet**) that's closest to the sun.

Period-luminosity curve: the graph that enables one to find the distance to a **cepheid variable.** It places **absolute magnitude** (brightness) on the vertical axis and period (days to complete a cycle) on the horizontal axis.

Photometry: the measurement of the properties of a light source. In astronomy, it pertains to the measurement of the brightness and colors of stars that, in turn, are indicators of stellar surface temperature.

Photosphere: the few-hundred-mile thick innermost layer of solar atmosphere that constitutes the sun's surface.

Planetesimals: ancient chunks of matter that originated with the formation of the **solar system** but never came together to form a planet.

Plasma: a substance made of ions (electrically charged atoms) and electrons that exists at extremely hot temperatures.

Plasma theory: the theory that the universe was born out of electrical and magnetic phenomena involving **plasma.**

Probe. *See* **Space probe**

Prominence: a high-density cloud of gas projecting outward from the sun's surface.

Propellant: an energy source for **rocket**s that consists of fuel and an oxidizer. Types of fuel include alcohol, kerosene, liquid hydrogen, and hydrazine. The oxidizer may be nitrogen tetroxide or liquid oxygen.

Proper motion: the apparent motion of a star resulting from both its actual movement in space and the shift in its position relative to Earth.

Protoplanet: the earliest form of a planet, plus its moons, formed by the combination of **planetesimals.**

Ptolemaic model. *See* **Geocentric model**

Pulsar: a rapidly spinning, blinking **neutron star.**

Q

Quadrant: an ancient instrument used for measuring the positions of stars.

Quantum mechanics: the study of the behavior of subatomic particles.

Quasars: extremely bright, star-like sources of **radio wave**s that are the oldest known objects in the universe.

R

Radiation: energy emitted in the form of waves or particles.

Radio astronomy: the study of objects in space by observing the **radio wave**s they emit.

Radio interferometer: a system of multiple **radio telescope**s linked electronically that act as a single telescope with a diameter equal to the area separating them. Powerful computers combine their information and create detailed pictures of objects in space.

Radio telescope: an instrument consisting of a large concave dish with an antenna at the center, tuned to a certain **wavelength**. It receives and processes **radio wave**s and produces a picture of the source emitting the radio waves.

Radio wave: the longest form of **electromagnetic radiation,** measuring up to six miles from peak to peak.

Red dwarf: a star that is 10 to 70 percent smaller in mass and much cooler than the sun.

Red giant: the stage in which an average-sized star (like our sun) spends the final 10 percent of its lifetime. Its surface temperature drops and its diameter expands to ten to one thousand times that of the sun.

Red-shift: the shift of an object's light **spectrum** toward the red-end of the visible light range—an indication that the object is moving away from the observer.

Reflector telescope: a telescope that uses mirrors to bring light rays into focus. It works by directing light from an opening at one end of a tube to a mirror at the far end. The light is then reflected back to a smaller mirror and directed to an eyepiece on the side of the tube.

Refractor telescope: the simplest type of telescope; light enters through one end of a tube and passes through a glass lens, which bends the light rays and brings them into focus. The light then strikes an eyepiece, which acts as a magnifying glass.

Retrograde motion: the perceived backward motion of the outer planets (those farther from the sun than Earth) as Earth overtakes them along their respective orbits around the sun.

Rocket: a tube-like device containing explosive material which, on being ignited, releases gases that propel the device through the air.

S

Schmidt telescope: a combined refractor-reflector telescope that has a specially shaped thin glass lens at one end of a tube and a mirror at the other.

Service module: the section of Apollo spacecraft in which supplies and equipment are carried.

Sextant: an early navigational instrument used to measure the angle from the horizon to a celestial body.

Seyfert galaxy: a fast-moving, spiral-shaped **galaxy** characterized by an exceptionally bright nucleus.

Singularity: the single point at which pressure and density are infinite.

Solar eclipse: the complete or partial blocking of the sun that occurs when the moon's orbit takes it in front of Earth.

Solar system: the sun plus all its orbiting bodies, including the planets, moons, **comet**s, **asteroid**s, **meteoroid**s, and particles of dust and debris.

Solar telescope: a modified reflecting or refracting telescope capable of directly observing the sun.

Solar wind: electrically charged subatomic particles that flow out from the sun.

Solstices: the two days each year when the sun is at its highest and its lowest points in the sky.

Soviet Union: the former country in Northern Asia and Eastern Europe that in 1991 broke up into the independent states of Armenia, Azerbaijan, Belarus, Estonia, Georgia, Kazakhstan, Kyrgyzstan, Latvia, Lithuania, Moldova, Russia, Tajikistan, Turkmenistan, Ukraine, and Uzbekistan.

Space age: the modern historical period beginning with the launch of *Sputnik 1* in 1957 and continuing to the present, characterized by space travel and exploration.

Space probe: an unpiloted spacecraft that leaves Earth's orbit to explore the moon, other bodies, or outer space.

Space race: the twenty-year-long contest, from the mid-1950s to the mid-1970s, for superiority in space travel and exploration, between the United States and the **Soviet Union.**

Space shuttle: a reusable winged space plane that transports astronauts and equipment into space and back.

Space station: an orbiting spacecraft designed to sustain humans for periods of up to several months.

Space telescope: a telescope placed on board a satellite that can make observations free from interference of Earth's atmosphere.

Space walk. *See* **Extravehicular activity (EVA)**

Spacetime: a four-dimensional construct that unites the three dimensions of space (length, width, and height) and a fourth dimension, time.

Special theory of relativity: Albert Einstein's theory—applicable to situations in which the rate of motion is constant—that space and time are not fixed, but change depending on how fast and in what direction the observer is moving.

Spectrograph: an instrument that photographs light **spectra** of celestial objects, making it possible to learn their temperature and chemical composition.

Spectrohelioscope: a combined telescope and **spectroscope** that breaks down sunlight into a colorful display of the sun's chemical components.

Spectroscope: an instrument used to break down **radiation** into its component **wavelength**s.

Spectroscopic binary star: a **binary star** system that appears as one star that produces two different light **spectra.**

Spectroscopy: the process of separating the light of an object (generally, a star) into its component colors so that the various elements present within that object can be identified.

Spectra. *See* **Spectrum**

Spectrum: the range of individual **wavelength**s of **radiation** produced when light is broken down by the process of **spectroscopy.**

Speed of light: the speed at which light travels in a vacuum—186,282.397 miles per second.

Spicules: narrow gas jets that characterize the outer edge of the sun's **chromosphere.**

Spiral galaxy: a **galaxy** with old stars at the center, surrounded by a band of star clusters and an invisible cloud of **dark matter,** with arms spiraling out like a pinwheel.

Steady-state theory: the theory of the origin of the universe stating that all matter in the universe has been created continuously, at a constant rate throughout time.

Stellar nurseries: areas within glowing clouds of gas and dust where new stars are in formation.

Stellar spectrophotometry: the study of the intensity of a particular spectral line or series of spectral lines in a star's absorption or emission **spectrum.**

Stratosphere: the second-lowest layer of Earth's atmosphere, from about 9 to 40 miles above ground.

Sundial: a primitive instrument used to keep time by following the sun's passage across the sky.

Sunspot: a cool area of magnetic disturbance that forms a dark blemish on the surface of the sun.

Supergiant: the largest and brightest type of star, which has over fifteen times the **mass** of the sun and shines over one million times more brightly than the sun.

Supernova: the explosion of a massive star at the end of its lifetime, causing it to shine more brightly than the rest of the stars in the **galaxy** put together.

T

Thermosphere: the layer of Earth's atmosphere, between 50 and 200 miles above ground, in which temperatures reach 1800 degrees Fahrenheit.

Transit: the passage of an inner planet (Mercury or Venus) between the sun and Earth.

Tropical year: the time it takes Earth to complete an orbit around the sun.

Troposphere: the lowest layer of Earth's atmosphere, in which weather patterns are formed.

U

Ultraviolet radiation: electromagnetic radiation of a **wavelength** just shorter than the violet (shortest wavelength) end of visible light **spectrum.**

Umbra: the dark, central part of the moon's shadow that sweeps across Earth during a **solar eclipse.**

V

Van Allen belts: doughnut-shaped regions of charged particles encircling Earth.

Variable star: a star that varies in brightness over periods of time ranging from hours to years.

Visual binary star: a **binary star** system in which each star can be seen distinctly.

W

Wavelength: the distance between one peak of a wave of light, heat, or energy and the next corresponding peak.

White dwarf: the cooling, shrunken core remaining after a medium-sized star ceases to burn.

X

X-ray: electromagnetic radiation of a **wavelength** shorter than **ultraviolet radiation** but longer than **gamma ray**s that can penetrate solids and produce an electrical charge in gases.

Picture Credits

The photographs and illustrations appearing in *Astronomy & Space: From the Big Bang to the Big Crunch* were received from the following sources:

On the cover: Hans Bethe (**AP/Wide World Photos. Reproduced by permission.**); Annie Jump Cannon (**UPI/Corbis-Bettmann. Reproduced by permission.**); Percival Lowell (**Lowell Observatory. Reproduced by permission.**); *Atlantis* space shuttle (**Corbis-Bettmann. Reproduced by permission.**).

Corbis-Bettmann. Reproduced by permission.: pp. 1, 18, 27, 28, 32, 34, 39, 41, 43, 48, 52, 69, 74, 80, 84, 111, 142, 154, 157, 178, 181, 215, 217, 262, 265, 295, 297, 309, 310, 325, 385, 413, 436, 459; **UPI/Corbis-Bettmann. Reproduced by permission.:** pp. 3, 30, 82, 91, 95, 139, 141, 162, 163, 168, 170, 186, 189, 243, 244, 251, 255, 284, 286, 301, 320, 330, 381, 392, 429, 508, 517, 533, 540, 547, 551, 559, 601, 610, 618, 658; **AP/Wide World Photos. Reproduced by permission.:** pp. 5, 24, 45, 54, 57, 93, 103, 129, 175, 176, 191, 202, 205, 208, 213, 269, 303, 322, 327, 352, 360, 408, 420, 424, 492, 497, 500, 505, 510, 519, 585, 588, 637, 645, 664, 669, 675, 677, 689, 697, 700, 704; **Frank Rossotto/Stocktrek Photo Agency. Reproduced by permission.:** pp. 37, 64, 88, 97, 126, 135, 148, 150, 173, 375, 383, 388, 405, 457, 488, 529, 570, 615, 625, 655, 672, 684, 691; **Mullard Radio Astronomy Laboratory/Science Photo Library, National Audubon Society/Photo Researchers, Inc. Reproduced by permission.:** p. 62; **Courtesy of the Library of Congress:** pp. 68, 514, 648; **Archive Photos. Reproduced by permission.:** pp. 71, 166, 258, 307, 315, 343, 394, 398, 544, 634; **Chris Butler/Science Photo Library, National Audubon Society/Photo Researchers, Inc. Reproduced**

by permission.: pp. 77, 502; **Frank Rossotto. Reproduced by permission.**: pp. 101, 346, 350, 354; **Stav Birnbaum Collection/Corbis-Bettmann. Reproduced by permission.**: p. 109; **Tommaso Guicciardini/INFN/Science Photo Library, National Audubon Society/Photo Researchers, Inc. Reproduced by permission.**: pp. 116, 410; **Dr. Charles Alcock, Macho Collaboration/Science Photo Library, National Audubon Society/Photo Researchers, Inc. Reproduced by permission.**: p. 124; **Illustrations reprinted by permission of Robert L. Wolke**: p. 146; **SETI Institute/Science Photo Library, National Audubon Society/Photo Researchers, Inc. Reproduced by permission.**: p. 158; **Courtesy of U.S. National Aeronautics and Space Administration (NASA)**: p. 194; **Hans & Cassidy. Courtesy of Gale Research.**: pp. 196, 537; **Mehau Kulyk/Science Photo Library, National Audubon Society/Photo Researchers, Inc. Reproduced by permission.**: p. 219; **Science Photo Library, National Audubon Society/Photo Researchers, Inc. Reproduced by permission.**: pp. 260, 552, 567; **© NASA, National Audubon Society Collection/Photo Researchers, Inc. Reproduced with permission.**: p. 275; **JLM Visuals. Reproduced by permission.**: pp. 289, 640, 641; **Courtesy of National Optical Astronomy Observatories**: p. 299; **Royal Observatory, Edinburgh/Science Photo Library, National Audubon Society/Photo Researchers, Inc. Reproduced by permission.**: p. 312; **Lowell Observatory. Reproduced by permission.**: p. 332; **Sovfoto/Eastfoto. Reproduced by permission.**: p. 339; **Reuters/Corbis-Bettmann. Reproduced by permission.**: p. 341; **The Bettmann Archive. Reproduced by permission.**: pp. 363, 416; **UPI/Bettmann. Reproduced by permission.**: pp. 367, 370, 378, 438, 441, 462, 522, 549, 599, 613, 616, 630, 662, 681; **NASA. Reproduced with permission.**: pp. 454, 581; **Julian Baum/Science Photo Library, National Audubon Society/Photo Researchers, Inc. Reproduced by permission.**: pp. 564, 628; **Reuters/Bettmann. Reproduced by permission.**: p. 577; **Finley Holiday Film/U.S. National Aeronautics and Space Administration. Reproduced by permission.**: p. 595; **David A. Hardy/Science Photo Library, National Audubon Society/Photo Researchers, Inc. Reproduced by permission.**: p. 621; **Courtesy of the University of Wyoming**: p. 693.

Hess, Victor (1883–1964)
Austrian-American astronomer

Victor Franz Hess was born and educated in Austria. He went to the University of Graz and earned his Ph.D. in 1906. He was then hired onto the faculty of the Vienna Academy of Sciences. Hess is best known for his discovery of **cosmic ray**s.

Hess became interested in a mysterious radiation that scientists had found in the ground and in the Earth's atmosphere. This radiation produced an electric charge in an **electroscope**—a tool used to detect charged particles—even in a sealed container.

Hess believed that the radiation was coming from the ground and that at a certain altitude it would no longer be detectable. To test his theory, Hess took a series of high-altitude hot-air balloon flights with an electroscope on board in 1912. His balloon reached an altitude of nearly 6 miles (10 kilometers). He made ten trips at night and one during a **solar eclipse,** to eliminate the sun as a possible source of the radiation.

To his surprise, Hess found that the higher he went, the stronger the radiation became. At the highest point he reached, the radiation was eight times as strong as on the Earth's surface. This discovery led Hess to believe that the radiation was coming from outer space. In later years, scientists confirmed this theory and named the energy cosmic rays.

Victor Hess.

We now know that cosmic rays consist of high-energy particles that constantly bombard Earth from all directions. They bring trillions of atomic nuclei into the Earth's atmosphere at a rate of 90 percent the **speed of light.**

Most cosmic rays are high-speed protons (hydrogen atoms that have lost an electron) although they also include the nuclei of all known elements. Astronomers now believe that they probably come from **supernova** explosions or **neutron star**s.

For his work on cosmic rays Hess was awarded the Nobel Prize in physics in 1936.

See also **Cosmic rays**

Hewish, Antony (1924–)

British astronomer

Antony Hewish was born in Cornwall, England. He attended King's College and later, Cambridge University. After graduating from Cambridge in 1948, he worked for a short time in the telecommunications industry. He then returned to Cambridge as a professor and joined a team conducting research in **radio astronomy.**

Hewish first used **radio telescope**s (instruments that detect **radio waves** in space) to study the sun's atmosphere. He determined the density of electrons in the sun's **corona,** or outer atmosphere, and observed the clouds of gas surrounding the sun.

After 1950, more powerful instruments were developed that made it possible to study radio sources farther away than the sun. Hewish was specifically interested in how radio signals from distant objects were received here on Earth, and the factors—such as gas in the Earth's atmosphere—that interfered with them.

In 1965, Hewish designed a new kind of radio telescope that used a scraggly wire antenna covering an area the size of a football field. Its purpose was to detect **quasar**s, extremely distant and bright starlike objects. The telescope picked up faint and rapidly changing radio signals and recorded them on long rolls of paper.

Antony Hewish.

Hewish and his colleague Martin Ryle were assisted in their research by a graduate student named Jocelyn Bell Burnell. Bell Burnell's job was to review every mark etched out on the paper. In August 1967, she noticed some strange markings. At first she and Hewish thought the markings were caused by interference from local amateur radio operators or other electrical interference. Once they ruled out that possibility, they looked to the sky to find the source.

The Discovery of Pulsars

Hewish and Bell Burnell began to monitor the signals with a high-speed recorder and learned that the signals went on and off regularly, about every 1.3 seconds. This discovery was mysterious because prior to that time the only recorded signals coming from space were continuous ones. While Hewish and Bell Burnell continued searching, they joked that the signals could be a form of extraterrestrial communication, and they named the mystery markings LGM, for Little Green Men.

Soon Bell Burnell found three other pulsating sources, and she and Hewish renamed the objects "**pulsar**s," short for "pulsating radio source." Hewish hypothesized that pulsars might be **white dwarf** stars (the cooling core of a burnt-out star) or **neutron star**s (the tightly packed, neutron-filled remains of a star). By the end of the following year, astronomers Thomas Gold and Franco Pacini determined that the pulsar signals are due to rapidly rotating neutron stars.

Neutron stars are incredibly dense. They may only be about 12 miles (about 19 kilometers) across but contain the **mass** of two suns. The spinning of a neutron star intensifies its **magnetic field,** causing the star to act as a giant magnet. It emits radiation from its magnetic poles, and if its **magnetic axis** is tilted in a certain way, the rotating star's on-and-off signal may be visible from Earth.

More than 450 pulsars have now been catalogued, including many in spots where a **supernova** is known to have occurred. Astronomers have calculated that a new pulsar is formed approximately every thirty years, when the core of an exploding star collapses and becomes a neutron star. Current estimates are that over one hundred thousand active pulsars may exist in our **galaxy.**

Hewish later proposed a pulsar-based system of space navigation, using the locations of three pulsars as reference points to keep space vehicles on course.

In 1974, Hewish and Ryle won the Nobel Prize for the discovery of pulsars. Although the Nobel committee did not officially recognize Bell Burnell, she received much attention for what many considered to be her discovery.

See also **Bell Burnell, Jocelyn** and **Pulsar**

High Energy Astrophysical Observatories

Between the years 1977 and 1982, the National Aeronautics and Space Administration (NASA) operated three High Energy Astrophysical Observatories (HEAO) in space. The first two of these satellite missions studied sources **X-ray** emissions (short wavelength, high-energy radiation produced by intensely hot material), while the third focused on **gamma ray**s and **cosmic ray**s.

X-ray astronomy and **gamma-ray astronomy** are both relatively new fields, involving the study of objects in space that emit X-rays and gamma rays, respectively. Since most space-based X-rays and gamma rays are prevented by our atmosphere from reaching Earth, the best place from which to observe them is in space. This fact led NASA in the early 1970s, to begin placing telescopes in space to study these and other types of **electromagnetic radiation** such as **infrared** and **ultraviolet radiation.**

The first satellite of the HEAO series was launched in August 1977 and swept the entire sky for X-rays for two and a half years before running out of fuel in January 1979. Its primary mission was to conduct a general survey of the X-ray sky, constantly monitoring X-ray sources, including individual stars, entire **galaxies,** and **pulsar**s. In March 1979, HEAO-1 burned up during re-entry into the Earth's atmosphere.

The second HEAO, also known as the Einstein Observatory, operated from November 1978 to April 1981. It contained a new type of X-ray telescope, called a "grazing incidence telescope," which created X-ray images about one thousand times more detailed than any previous instruments. The Einstein Observatory made over five thousand specific observations, producing maps of massive X-ray sources such as clusters of galaxies and **supernova**e remains. It also made the startling discovery that X-rays are emitted by nearly every star.

HEAO-3 was launched in September 1979 and contained several experiments, all of which ceased functioning between 1980 and 1982. Some of the instruments measured the **mass,** electrical charge, and energy of cosmic rays. Other pieces of equipment on the satellite searched for gamma rays from solar **flare**s, as well as from other sources.

See also **Cosmic rays**; **Gamma ray astronomy**; **Space telescope**; and **X-ray astronomy**

Hipparcos

Hipparcos was one of the least glamorous, yet most effective, satellites to be launched in the 1990s. The High Precision Parallax Collecting Satellite (Hipparcos for short) of the European Space Agency (ESA) was launched in August 1989. It spent four years making precise measurements of the position and motion of over one hundred thousand stars.

Charting stars is something that astronomers have done since the beginning of recorded history. So why did the ESA spend hundreds of millions of dollars to send a machine into space to do what humans have been doing for thousands of years?

The answer is similar to the reason for all **space telescope**s, that is, that the view from space is clearer than it is from Earth. The accuracy of ground-based instruments is limited by turbulence in the Earth's atmosphere, which scatters incoming **electromagnetic radiation.** Light shining from a distant star seems to dance around when examined through a telescope on Earth, making it difficult to obtain measurements with a high degree of accuracy. A space-based system, like *Hipparcos,* does a much better job.

While the satellite is called "Hipparcos" it was named for Hipparchus, the brilliant Greek astronomer of the second century B.C. Hipparchus is best remembered for his creation of instruments for making astronomical measurements. His instruments were used for seventeen hundred years before the invention of the telescope. With his basic tools, Hipparchus determined the distance to the moon as twenty-nine and one-half Earth-diameters away, very close to today's accepted value of thirty Earth-diameters. Hipparchus also constructed an atlas of the stars and categorized the stars by brightness.

Hipparcos, a half-ton satellite, was propelled into space by an Ariane **rocket.** Because of a faulty launch engine, *Hipparcos* was not boosted high enough to reach its intended orbit. Instead, it fell into a lower orbit around the Earth that resulted in the planned two and one-half year mission being extended to four years.

Astronomers are now in the process of compiling the data collected by *Hipparcos.* The *Hipparcos* catalogue, as it will be called, is expected to shed new light on the structure of the universe and our place within it.

Hogg, Helen Sawyer (1905–)

American astronomer

Helen Sawyer was first introduced to stargazing by her mother when she was a child. These early sessions plus an astronomy class at Mount Holyoke College in South Hadley, Massachusetts, led Sawyer to her life's work of studying the **cosmos.** Sawyer went to graduate school at Radcliffe College in Cambridge, Massachusetts, and while there began working with Harvard professor Harlow Shapley on a study of **globular cluster**s, clusters of stars within a **galaxy.**

The main reason astronomers find globular clusters interesting is that they contain **cepheid variable** stars. Cepheid variables are considered to be "astronomical yardsticks" because they can be used to determine distances in space. Shapley was using globular clusters to measure the size of the **Milky Way** galaxy. He found that our galaxy is much larger than previously believed and that the sun is not at its center.

While at Harvard, Sawyer met her future husband, Frank Hogg, who was researching **stellar spectrophotometry,** the **spectra** of light given off by stars. She combined his specialty with her own work on globular clusters and spent countless hours making long time-exposure photographs of globular clusters. In the process she discovered 142 new **variable star**s.

Variable stars change in brightness over time. For most stars these changes occur very slowly, over a period of months or even years. For other variables the changes occur in a matter of hours. Cepheid variables, blinking yellow **supergiant** stars, are a special class of variables. A cepheid's period of light variation is related to its brightness at a constant distance from Earth, which is the reason astronomers use these stars as mile-markers in space.

In 1939, Helen Sawyer Hogg created the first complete listing of the known 1,116 variable stars in our galaxy. In 1955, she updated this catalogue, adding 329 new variables, one-third of which she had discovered herself.

See also **Shapley, Harlow** and **Variable stars**

Hooker Telescope

The Hooker Telescope is one of the oldest and largest telescopes still in operation today. It was completed in 1917 at Mount Wilson Observatory, located in the San Gabriel Mountains outside of Pasadena, California. With a primary mirror 100 inches (254 centimeters) in diameter, the Hooker was the world's largest and most powerful telescope for its first thirty years.

It was at the Hooker Telescope that astronomer Edwin Hubble made his revolutionary discovery that there are **galaxies** in the universe outside of our own **Milky Way.** He also determined that these galaxies are moving away from one another. These findings led to two conclusions: first, that the universe is a much larger place than previously thought; and second, that it is expanding.

The Hooker Telescope was the brainchild of pioneering astronomer and director of the Mount Wilson Observatory, George Hale. Hale was the driving force behind the creation of four telescopes, each surpassing the last as the world's largest.

Hale's first record-breaking telescope was the 40-inch (102-centimeter) **refractor telescope** at Yerkes Observatory in Wisconsin. Hale served as director at Yerkes between 1877 and 1903. In his next position, at Mount Wilson in 1908, Hale assembled a **reflector telescope** with a 60-inch-diameter (152-centimeter-diameter) mirror.

The success of that project led to his planning an even bigger telescope, one initially designed to have an 84-inch (213-centimeter) mirror. A grant from John D. Hooker, philanthropist and founder of the California Academy of Science, however, allowed for the construction of a telescope with a 100-inch (254-centimeter) mirror. Subjected to building delays due to World War I, the Hooker Telescope took nearly ten years to complete.

Telescope-builders encountered numerous obstacles in trying to cast a mirror of the size needed for the Hooker. They had to use three different ladles to pour the melted glass, which created temperature differences, resulting in the formation of bubbles in the hardened glass. It took four attempts in order to produce a suitable disk. The next stage—the grinding and polishing of the glass into a mirror—took six years.

In 1917, a worried group of astronomers at Mount Wilson prepared to test the new instrument. To their dismay, they found the telescope did not function at all. They then realized that the problem was a temperature factor, since the dome had been left open all day. Once the dome had cooled to nighttime temperatures, they tested the telescope again. This time it worked beautifully.

Hale's fourth telescope, which was completed in 1947, ten years after his death, bears his name. The 200-inch (508-centimeter) Hale Telescope was constructed at Palomar Observatory, some 90 miles (140 kilometers) from Mount Wilson.

The Hooker Telescope remains to this day Mount Wilson's primary instrument. It has been in use continuously except for the period from 1985 to 1995, when it was being refurbished. Recently it was equipped with an advanced form of technology known as **adaptive optics**—a system that makes minute adjustments to the shape of the mirror within hundredths of a second, to correct distortions that result from disturbances in the atmosphere.

See also **Hale, George**; **Hale Telescope**; **Mount Wilson Observatory**; and **Optical telescope**

Hoyle, Fred (1915–)
English astronomer

Fred Hoyle was born in Yorkshire, England. He attended Emmanuel College at Cambridge and was then hired to teach mathematics at Cambridge University. Later he moved to the United States to take a job as a professor of astronomy and philosophy at Cornell University in Ithaca, New York.

Hoyle has made detailed studies of the nuclear reactions that take place in the core of a star. He has also researched the gravitational, electrical, and nuclear fields of stars and the various elements formed within them.

Hoyle has written several books on stars, both technical and for general readers, as well as a number of science fiction stories and even a script for an opera.

In 1948, Hoyle joined the debate between steady-state and big bang theorists on how the universe began. He wrote several books siding with steady-state proponents Thomas Gold and Hermann Bondi. The **steady-state theory** claims that the universe has always been essentially the same as it is today, and that it will continue that way forever. Taking into account proof that the universe is expanding, the theory states that as matter

Fred Hoyle relaxes at home, October 1964.

in space moves apart, new matter is created to fill in the gaps. Hoyle calculated that only one new atom per century would have to be added to a structure the size of a skyscraper to keep pace with the expansion of the universe. The theory also states that as older **galaxies** die, new galaxies take their place, and that the structure of the universe is unaffected.

The **big bang theory,** ironically, got its name from an off-hand remark made by Hoyle on a radio show in England. Hoyle was not very happy about this turn of events and avoided the term from then on. The big bang theory describes a universe that was born many billions of years ago from a single point that exploded in a "big bang." Out of this explosion came the building blocks of stars, planets, and other celestial bodies. This theory, which includes the notion of a constantly evolving universe, was bolstered by Edwin Hubble, who in 1929, found proof that all matter in space is moving away from all other matter.

Hoyle found it impossible personally to accept the concept that the universe was created instantly, out of nothing, by a mysterious bang. He thought the idea that matter was created continuously over time was more realistic.

For two decades, the steady-state and big bang theories were considered equally valid explanations as to how the universe began. But then three pieces of new evidence shifted the balance toward the big bang theory.

The first piece of evidence was the discovery of **quasar**s in 1963. These extremely bright objects occur only at the farthest reaches from Earth. The fact that they are not scattered throughout the universe suggests that they must have been formed long ago and not continuously over time, as the steady-state theory would dictate.

The next year, radio astronomers found proof of the "big bang" itself. They found a background radiation temperature in the universe of about 3 degrees above **absolute zero.** This temperature is just what astronomer George Gamow had predicted, assuming that a big bang had occurred billions of years ago. Hoyle remained skeptical, however, and suggested that the observed radiation was coming from another universe bordering on our own.

The most important piece of evidence was found in 1992, when the National Aeronautics and Space Administration's *Cosmic Background Explorer* (*COBE*) satellite looked fifteen billion **light-year**s into space (the same as looking fifteen billion years into the past) and detected tiny temperature changes in the cosmic background radiation. This evidence points to gravitational disturbances in the early universe, or proof that the universe has changed over time.

This last piece of evidence appears to have seriously weakened the steady-state theory for the explanation of how the universe began, at least for now.

Hoyle has also offered theories about how both the **solar system** and life on Earth began. He proposes that the solar system was formed out of the remains of an exploded star that was once paired with our sun. And he believes that life on Earth began with organic compounds found in the **interstellar medium,** that were carried to Earth by **comet**s.

See also **Big bang theory**; *Cosmic Background Explorer*; **Gamow, George**; **Gold, Thomas**; and **Steady-state theory**

Hubble, Edwin (1889–1953)

American astronomer

Edwin Powell Hubble's work profoundly changed our concept of the universe and our place in it. He was the first astronomer to detect **galaxies** outside of our own, opening our eyes to the reality that the **Milky Way** is just one galaxy among many. The presence of other galaxies also meant that the universe is much larger than anyone had previously imagined. Hubble reshaped our understanding of the **cosmos** in much the same way that Copernicus did when he announced that the Earth was not the center of the **solar system.**

Hubble was born in Marshfield, Missouri. He was awarded a scholarship to the University of Chicago, where he studied with physicist Robert A. Millikan (known for his work on **cosmic rays**) and astronomer George Hale. Hubble's first love was football, but his mother talked him out of playing the sport in college. Hubble was also a powerful boxer, and he continued to participate in that sport for many years. He even received a challenge one from world heavyweight champion Jack Johnson, which he did not accept.

After completing degrees in mathematics and astronomy, Hubble went to Oxford University in England as a Rhodes scholar, where he studied law. That experience left him speaking with an English accent for the rest of his life.

Hubble returned to the United States in 1913 and set up a law office in Louisville, Kentucky. But his old interests kept tugging at him and the next year he closed up shop and returned to the University of Chicago to begin a graduate program in astronomy. Hubble later compared astronomy to religion and said that after practicing law for a year he "got the calling" for astronomy.

After earning his Ph.D., Hubble was offered a job at Mount Wilson Observatory in California by his old professor George Hale. He accepted the position, but World War I broke out and Hubble enlisted in the army. Hubble served for two years in France and was wounded in the arm before he came back to Mount Wilson in 1919. He arrived just as the Hooker Telescope (the world's largest at 100 inches, or 254 centimeters, across) was completed and ready for use.

Before Hubble's time, scientists had assumed that the Milky Way was the only galaxy and that it measured only a few thousand **light-year**s across. The Hooker telescope and other powerful telescopes created in the 1920s were instrumental in changing this notion. It was while looking through the Hooker telescope that Hubble and his assistant Milton Humason discovered dozens of galaxies.

Hubble Studies Nebulae

At Mount Wilson, Hubble resumed the study of **nebula**e (clouds of gas and dust) he had begun as a graduate student. In an effort to determine the nature of these fuzzy spots of light, he photographed them, broke down the light they produced into its component wavelengths, studied their shapes, and kept careful notes. The most significant question that arose during this research was whether or not these nebulae were part of our galaxy.

To answer this question, Hubble identified twelve **cepheid variable** stars in one nebula in a region of space called "Andromeda." Astronomers Henrietta Swan Leavitt and Harlow Shapley had recently demonstrated how to use cepheids (blinking yellow **supergiant**s) as distance markers. Hubble applied their discoveries to determine the distance to his twelve stars and learned that they were at least eight hundred thousand light-years away. This distance was much greater than the farthest reaches of the Milky Way. Thus he concluded that the Andromeda was a separate galaxy.

Hubble went on to study and describe all the galaxies he could find. He divided them into two categories based on their shape: spiral and elliptical (oval). He also studied their locations and discovered that they were distributed evenly in space.

Opposite page:
Edwin Hubble looks
through the 48-inch
(122-centimeter)
Oschin Telescope at
Palomar
Observatory in June
1949.

Humason photographed the distant galaxies and studied the range of wavelengths of light they emitted. He found that the light from distant galaxies is shifted toward the red end of the visible **spectrum,** which indicated they were moving away from the observer. This indicator of motion is called **red-shift.** Further study showed that some of these galaxies were moving at a rate of one-seventh the **speed of light.**

In 1929, Hubble developed a famous equation that has come to be known as **Hubble's Law.** Hubble's Law says that the more distant a galaxy is, the faster it is moving away from our galaxy. The law is important, therefore, because it describes the expansion of the universe.

The information collected by Hubble and Humason supported the **big bang theory** of the beginning of the universe. The movement of galaxies away from one another is consistent with the idea that the universe began as a single point, billions of years ago, and that a huge explosion resulted in matter being created and scattered over great distances. The work of these two astronomers is widely credited with ushering in the era of modern **cosmology,** the study of the origin, evolution, and structure of the universe.

In 1949, a telescope twice as powerful as the Hooker, called the Hale Telescope, went into operation at another California observatory, Palomar Observatory. German-born American astronomer Walter Baade used it to measure more accurately the distance to the Andromeda galaxy and found it was about two million light-years away, or more than twice the distance Hubble had thought.

This discovery had implications beyond the Andromeda galaxy. If this particular galaxy was farther away, then the galaxies moving away from it were also farther away, indicating that the universe was even larger than Hubble had thought. And since looking at Andromeda two million light-years away is like looking two million years into the past, scientists had to conclude that the universe was also older than previously estimated.

Around this time, Hubble's health began to fail. While preparing for an excursion to Mount Palomar, the sixty-four-year-old Hubble suffered a stroke and died.

Edwin Hubble's name lives on in the Hubble Space Telescope, an observatory in space launched by the National Aeronautics and Space Administration (NASA) in 1990. In early 1996, this telescope made photographs of fifteen hundred very distant galaxies in the process of formation, indicating that the number of galaxies in the universe is far greater than anyone had ever predicted. Astronomers now estimate the number of galaxies to be approximately fifty billion.

See also **Andromeda galaxy**; **Baade, Walter**; **Big bang theory**; **Galaxy**; and **Hubble Space Telescope**

Hubble Space Telescope

In April 1990, the Hubble Space Telescope (HST) was launched by the **space shuttle** *Discovery.* Two months later, a serious flaw was discovered in the telescope's mirror. The HST, which once promised to revolutionize our view of the universe, instead earned the nickname "techno-turkey" and was viewed by critics as an example of wasted tax dollars. Three years later, however, the problem was corrected by astronauts from the space shuttle *Endeavour.* The HST now functions even better than originally intended. It produces spectacular views of **galaxies** and **nebula**e and a host of objects at a greater distance than we have ever seen before.

The original proposal for a telescope in space was drawn up by National Aeronautics and Space Administration (NASA) officials in the early 1970s. Congressional complaints over the project's complexity and cost led to the development of a less ambitious plan in 1976. The modified plan was then accepted by Congress. The decision was then made to name the **space telescope** for Edwin Hubble, the astronomer who first discovered the existence of galaxies outside our own. The following year, the European Space Agency (ESA) joined the United States as a partner, with an agreement to supply 15 percent of the equipment needed for the HST in exchange for 15 percent of the observing time.

In 1985, after eight years of construction, the 1.5 billion dollar HST was ready for launch. But then, in January 1986, came the explosion of the space shuttle *Challenger,* an accident that led to the grounding of the entire shuttle fleet for the next two years and eight months. The HST launch was delayed until April 24, 1990, when it was finally granted a spot on the space shuttle *Discovery.*

Problems With the HST Mirror

That June, NASA scientists learned that the telescope had a tiny but significant flaw. The curve in its 94.5-inch-diameter (240-centimeter-diameter) main mirror was off by just a fraction of a hair's width. Yet that flaw was enough to cause light to reflect away from the center of the mirror. As a result of this problem, the HST produced blurry images. Although certain experiments could still be carried out, the situation was clearly a disappointment to those who had eagerly anticipated receiving the clearest pictures yet of the universe.

Plans were quickly devised to fix the telescope. Principal among these plans was the development of Corrective Optics Space Telescope Axial Replacement (COSTAR), a group of three coin-sized mirrors that, when placed around the main mirror, bring the light into proper focus.

The necessary repairs to HST were made in early December 1993 by four astronauts from the space shuttle *Endeavour.* They caught up with the HST two days after the launch of *Endeavour* and pulled it into the shuttle's cargo bay. Alternating pairs of astronauts then spent nearly a week fixing the telescope. In addition to attaching COSTAR, the astronauts in-

*Photo taken of the
Hubble Space
Telescope during a
servicing mission.*

stalled a new camera and solar arrays (for power generation), and replaced two pairs of **gyroscope**s.

For the next two weeks, while the instruments adjusted to new atmospheric conditions, scientists anxiously awaited the results. Then at one o'clock in the morning on December 18, scientists at the Space Telescope Science Institute in Baltimore, Maryland, crowded into a room to catch a glimpse of Hubble's first post-operation image. A crystal-clear star appeared on the monitor and cheers filled the air. In a published report, Hubble program scientist Edward Weiler said that the telescope had been "fixed beyond our wildest expectations."

Now the HST regularly makes headlines with its startling discoveries. For instance, it has captured detailed images of stars in various stages of evolution, from newborns still surrounded by dusty disks, to those in the last throes of life casting off their atmospheres. It has detected about fifteen hundred extremely old, distant galaxies in a patch of space that was previously considered "empty." Presently, scientists are using the HST to measure distances to other galaxies in order to come up with a precise value for the Hubble constant, the rate at which the universe is expanding. Given that value, they will be able to determine, with greater accuracy than ever before, the age of the universe.

See also Endeavour; **Hubble, Edwin**; **Space telescope**; and **Stellar evolution**

Huggins, William (1824–1910)
English astronomer

William Huggins was the father of stellar **spectroscopy,** the study of light given off by stars. In 1856, he built his own observatory and began photographing stars in order to break their light down into its component wavelengths.

Visible light includes a **spectrum** of colors with red on one end and violet on the other (the colors of the rainbow). Atoms give off and absorb light at various wavelengths. A **spectroscope,** a simple instrument containing a prism surrounded by two lenses, produces a spectrum of the light that enters its chamber. The spectrum can either appear as a series of dark lines indicating the wavelengths at which the light is or absorbed, or a series of bright lines indicating the wavelengths at which light is emitted. The light of an element, when passed through a spectroscope, produces a signature spectrum that identifies the element. In the same manner, the spectrum of starlight indicates which elements are present in a star's atmosphere.

Huggins used a spectroscope to determine that celestial bodies contain some of the same elements that exist on Earth. For instance, he found oxygen present in the spectrum of a star and carbon compounds in the spectrum of a **comet.** Likewise, he studied the spectrum of a **nova** (a star that suddenly becomes very bright) and found that it contained hydrogen. These findings disproved the hypothesis, made by Aristotle twenty-one hundred years earlier, that objects in space were made of a special material not found on Earth.

Huggins observed the spectrum of a bright patch in the sky called a **nebula** and learned that it was made up of gasses, not stars, as had always been assumed. He was not successful, however, in his attempt to study the **spectra** of planets. The reason for this failure is that planets do not generate their own light, but merely reflect the sun's light.

William Huggins.

Huggins was among the first to use time-exposure photographs. This method allows light from a faint object to be collected over a long period of time, thus magnifying its brightness. In this way he was able to record the spectra of very distant matter, including stars, comets, nebulae, and others.

By obtaining the spectrum of an object, Huggins showed, one can also determine its movement. He was able to detect motion by studying any shift of **absorption lines,** toward one end or the other of the spectrum. Huggins found that when light waves given off by an object are shifted toward the red end of the visible light spectrum, this means the object is moving away from the observer. Just the opposite is true for a **blue-shift**ed object. It is moving closer. Huggins also established that the degree of shift indicates the object's speed.

See also **Spectroscopy**

Humason, Milton (1891–1972)

American astronomer

Milton La Salle Humason, equipped with only persistence, a pleasant personality, and a devotion to astronomy, overcame his lack of education to become one of this country's most noteworthy astronomers. Originally from Dodge Center, Minnesota, Humason attended summer camp at Mount Wilson Observatory in California when he was fourteen years old. Humason was so fascinated by what he saw that he soon dropped out of school and returned to the mountain.

For a few years, Humason worked as a mule driver, bringing supplies up and down the mountain. In 1911, he left the observatory and went to work for a relative. However, a notice that the observatory was seeking a janitor brought him back six years later. Humason's interest in astronomy came to the attention of astronomers George Hale and Edwin Hubble, who hired him as a member of the science staff.

Humason's first project, to search for a planet beyond Neptune, was not successful. He was actually searching the correct part of the sky, but could not see Pluto because of a defect in his equipment.

Humason is best known for his work with Hubble on the discovery of **galaxies** outside of the **Milky Way** and the gathering of information supporting the theory that universe was expanding.

Humason was assigned to assist Hubble by photographing hundreds of distant galaxies and determining the speed at which they were moving away from one another. The speed with which a galaxy is moving can be determined by observing the light **spectrum** emitted by a galaxy. The degree to which the spectrum is shifted toward the red end (known as the **red-shift**) indicates the speed at which a galaxy is moving away from us.

Photographing the galaxies was in itself no easy task. After finding a faint galaxy among the billions of stars, Humason had to position a **spectroscope** carefully and hold it steady all night long. For the faintest galaxies this took even longer, sometimes several nights. Humason had to withstand cold weather and fatigue to get the job done.

In 1956, Humason, working with others, refined **Hubble's Law.** This law defines a distance-to-speed relationship, showing that the more distant a galaxy is, the faster it is moving away from our galaxy. Humason and his colleagues updated this law take into account the idea that galaxies traveled at faster speeds in the distant past. It makes the law more consistent with the **big bang theory** of the beginning of the universe.

Humason is probably the only person in recent history to progress from mule driver to janitor to full astronomer at one of the world's most prestigious observatories.

See also **Hubble, Edwin**

Huygens, Christiaan (1629–1695)
Dutch astronomer, physicist, and mathematician

Although Christiaan Huygens did not receive much attention during his lifetime, he is recognized today as one of the most brilliant scientists in history. His work was crucial to the development of the modern sciences of mechanics, physics, and astronomy.

Huygens was born in The Hague, Netherlands, in 1629. His father, a diplomat and poet, believed in the value of a classical education and arranged for Huygens' private training in mathematics, languages, literature, and music. René Descartes, the famous mathematician-philosopher, was a family friend and taught the young Huygens about the "mechanistic" philosophy of nature. That philosophy says that occurrences are caused by matter influencing other matter. Descartes convinced Huygens that all the great mysteries of nature would one day be explained by science.

Christiaan Huygens.

At age sixteen, Huygens left home to attend college, but was not satisfied with the education he received at two different Dutch institutions. Four years later, he returned to his home town. Supported by his wealthy father, he began conducting his own research in astronomy, physics, and applied mathematics.

One of his first and most successful projects was grinding telescope lenses. By 1655, he had produced lenses of the highest clarity. Looking through his lenses, he discovered a large moon circling Saturn, which he named Titan.

Huygens then began placing his lenses into very long telescopes—up to 23 feet (7 meters) in length—resulting in even greater magnification. Using these instruments, he was able to chart the surface features of Mars. He also discovered the Great Orion **nebula,** a multi-colored cloud of hot gas in the Orion **constellation.**

Perhaps Huygens' greatest accomplishment using the long telescopes was his discovery of Saturn's ring. To less sophisticated telescopes, the ring appeared as two small planets, one on either side of Saturn. Huygens wrote in 1658: "It [Saturn] is surrounded by a thin, flat ring, nowhere touching, and inclined to the ecliptic." (The ecliptic is the orbital plane in which all the planets except Pluto travel as they orbit around the sun.)

Astronomers at the time, however, were skeptical about this theory. Huygens studied Saturn over a period of time and explained how the changing angle of the planet's tilt (relative to Earth as both planets revolved around the sun) caused the ring's changing appearance. He predicted that in the summer of 1671 Saturn's ring would be inclined so that it would be edge-on to Earth, and that such a thin slice would not be visible using telescopes of the day. He was correct, and thus had proved his "ring" theory correct.

Huygens' Research On Clocks

Also in the 1660s, Huygens was working on the development of an accurate clock. Ships' navigators needed timepieces on which they could rely, and up until that point, clocks were very inaccurate. Existing clocks were operated by a weight that fell slowly but irregularly, causing gears to turn and move the clock's hands.

Huygens experimented with a theory developed by Galileo Galilei years earlier, suggesting that a swinging pendulum would take the same amount of time to move in one direction as it did to return (an effect Galileo called isochronicity). Galileo felt that a pendulum could be used to keep time but was unable to prove it.

Huygens discovered that isochronicity could be achieved only if the arc made by a swinging pendulum was not quite circular. He then built a pendulum into a weight-driven clock. The pendulum swung exactly once each second, regulating the movement of the clock's hands. A falling weight drove the gears and kept the pendulum from being slowed down by air resistance and friction. Pendulum clocks, and the grandfather clock design in particular, caught on quickly throughout Europe.

Through his experiments with pendulums, Huygens learned more general facts about motion and the forces that act upon a moving object. He developed the Law of the Conservation of Momentum, which says that the energy of a moving object remains constant until the object is stopped or its direction is changed.

Huygens' later work involved the nature of light. During Huygens' lifetime, most European scientists, including Isaac Newton, suggested that light was composed of particles. Using a prism to split light into the colors of the rainbow, Newton concluded that white light must be the result of all the colored particles of light coming together in a vacuum. Huygens, remembering Descartes' mechanistic philosophy of nature, said that it was highly unlikely that a group of particles would independently assemble in a vacuum. In 1690, Huygens suggested instead that light was made up of a series of waves, similar to sound waves, that traveled through an invisible substance called ether.

Very few scientists at the time believed Huygens' wave theory of light, particularly the part about ether. Newton had become a very important figure in the scientific community and his particle theory was the most widely accepted explanation of the nature of light. It was not until the nineteenth century that another scientist, Thomas Young, picked up where Huygens left off with the wave theory. But this time he left out the concept of ether.

At the time of Huygens' death, his work was all but forgotten. He was a recluse who took no students and rarely published his work. His accomplishments were dwarfed by those of Galileo and Newton, two giants who were making history with their discoveries immediately before and after Huygens. It was not until many years later that Huygens was recognized for his substantial contributions to science.

See also **Saturn**

Hypatia of Alexandria (A.D. 370–415)
Greek mathematician and philosopher

Although much information is missing about the life of Hypatia of Alexandria, she is regarded as the only important female scholar of ancient times. Hypatia, who lived at a time when women were treated as property, broke free from the norm and became the first woman to teach and analyze highly advanced mathematics.

Historians believe that Hypatia's father, Theon of Alexandria, was her teacher. Theon was the last recorded member of the Museum of Alexandria, the great learning center in Egypt resembling a large modern university with several schools, public auditoriums, and a famous library. Scholars came to the museum from all across the Roman Empire, Africa, India, southern Europe, and the Middle East to pore through the largest collection of books in the world, to listen to lectures, and to debate the latest philosophical and scientific theories. From the time of its construction in the third century B.C. until its destruction seven hundred years later, the museum was probably the world's most important scholarly institution.

Hypatia became a teacher at one of the museum's schools, called the Neoplatonic School of Philosophy, and became its director in the year 400. She was famous for her lively lectures and her books and articles on mathematics, philosophy, and a number of other subjects.

Although very few written records remain, it appears that Hypatia invented or helped invent the **astrolabe,** an instrument used by astronomers to observe the positions of the stars. With some adjustments, the astrolabe has also been used for timekeeping, navigation, and surveying.

Hypatia of Alexandria.

It is likely that Hypatia worked on this project and others with Synesius of Cyrene, a scholar who had attended Hypatia's classes. Letters from Synesius to Hypatia that have survived the years indicate that the two of them also worked together to invent a brass hydrometer (used to measure specific **gravity,**) and a hydroscope (used to observe objects under water).

Hypatia was the last scientist to work at the museum's library. Her life came to a terrible end at the age of forty-five, when she was murdered by an angry mob. Although no one is sure of the reason for this attack, many historians believe that members of Alexandria's Christian community disliked Hypatia for her independence and her pagan beliefs. Another theory suggests that she was caught up in a political and religious rivalry between Orestes, the pagan

**Hypatia of
Alexandria**

governor of Alexandria of whom she was a vocal supporter, and Cyril, the city's bishop.

After Hypatia's death, her works were destroyed along with those of many other great thinkers when mobs burned the library. The record of her life and accomplishments has only been pieced together from letters between Hypatia and her colleagues.

See also **Ancient Greek astronomy**

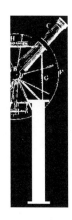

Inflationary theory

The **inflationary theory** is a recent addition to the **big bang theory.** It attempts to answer questions such as why matter is so evenly distributed throughout the universe. It was developed in 1980 by American astronomer Alan Guth and says, in short, that at its earliest stages, the universe expanded at a rate much faster than it is expanding today.

The big bang theory states that the universe began as a single point billions of years ago, and that a huge explosion resulted in matter being created and scattered over great distances. The first proof of this theory was offered in the 1920s by American astronomer Edwin Hubble, who showed that **galaxies** are moving away from one another and that the universe is expanding.

In the 1960s, Russian-born American astronomer George Gamow predicted that the big bang itself would have left traces of background radiation that could be detected even after many billions of years. He estimated that the radiation, by the present time, would have cooled to just a few degrees above **absolute zero.** He was later proven correct when astronomers Arno Penzias and Robert Wilson discovered that the universe has a background temperature of about -274 degrees Fahrenheit (-273 degrees Celsius), or about 3 degrees above absolute zero.

Twenty years later at Stanford University, Guth suggested that in the split-second following the big bang (the inflationary period), the universe ballooned out in all directions, becoming many billions of times its original size. This ballooning, the theory goes, occurred due to a tiny change in an energy field in the vacuum of space. It resulted in the creation of both the observable universe (the fifteen billion or so light years in all directions that can be observed from Earth) and the invisible universe (which we cannot detect but is many times the size of the observable universe and could be made up of anything, even anti-matter particles).

The idea that we can look only at a small slice of the universe explains why space appears "flat" to us. The universe is thought to be curved, perhaps with a spherical shape, like the Earth. But also like on Earth, the small area visible from any one point appears to be flat.

The inflationary theory also addresses the question of **homogeneity,** or sameness, of temperature and density in space, wherever you look. Galaxies, for instance, are evenly distributed throughout the observable universe. This fact has long had scientists wondering how matter could have interacted to become evenly placed throughout the huge expanse of the universe.

According to the inflationary theory, the universe was the size of a proton just before the inflation. Within this space were trillions of particles, all interacting to produce the big bang. The rest of the particles that eventually came together to form objects came from the energy released in the explosion. Thus, the theory goes, all matter in the observable universe began at the same place and was evenly spread out as that place inflated.

In 1984, the inflationary theory was further refined by A. D. Linde, Paul J. Steinhardt, and Andreas Albrecht, three astronomers who calculated that the period of ballooning-out was longer than Guth had stated. This theory closely matches what is continuously being learned about the universe, and is widely accepted among astronomers.

See also **Big bang theory**

Infrared Astronomical Satellite

Opposite page:
*The Infrared
Astronomical
Satellite undergoes
integration and
testing in the
Netherlands, 1983.*

In 1983, an international group consisting of the United States, Great Britain, and the Netherlands launched into orbit its Infrared Astronomical Satellite (IRAS). Over a span of seven months, IRAS surveyed the entire sky twice, discovering nearly 250 objects (including many new infrared **galaxies**) and learning about the formation of planets and stars. After that,

the satellite ran out of coolant and ceased to function. The coolant was needed to keep the instruments on board from overheating. Once it was used up, the mission was over.

IRAS and other infrared satellites constitute the space-based portion of the relatively new field of **infrared astronomy.** Scientists have long known that **electromagnetic radiation** in the infrared wavelength range is emitted by many objects in space and that an infrared picture of the sky would differ greatly from the image produced by visible light. Simple devices were invented in the 1960s and 1970s to measure a narrow wavelength range of **infrared radiation,** but those devices were laborious in exposure time and in the piecing together of thousands of images into a single image. It was not until the early 1980s that the technology was available to make a much more complete study of the infrared sky. And whereas ground-based telescopes, particularly those placed at high altitudes, can find relatively strong sources of infrared radiation, their space-based counterparts have produced results nothing short of spectacular.

The main instrument aboard IRAS was a 23-inch-wide (58-centimeter-wide) **reflector telescope,** which detected the infrared radiation and displayed it on sixty-four semiconductor panels. Since infrared radiation is essentially heat and the instruments had to be kept cool, the equipment area was surrounded by a large flask of liquid helium. Liquid helium absorbs heat and then boils away, little at a time. To slow the boiling process, keeping the instruments cool as long as possible, the entire flask was wrapped in many layers of insulation and covered by a sunshade. The helium, in this design, was supposed to last three hundred days, but was actually used up in about two-thirds of that time.

Discoveries Made by IRAS

One of IRAS' most important finds was regions of the **Milky Way** in which new stars are being formed. Such regions are known as **stellar nurseries.** The satellite first located numerous bright glowing clouds of heated dust, but its instruments were only able to penetrate partway. Radiation from young stars was blocked by dust at the center of the clouds. Astronomers then used Earth-based infrared detectors to examine the cores of those clouds. The Earth-based instruments were more efficient in this case. This is because the IRAS' detectors were tuned to radiation in the longest end of the range of infrared wavelengths (called "far-infrared" wavelengths). The infrared light at the cores of the clouds shines in "near-infrared" wavelengths. Thus, the ground-based telescopes that were tuned to near-infrared wavelengths were able to penetrated the cores. In this way, the ground telescopes were able to construct complete images of several stellar nurseries and gained a much better understanding of the evolution of our galaxy.

IRAS also discovered six new **comet**s and huge invisible tails on the previously discovered Comet Tempel-2. Particularly exciting finds included a number of dust shells, each surrounding an individual star, that may have something to do with the formation of planets. Finally, IRAS learned that many galaxies are strong sources of infrared radiation and that some, called starburst galaxies, shine even more brightly in infrared light than they do in visible light.

The United States provided the telescope for this international project, as well as the launch site. The Netherlands produced the spacecraft and certain on-board equipment. Great Britain was responsible for tracking and controlling IRAS, once it reached orbit. The data from IRAS was analyzed and compiled into catalogues at the National Aeronautics and Space Administration's Jet Propulsion Laboratory in California.

In late 1995, the European Space Agency (ESA) launched the Infrared Space Observatory (ISO) to continue the work begun by IRAS.

See also **Infrared astronomy**; **Infrared Space Observatory**; and **Space telescope**

Infrared astronomy

The recent development of **infrared astronomy** has led to the discovery of many new stars, **galaxies, asteroid**s, and **quasar**s. Infrared astronomy involves the use of special telescopes that detect **electromagnetic radiation** at infrared wavelengths. Although astronomers had long known about the potential of studying space by means of infrared waves, the necessary equipment was not produced until the 1970s. Then in the 1980s, large infrared detectors were developed for the military. Astronomers were able to modify these instruments for their own use, which vastly improved the quality of infrared astronomy technology.

Two types of infrared telescopes exist: those on the ground and those carried into space by satellites. The use of ground-based telescopes is somewhat limited because carbon dioxide and water in the atmosphere absorb much of the incoming **infrared radiation.** The best observations are made at high altitudes in places with dry climates. An obvious advantage of infrared telescopes over optical ones is that, since they are not picking up visible light, they can be used during the day as well as at night. This feature gives astronomers more time to make observations.

Infrared telescopes in space have the advantage of being able to pick up much of the infrared radiation that is blocked out by the Earth's atmosphere. In 1983, an international group made up of the United States, Great Britain, and the Netherlands, launched into orbit its Infrared Astronomical Satellite (IRAS). This satellite has uncovered never-before-seen parts of the **Milky Way.** Some of these areas had been hidden from view by clouds, but infrared radiation passes right through those clouds.

Discoveries With Infrared Telescopes

What astronomers found were areas where new stars are forming, known as **stellar nurseries.** IRAS first located numerous bright glowing clouds of heated dust, providing a partial view of the stars within. But the dust still hid from sight the center of the cloud, where stars are actually created. Astronomers were able to use Earth-based infrared detectors to penetrate the cores of the clouds IRAS had found. Scientists now have complete pictures of several stellar nurseries and a much better understanding of the evolution of galaxies.

With the aid of infrared telescopes, astronomers have also located a number of new galaxies, many too far away to be seen by visible light. Some of these are **dwarf galaxies,** which are more plentiful, but contain fewer stars, than visible galaxies. The discovery of dwarf galaxies has led to a new theory of galactic evolution. According to that theory, infrared dwarf galaxies once dominated the universe and then came together over time to form visible galaxies, like our own.

With the growing use of infrared astronomy, scientists have learned that galaxies contain many more stars than had ever been imagined. Infrared telescopes are able to detect radiation from relatively cool stars, which give off no visible light. Many of these stars are the size of the sun. These discoveries have drastically changed calculations made by scientists of the total **mass** in the universe.

Infrared detectors are also useful for observing far-away objects such as **quasar**s. Quasars have large **red-shift**s, which indicate that they are moving away from Earth at high speeds. In a red-shifted object, the waves of radiation are lengthened and shifted toward the red end of the **spec-**

trum. Since the red-shift of quasars is so great, their visible light gets stretched into infrared wavelengths. Whereas these infrared wavelengths are undetectable with optical telescopes, they are easily viewed with an infrared telescope.

See also **Infrared Astronomical Satellite**

Infrared Space Observatory

In November 1995, the European Space Agency (ESA) launched the most recent in a series of space-based infrared telescopes, the Infrared Space Observatory (ISO). This satellite project, which is expected to shed new light on the formation of the **solar system,** has attracted the participation of over one thousand astronomers from Europe, the United States, and Japan.

On November 28, ISO's telescope lens was uncovered for the first time. It immediately focused on the nearby Whirlpool **galaxy,** specifically on areas of star formation in the **spiral galaxy**'s arms. By the time ISO's mission is over in November 1997, it will have studied many objects within and beyond our galaxy, including several that are invisible to optical telescopes.

ISO is the successor to the Infrared Astronomical Satellite (IRAS), an orbiting infrared observatory launched in 1983 by the United States, Great Britain, and the Netherlands. Unlike IRAS, which undertook a general survey of the entire sky, ISO will study smaller regions in greater detail.

ISO, IRAS, and other satellite projects constitute the space-based portion of the relatively new field of **infrared astronomy.** By examining **electromagnetic radiation** in the infrared wavelength range, scientists obtain a much different picture of the sky than what can be seen in visible light. Whereas ground-based telescopes, particularly those placed at high altitudes, can find relatively strong sources of **infrared radiation,** their space-based counterparts can detect infrared light from a far greater range of sources and yield much sharper images.

The main instrument aboard ISO, like that on IRAS, is a 23-inch-wide (58-centimeter-wide) **reflector telescope** sensitive to infrared radiation. ISO also contains four other scientific instruments: a camera; a photometer, which measures the brightness and temperature of radiation at particular wavelengths; and two spectrometers, which break down incoming light and analyze the chemical composition of the objects producing the light. As with IRAS, ISO's instruments are cooled by a flask of liquid helium.

A highlight of ISO's early operation was the observation of a collision between two galaxies and the dust clouds formed during the collision. The dust clouds are visible only at infrared wavelengths. Astronomers believe that dust clouds formed in this way become breeding grounds for new stars, making them key elements in the evolution of galaxies. In one pair of colliding galaxies observed by ISO, the infrared emission was concentrated so heavily in such a small area of the sky, that astronomers suspect the presence of a **black hole.**

One of ISO's main objectives is to conduct a careful survey of star-forming regions in several galaxies. The reason for this objective, according to French astronomer Catherine Cesarsky, is that "Only by studying other galaxies can we fully understand our own galaxy, the **Milky Way,** and how it created conditions for life."

ISO is expected to cease functioning when its supply of liquid hydrogen runs out in November 1997.

See also **Infrared Astronomical Satellite**; **Infrared astronomy**; and **Space telescope**

Intelsat

In the early 1960s, the demand for global telephone and television connections was growing beyond the capability of existing technology. It was apparent that the trans-oceanic telephone lines and small communications satellites of individual nations were not sufficient for the continually increasing volume. Part of this need was addressed when the United States, in 1962, formed a worldwide communications satellite network of its own, called the Communications Satellite Corporation (Comsat).

Comsat, however, was never intended to serve the needs of the whole world. U.S. President John F. Kennedy recognized the need for a comprehensive, jointly owned international communications system in 1961, when he made a request for "the nations of the world to participate in a satellite system in the interests of world peace and closer brotherhood among people throughout the world." This statement led to the 1964 formation of the International Telecommunications Satellite Organization (Intelsat).

Intelsat has grown from its 11 original members to include, at present, over 130 nations. This non-profit organization now handles most of the world's international telephone and television communications, serving billions of people on every continent. If you have ever placed an overseas telephone call or watched the Olympics, tennis from Wimbledon, or news reports from Bosnia or the Middle East, then you have used Intelsat.

Intelsat consists of twenty satellites that circle the Earth in a **geosynchronous orbit,** a path that takes twenty-four hours to complete. Thus, each satellite always stays over a particular point on the Earth's surface and can receive signals from relay stations on the ground. Each satellite contains a receiver, an amplifier, and a transmitter, which are used to receive and send thousands of messages at a time.

An Intelsat 6 communications satellite.

Early Years of Intelsat

The first Intelsat satellite (and the world's first commercial communications satellite), called *Early Bird,* was launched in April 1965. It was a metal cylinder, just over 2 feet (0.6 meters) wide and 1.5 feet (0.5 meters) tall, encircled by a band of solar cells. This satellite, primitive by today's standards, could handle 240 telephone lines or 1 television channel at a time. *Early Bird* was in use for three-and-a-half years.

In 1967, three new satellites of the Intelsat 2 series were lifted into orbit. These were somewhat larger than the *Early Bird* and extended communications service to many parts of the world that the first satellite could not reach. The next year, in an attempt to keep pace with the growing demand for international communications, the first satellite of the Intelsat 3 series was launched. A total of eight satellites made up this series, although several of them experienced malfunctions. These satellites were each twice the size of one from the previous series and could manage 1,200 telephone calls or 4 television channels at a time.

Satellite design was revolutionized again in 1971 with the Intelsat 4 fleet. These machines stood over 16 feet (5 meters) tall with antennae extended and could carry 6,000 telephone circuits. Further, they were the first communication satellites capable of carrying color television signals. The more advanced models of the Intelsat 4A series began reaching orbit in 1975.

The 1980s saw the deployment of satellites of a different design. The Intelsat 5 satellites, instead of sporting the spinning drum configuration of earlier models, looked more like birds with long outstretched solar-panel wings. The extra power generated by this design enabled Intelsat 5 satellites to work harder. They could relay 15,000 telephone calls at a time. Between December 1980 and January 1989, thirteen of these satellites were successfully placed into orbit.

The five satellites of the Intelsat 6 group, which were launched between October 1989 and October 1991, returned to the cylindrical design. The second of that series, which malfunctioned, made headlines in May 1992 when it was repaired by the crew of the **space shuttle** *Endeavour.*

The most recent additions to the fleet have been the Intelsat 7 satellites. As of March 1996, seven of these had been lifted into orbit, with another one scheduled for launch in September 1996. These huge vessels, expected to last ten to fifteen years, can each handle up to 22,500 telephone calls and 3 television channels at a time, a huge advance from the *Early Bird*.

At present, eight satellites for the Intelsat 8 series are on order, due to be sent into space between summer 1996 and summer 1997.

See also **Communications satellite**

Interferometry

Scientists can accurately measure the dimensions of even the tiniest object using **interferometry.** This technique involves splitting a beam of light in two, bouncing both beams off a series of mirrors, and examining the pattern produced when the beams comes back together. If one beam is changed along its path, an interference pattern in the form of a series of colored lines, called spectral lines is produced. The spectral lines indicate the size of the object emitting the light, to the distance of a single wavelength. Interferometry can also be used to determine the size of distant stars and to measure the space between them.

The first interferometer was developed almost by accident in 1887 by American physicist Albert Michelson. Michelson and fellow scientist Edward Morley were attempting to prove that light travels through an invisible substance called ether, just as tides travel through water.

Although the experiments of Michelson and Morley failed to prove the existence of ether, they were an important step in the early development of the science of interferometry. Michelson had created an instrument capable of measuring distances with a high degree of accuracy. He recognized that interferometry had a range of uses.

One branch of interferometry, known as spatial interferometry, is applied primarily in the field of **radio astronomy,** but increasingly in optical astronomy, to provide a more detailed look at objects in space. This process requires a series of two or more telescopes, all focused on the same source. They are linked electronically so that the information collected by each one is transmitted to a central computer, which combines the data. The string of telescopes acts as a single telescope with a diameter equal to the area separating them. The result is an image with much finer detail than that of an image produced by any one telescope.

Perhaps the most famous **radio interferometer** in use today is the Very Large Array (VLA), constructed in 1977 in Socorro, New Mexico. The VLA of a series of twenty-seven **radio telescope**s, each about 75 feet (23 meters) in diameter. They move about on railroad tracks, arranged in a "Y" shape.

See also **Radio interferometer** and **Very Large Array**

International Space Station

The year 2002 is the scheduled grand opening of the International Space Station. Work is now proceeding on construction of the components for this permanent international laboratory in space. Once operational, six astronauts at a time will be able to spend periods of three to five months each, conducting scientific research on the **space station.**

The idea for this space station began with plans for a U.S. station, called *Freedom,* that never came to be. The creation of *Freedom* was first announced by President Ronald Reagan in 1984, who proposed that it be completed within the decade. At that time, it was estimated the station could be built for 8.5 billion dollars. It soon became apparent, however, that this price tag was grossly underestimated. Many congressional debates and budget cuts later, the project was canceled in the early 1990s.

National Aeronautics and Space Administration (NASA) officials then sought to do more with less by attracting international partners. As it now stands, the International Space Station is a joint venture of the United States, Russia, Canada, the fourteen member nations of the European Space Agency (ESA), and Japan. Thus far the other countries have pledged a total of 9 billion dollars, enabling the United States to reduce its own costs to 2.1 billion dollars annually.

In addition to most of the **space shuttle** flights for construction of the station, the United States is contributing the main laboratory, living quarters, and scientific equipment. Russia is supplying three research modules, a **service module** (containing controls and life support systems), a power generator, two Soyuz spacecraft that can be used for emergency evacuation, and training of astronauts on board its currently operating *Mir* space station. Canada is providing a robotic arm to be used for space station construction and repair. The ESA is furnishing a pressurized laboratory, and Japan is supplying a research laboratory.

The first portion of the space station is scheduled to be placed in orbit in November 1997. Seven months and four assembly missions later, the station should be ready for three people to begin living there. Scientific equipment is slated for delivery by the end of that year, at which point experiments can begin. After an estimated forty-four assembly missions, the station should be completed by June 2002. At that point it will measure 361 feet (110 meters) wide by 290 feet (88 meters) long and weigh 924,000 pounds (419,000 kilograms).

The scientific research to be conducted on the space station falls into three categories: medicine, industrial materials, and communications technology. Medical experiments will focus on the prevention and treatment of diseases of the heart, lungs, kidneys, bones, and brain, as well as studies of cancer, diabetes, immune system disorders, and other illnesses. The station will also be used for testing new polymers and combinations of metals that can be used for anything from contact lenses to building materials, and the development of semiconductors for high-speed supercomputers.

In addition to its obvious scientific merits, the International Space Station is being looked to as a model of international cooperation for the twenty-first century.

See also **Mir** **space station** and **Space station**

International Ultraviolet Explorer

The Earth's atmosphere provides an effective filter for many types of cosmic radiation, including **ultraviolet radiation.** This effect is crucial for the survival of life on Earth because unlimited exposure to ultraviolet radiation would kill all organisms. On the other hand, the filtering effect of the atmosphere prevents scientists from observing objects in space that emit light with ultraviolet wavelengths. To overcome this problem, astronomers have placed ultraviolet telescopes, such as the International Ultraviolet Explorer (IUE), directly into space.

The IUE was launched on January 26, 1978, into a **geosynchronous orbit** 2,700 miles (4,344 kilometers) over the Atlantic Ocean. A geosynchronous orbit is one in which an object travels around the Earth in the same time that it takes the Earth to rotate once on its axis. Thus, the object always remains in the same position relative to any given point on the Earth's surface. This joint project of the United States, Great Britain, and the European Space Agency (ESA), was intended to function for only

**I n t e r -
n a t i o n a l
U l t r a v i o l e t
E x p l o r e r**

three to five years. Now in its eighteenth year of continuous operation, IUE holds the title of longest-lived astronomical satellite.

The IUE has provided a wealth of information on planets, stars, **galaxies, comet**s, the **interstellar medium,** and **quasar**s. It has also made detailed studies of **nova**e, **supernova**e, and the July 1994 collision of Comet Shoemaker-Levy with Jupiter.

International Support for the IUE

The idea of a space-based ultraviolet telescope was first proposed by professor Bob Wilson and his team at University College, London, in 1964 to the European Space Research Organization (ESRO), the forerunner to ESA. But the idea was rejected because of its cost. A scaled-down version of the project was again turned down in 1968. NASA became interested in the project at that time as a way to bridge the gap in ultraviolet astronomy experiments between the early ultraviolet satellites and the Hubble Space Telescope, slated for launch in the 1990s. Thus, in 1972, NASA made an agreement with Great Britain to build the IUE. A year later, ESRO joined the project. (ESRO's place was taken by ESA upon the latter agency's formation in 1975).

NASA agreed to provide much of the financing and the work for the project, including building the telescope and the 13.75-foot-long (4.2-meter-long) spacecraft, launching the spacecraft, and contributing a ground station at the Goddard Space Flight Center in Greenbelt, Maryland. ESA provided the solar panels (the IUE's power source) and contributed a second ground station, the Villafranca Satellite Tracking Station in Madrid, Spain. Great Britain supplied the ultraviolet detectors and data-analysis computer software. Ownership of the project is divided as follows: two-thirds belongs to NASA while the other third belongs to Great Britain and the ESA together. Two-thirds ownership entitles NASA to two-thirds of the observing time on the IUE.

The IUE is popular among astronomers because it operates like a ground based observatory. Hundreds of astronomers from many nations have scheduled observing time over the years at one of the two control stations. At these stations, data from the IUE is transmitted to visual screens via radio signals. Visitor choose the direction in which to aim the IUE, collect their data, and take it back to their laboratories for analysis.

Scientists now estimate that the IUE will remain in operation at least through the year 1997 and maybe into 1998.

See also **Space telescope** and **Ultraviolet astronomy**

Interstellar medium

For the most part, the **interstellar medium**—the space between the stars—is just that: space. It consists of vast stretches of nearly empty space; the vacuum of the universe. It would be totally empty if not for a smattering of gas atoms and tiny solid particles.

On average, the interstellar medium in our region of the **galaxy** holds about one atom of gas per cubic centimeter and 25 to 50 microscopic solid particles per cubic kilometer. In contrast, the air at sea level on Earth contains about 1,019 molecules of gas per cubic centimeter.

In some regions of space, however, the concentration of interstellar matter is thousands of times greater than average. Where there is a large enough concentration of gas and particles (particles are also called **cosmic dust**), they form clouds. Most of the time these clouds are so thin they are invisible. But at other times they are dense enough to be seen, in which cases they are called **nebula**e.

Cosmic Dust

Cosmic dust accounts for only 1 percent of the total **mass** in the interstellar medium, the other 99 percent being gas. The dust is believed to be made primarily of carbon and silicate material (silicon, oxygen, and metallic ions), possibly with frozen water and ammonia, and solid carbon dioxide. A "dark nebula" is a relatively dense cloud of cosmic dust. What makes the nebula dark is that much of the starlight in its path is either absorbed or reflected by dust particles. When starlight is reflected, it shines off in every way, meaning only a small percentage is sent in the direction of Earth. This process effectively blocks most of the starlight from Earth's view.

One famous dark nebula is called the "dark rift." It consists of a long dark band across the **Milky Way.** Our galaxy also has many small dark patches of concentrated particles, called **globule**s. They can be seen when silhouetted against the surrounding starlight or glowing nebulae.

Even individual particles of cosmic dust affect the quality of starlight. Random dust particles absorb or reflect some light from various stars, causing them to appear far dimmer than they actually are. It has even been theorized that without the presence of cosmic dust, the Milky Way would shine so brightly that it would be light enough on Earth to read, even at night.

Most dark nebulae resemble slightly shimmering, dark curtains. However, in cases where a dense cloud of dust is situated near a particularly bright star, the scattering of light may be more pronounced, forming a "reflection nebula." This is a region where the light is reflected so that it illuminates the dust itself.

Interstellar Gas

In contrast to solid particles, interstellar gas is transparent. Hydrogen accounts for about three-quarters of the gas. The rest is helium plus trace amounts of nitrogen, oxygen, carbon, sulfur, and possibly other elements.

While interstellar gas is generally cold, the gas near very hot stars becomes heated and ionized (electrically charged) by **ultraviolet radiation** given off by those stars. The glowing areas of ionized gas are called "emission nebulae." Two well-known examples of emission nebulae are the Orion nebula, visible through binoculars just south of the hunter's belt in the **constellation** of the same name, and the Lagoon nebula in the constellation Sagittarius. The Orion nebula is punctuated by dark patches of cosmic dust.

Interstellar space also contains over sixty types of polyatomic (containing more than one atom) molecules. The substance formed in the greatest abundance is molecular hydrogen (H_2); others include water, carbon monoxide, and ammonia. Since these molecules are broken down by starlight, they are found primarily in dense, dark nebulae, where they are protected from the light by cosmic dust. These nebulae—known as **molecular cloud**s—are enormous. They stretch across several **light year**s and are one thousand to one million times as massive as the sun.

Various theories have been proposed as to the origins of interstellar matter. Some matter has been ejected into space by stars, particularly from stars in the final stages of their life. We know that as a star depletes the supply of fuel on its surface, the chemical composition of the surrounding interstellar medium is altered. Massive **red giant** stars have been observed ejecting matter, probably composed of heavy elements such as aluminum, calcium and titanium. This material may then condense into solid particles, which combine with hydrogen, oxygen, carbon, and nitrogen when they enter interstellar clouds.

It is also possible that interstellar matter represents material not formed into stars when the galaxy condensed billions of years ago. Evidence supporting this theory can be found in the fact that new stars are born within clouds of interstellar gas and dust.

See also **Molecular cloud**; **Nebula**; **Red giant star**; and **Stellar evolution**

Jansky, Karl (1905–1950)
American radio engineer

Karl Jansky became the father of **radio astronomy** quite by accident. Jansky was born in Oklahoma and studied engineering at the University of Wisconsin. In 1928, he went to work for Bell Telephone Laboratories, where he was assigned to find the source of interference that was disrupting radio calls across the Atlantic Ocean. This assignment led Jansky to discover that objects in space give off **radio wave**s.

Jansky constructed an antenna from wood and brass to detect radio signals at a specific frequency. He mounted the antenna on wheels from a Model-T Ford, so he could rotate it. Jansky found that signals were coming from three sources but could identify only two, one nearby and one more distant. The third, a mystery source, produced a steady hiss. Although it did not interfere with telephone calls, Jansky was intrigued and continued to search for its origin.

The intensity of the unknown signal varied at different times during the day, which first led Jansky to suspect that the sun was the source of the signal. He gathered information for several months and noticed that the signal came on strongest about four minutes earlier each day. He discussed the matter with a friend, who recognized that the four-minute variation was a function of sidereal time, that is, time measured by the Earth's rotation with respect to the stars. (A sidereal day is different than a solar day. A sidereal day is simply the time it takes for the Earth to complete one rotation about its axis. A solar day, which is about four minutes longer than a sidereal day, is the length of time from one sunrise to the next. The

length of a day is dependent upon two types of Earthly motion: its orbit around the sun and its rotation upon its axis.)

Because of the four-minute difference in its daily pattern, Jansky ruled out the sun as the possible source. The signal seemed instead to be coming from the **constellation** Sagittarius in the southern **Milky Way.** But since the sun itself is a star, Jansky decided that the stars were not the source. He then guessed correctly that the signal was coming from interstellar gas and dust.

Jansky's discovery attracted a lot of attention in 1933. He argued for the construction of a larger receiver, 100 feet (30 meters) across, with which to make more complete observations. Bell Laboratories, however, was not interested in the project since astronomy was not related to their line of work. Jansky then approached universities but could not convince scientists of the importance of his findings.

Jansky died at the age of forty-five from a stroke brought on by a liver ailment. The world had to wait until amateur astronomer Grote Reber built his own radio dish in 1937 to learn more about the new field of radio astronomy.

See also **Radio astronomy**

Jemison, Mae (1956–)

American astronaut

It often takes a determined individual to cross the barriers of discrimination that confront women and racial minorities in our country. And it takes a very physically fit and well-trained scientist to become an astronaut. To accomplish all of the above, and to become the first Black woman in space, requires an especially capable person. That person is Mae Jemison.

To describe Jemison simply as an astronaut is to ignore the many other aspects of her life. Jemison is a medical doctor who also holds degrees in chemical engineering and African and Afro-American Studies. As a medical student, she worked and studied in Cuba, Kenya, and at a Cambodian refugee camp in Thailand. And as a Peace Corps volunteer, she spent two and one-half years practicing medicine in the West African countries of Sierra Leone and Liberia.

*Opposite page:
Karl Jansky, at the
Bell Telephone
Laboratories
Station, with one of
the instruments he
used to detect radio
impulses in the
Milky Way.*

Jemison is a self-proclaimed "womanist," meaning she has well-defined feminist beliefs. In addition to taking the pro-choice side of the abortion debate, she advocates expanding the opportunities available to women.

Mae Carol Jemison was born in 1956 in Decatur, Alabama, and grew up on the south side of Chicago, Illinois. Her father was a carpenter and roofer, and her mother was a schoolteacher. Jemison has an older sister who is a child psychiatrist and an older brother who is real estate broker.

From the time she was a youngster, Jemison was very interested in astronomy and space. She always believed she would one day travel in space, despite the fact that until recently there were no Black or female astronauts.

After graduating from Morgan Park High School in Chicago in 1973, Jemison received a scholarship to attend Stanford University in California. There she majored in both chemical engineering and African and Afro-American Studies. In addition to excelling in her studies, Jemison took part in a wide range of extracurricular activities, one of which was to serve as the first female leader of the Black Student Union.

After graduating from Stanford in 1977, Jemison went on to study medicine at Cornell University Medical College in New York City. On receiving her medical degree four years later, she headed back to the West Coast. Jemison worked first as an intern and then as a general practitioner in the Los Angeles area until she left for her Peace Corps assignment in 1983.

Jemison Chosen To Be an Astronaut

When Jemison returned to the United States in 1985, she was hired as a physician with a health maintenance organization. Jemison remained in that position only until February 1987. She left her job when she found out she was one of the fifteen individuals (out of two thousand applicants) accepted by the National Aeronautics and Space Administration (NASA) to enter the astronaut training program, the first Black woman ever to receive that honor.

Jemison spent the next year learning about the **space shuttle** program and preparing for the difficulties of life in space. By August 1988, she had become a fully qualified mission specialist, ready to serve on shuttle missions.

Jemison spent the next five years working at NASA before she was selected to join a shuttle crew. She was assigned to the September 12,

*Opposite page:
Astronaut Mae
Jemison performs a
pre-flight switch
check in the space
shuttle Atlantis,
May 5, 1989.*

1992, mission of the space shuttle *Endeavour,* which carried on board the Japanese Spacelab laboratory. During the eight-day journey, Jemison conducted experiments on space sickness (an illness suffered by about half of all astronauts during their first few days in space), the loss of calcium from bones, tissue growth, and the effects of weightlessness. In addition, Jemison gave a fifteen-minute presentation telecast live to sixty children gathered at the Museum of Science and Industry in Chicago. "I'm closer to the stars," said Jemison, "somewhere I've always dreamed to be."

As the first Black woman in space, Jemison has become something of a celebrity. She is considered, naturally, a role model for Black youth. "When I'm asked about the relevance to Black people of what I do, I take that as an affront," said Jemison in a published report. "It presupposes that Black people have never been involved in exploring the heavens, but this is not so. Ancient African empires—Mali, Songhai, Egypt—had scientists, astronomers. The fact is that space and its resources belong to all of us, not to any one group."

Jemison resigned from NASA in 1993 and founded a company called the Jemison Group, which develops and sells advanced technologies. Jemison is single and lives in Houston, Texas with her cat, Sneeze.

Jupiter

On December 7, 1995, a **probe** the size of an average backyard barbecue grill dropped from the spacecraft *Galileo* and entered Jupiter's atmosphere at a speed of 106,000 miles (170,554 kilometers) per hour. Within two minutes it slowed to 100 miles (161 kilometers) per hour. Soon after, the probe released a parachute and it floated downward to the planet's hot surface. As it fell, intense winds blew it 300 miles (483 kilometers) horizontally. The probe spent fifty-eight minutes taking extremely detailed pictures of the giant planet until its cameras stopped working at an altitude of about 100 miles below the top of Jupiter's cloud cover. Eight hours later, the probe was completely vaporized as temperatures reached 3,400 degrees Fahrenheit (1,870 degrees Celsius).

The mini-probe traveled aboard the larger *Galileo* probe for six years and over half a billion miles to reach its destination. It sent back information that confirms some of what scientists have believed about Jupiter, but contradicts other predictions. Those who designed the probe are quick to

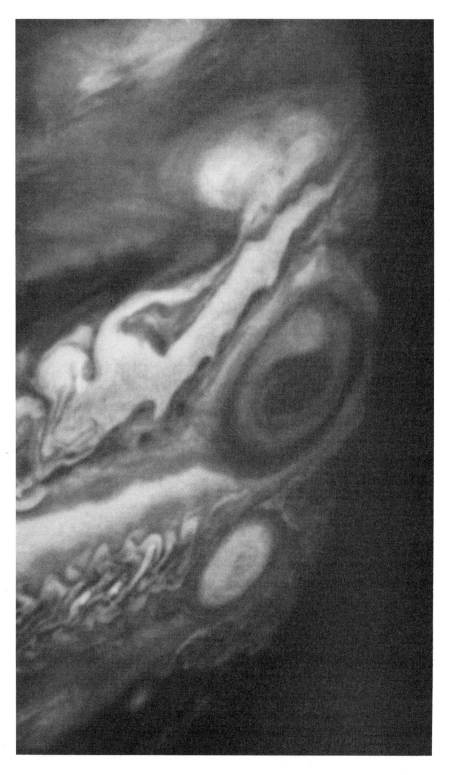

Jupiter, with a view of the Great Red Spot. This swirling storm covers an area large enough to cover two Earths.

remind us that it collected information from only one spot on the huge planet, and that general conclusions about the planet as a whole should not be drawn from its findings. This experience would be like having a Martian probe land in the Atlantic Ocean and observers concluding that all of Earth is covered by water.

What the probe discovered first was a belt of radiation 31,000 miles (49,900 kilometers) above Jupiter's clouds, containing the strongest **radio waves** in the **solar system.** It next encountered Jupiter's swirling clouds and found that they contain water, helium, hydrogen, carbon, sulfur, and neon, but in much smaller quantities than expected. It also found gaseous krypton and xenon, but in greater amounts than previously estimated.

Scientists had predicted that the probe would encounter three or four dense cloud layers of ammonia, hydrogen sulfide, and water, but instead it found only thin, hazy clouds. And the probe detected only faint signs of lightning at least 600 miles (965 kilometers) away, far less than expected. The probe found that lightning on Jupiter occurs only one-tenth as often as it does on Earth.

The probe did not survive long enough to gather information on Jupiter's core. Astronomers believe that the planet has a rocky core made of material similar to Earth, but with a diameter about five or ten times than that of Earth's core. The core's temperature may be as hot as 18,000 degrees Fahrenheit (9,820 degrees Celsius), with pressures two million times those at the Earth's surface. Scientists believe that a layer of compressed hydrogen surrounds the core. Hydrogen in this layer may act like a metal and may be the cause of Jupiter's intense **magnetic field** (five times greater than the sun's).

Perhaps the biggest surprise uncovered by the probe was the lack of water on the planet. Again, overall conclusions can not be drawn from one sampling. But if it turns out that Jupiter is not the watery planet scientists have always assumed, then there is little chance of finding life there.

Physical Properties of Jupiter

Jupiter is by far the largest planet in our solar system. It is thirteen hundred times larger than Earth, with three hundred times Earth's **mass.** It has a diameter of 85,000 miles (136,765 kilometers), while the Earth's diameter is just over 7,900 miles (12,700 kilometers) at the equator. With its sixteen moons, Jupiter is considered a mini-solar system of its own. Jupiter is often the brightest object in the sky after the sun and Venus. For some unknown reason, it reflects light that is twice as intense as the sunlight that strikes it.

Through a telescope, Jupiter looks like a globe of colorful swirling bands. These bands may be a result of Jupiter's fast rotation. One day on Jupiter lasts only ten hours (compared to a rotational period of twenty-four hours for the Earth).

Jupiter's most outstanding feature is its bright Great Red Spot. The spot is actually a swirling, windy storm over 8,500 miles (13,680 kilometers) wide and 16,000 miles (25,745 kilometers) long, an area large enough to cover two Earths. The spot may get its red color from sulfur or phosphorus, but no one is sure. Beneath it lie three white oval areas. Each is a storm about the size of Mars.

One reason Jupiter is considered such an important object for study is that scientists believe it may hold information about the birth of the solar system. "Jupiter is a giant ruin left over from events we hardly understand," said astronomer Toby Owen of the University of Hawaii in late 1995. "It's like opening a tube that has been sealed for four and one-half billion years."

One theory about the planet's origin is that Jupiter is made of the original gas and dust that came together to form the sun and planets. Since Jupiter is so far from the sun, its components may have undergone little or no change. A more recent theory, however, states that Jupiter was formed from ice and rock from **comet**s, and that it grew by attracting other matter around it.

Astronomers have been observing Jupiter since the beginning of recorded time. In 1610, Galileo Galilei looked through his homemade telescope and saw four moons orbiting a yellow-and-brown striped planet.

Much more recently, in 1979, the *Voyager* **space probe**s passed by Jupiter and took pictures of the planet's swirling colors and volcanic moons, as well as a previously undiscovered ring surrounding the planet. Those discoveries merely heightened the curiosity of the scientific community, which eagerly awaited the *Galileo* and its promise of photos one thousand times more detailed than those of its predecessor.

The 2.5-ton (2.3-metric ton) *Galileo* probe was launched aboard the **space shuttle** *Atlantis* in 1989. It will continue to orbit Jupiter and eight of its moons through late 1997, sending information back to Earth.

See also **Galileo** and **Voyager program**

Kennedy Space Center

Kennedy Space Center (KSC) is a 140,000-acre stretch of land and water at Cape Canaveral, on Florida's Atlantic Coast, and has been and continues to be the launch site of most U.S. spacecraft.

KSC operates under the control of the National Aeronautics and Space Administration (NASA), the government organization created in 1958 to run America's space program. The space center, which was named in honor of slain President John F. Kennedy, is home to both NASA and U.S. Air Force facilities. While NASA activities are based on the site's northern half and an Air Force station occupies the southern half, the two operations share some equipment and launch pads.

The KSC site was originally used as a missile range following World War II. Cape Canaveral was selected for that purpose because of the nearby string of islands from which missiles could be tracked. It was later determined to be a good site for spacecraft launches as well, because of its good weather and closeness to the ocean, into which used **rocket** fuel tanks and other components fall during launch.

In 1958, when NASA engineers were preparing to send into space the first U.S. artificial satellite, *Explorer 1,* KSC was the obvious choice for the launch site. Besides the existence of missile launch facilities, the site had another factor working in its favor: it is close to the equator. Being close to the equator is an advantage in a rocket launch because the Earth rotates fastest (from west to east) at the equator. Thus, if the rocket is launched toward the east it receives an extra push from the Earth's rotational movement.

KSC Structures

Numerous structures are located at KSC. The majority of these structures are launch pads and large buildings. Launch pads have sprung up like mushrooms over the years, since they must be custom-built for each type of rocket and spacecraft. The advent of the **space shuttle** has meant the construction of a whole new breed of launch facilities, as well as a 3-mile (5-kilometer) runway used for shuttle landings. Meanwhile, some of the earliest launch pads have now been torn down and others, unused for decades, sit rusting in the salty sea breeze.

The space center's gigantic buildings are used for the construction of large rockets. While smaller rockets are assembled directly on the launch pad, the larger rockets are put together first and then transported to the pad in one piece. Titan rockets are assembled inside KSC's Vertical Integration Building, a structure large enough to house four Titans at a time. The rockets are then placed on a train for the ride to the launchpad.

The giant Saturn rockets of the early days of space flight were assembled in the fifty-two-story Vehicle Assembly Building. They were then brought to the pad, a few miles away, by a huge vehicle called a "Crawler Transporter." That building today is used for assembly of the space shuttle.

Other U.S. launch centers, from which a small number of military and observational satellites have been sent into space, include Vandenberg Air Force Base in California and Wallops Island off the coast of Virginia.

See also **National Aeronautics and Space Administration**

Kepler, Johannes (1571–1630)

German astronomer

Johannes Kepler arrived at a career in astronomy after first studying religion, then teaching mathematics, and later practicing **astrology** (the supposed influence of planets and stars on the course of human affairs) and mysticism (a spiritual discipline). Working with data collected by Danish astronomer Tycho Brahe, Kepler made his greatest contribution to the field of astronomy, the laws of planetary motion.

Kepler was born in Weil, an area that is now part of southwestern Germany. His childhood was very unhappy due to an irritable mother and a violent father who abandoned the family when Kepler was only a teenager. The young Kepler struggled with a range of illnesses, including smallpox (which left him with crippled hands), and experienced poor vision. None of his physical problems could detract, however, from the fact that he had a brilliant mind.

Kepler obtained his bachelor's degree in theology (the study of religion) at age seventeen and continued his education in a master's program at the Protestant-run University of Tübingen. It was there that he became convinced of the **Copernican** (sun-centered) **model** of the **solar system.** Kepler also studied mathematics, and soon after he graduated in 1591 was hired to teach mathematics at the high school in Graz, Austria.

Kepler soon realized that teaching was not for him and took up astrology. He earned a living by producing **constellation** charts and casting horoscopes. In 1596, he published a book outlining the mystical relationship between objects in the solar system and geometric objects such as spheres and cubes. This book, entitled *Mysterium Cosmographicum (Mystery of the Universe)*, earned Kepler a degree of fame.

In 1600, Kepler received and accepted an offer to work with Tycho Brahe in Prague, Czechoslovakia. Kepler and Brahe had greatly different personal styles and never really got along. Brahe, an arrogant man who loved to show off his great wealth, constantly irritated the modest Kepler. The situation did not last long, however, as Brahe died just eighteen months after Kepler's arrival.

Johannes Kepler.

Kepler's Astronomical Research

After Brahe's death, Kepler succeeded him as the official imperial mathematician to the Holy Roman Emperor. This position gave him access to all of Brahe's records, including his sightings of Mars. Kepler took those notes and attempted to plot Mars' orbit. This task, which he estimated would take only eight days to complete, ended up taking him several years.

In 1604, Kepler took time off from this project to study a **supernova,** an exploding dying star. This star was nearly as bright as Venus and came to be known as Kepler's Star. Kepler also constructed his own telescope and verified Galileo's discovery of Jupiter's moons. He called them satellites, a word that is now used to describe any natural or human-made orbiting object.

Kepler had a difficult time constructing Mars' orbit because he assumed the planet's path was circular. No matter how many ways he tried, he could not make his calculations fit Brahe's observations. And because Brahe was known to be such a perfectionist, Kepler never doubted the accuracy of his mentor's notes. Finally, Kepler re-calculated the orbit of Mars assuming that the planet followed an elliptical, instead of circular, path. Brahe's observations now matched perfectly.

This discovery led to Kepler's 1609 publication of his first two laws of planetary motion. The first law states that a planet travels around the sun on an elliptical path. The second law says that a planet moves faster when closer to the sun and slower when farther away.

Ten years later Kepler added a third law of planetary motion. This law makes it possible to calculate a planet's relative distance from the sun knowing its period of revolution. Specifically the law states that the cube of a planet's average distance from the sun is equal to the square of the time it takes that planet to complete its orbit.

In the same year, Kepler published a book on **comet**s, which contained some information that was accurate and some that was wrong. Kepler was correct in supporting Brahe's theory that comets are objects in space and not occurrences in the Earth's atmosphere, like thunderstorms. But he was wrong in stating that a comet travels in a straight line, coming from and disappearing into infinity. (It was not until 1695 that English astronomer Edmond Halley discovered that comets, like planets, follow elliptical orbits around the sun.)

In 1626, Kepler moved to Ulm, Germany, where he published his final book, *The Rudolphine Tables*. This catalogue of the movement of planets was used by astronomers throughout the next century.

Kepler died, following a short illness, at the age of fifty-nine.

See also **Planetary motion**

Kirchhoff, Gustav (1824–1887)
German physicist

Gustav Robert Kirchhoff was the first scientist to apply **spectroscopy** to astronomical objects. Spectroscopy is the process of breaking down light into its **spectrum** of component colors. Two hundred years earlier, Isaac Newton had used a simple prism to split white light into a rainbow of colors. Working with chemist Robert Bunsen, Kirchhoff advanced this science to the point of being able to identify elements present in stars.

Kirchoff was born in Königsberg, Germany, in 1824. After completing high school, he attended the university in his hometown, where he earned outstanding academic marks. While a student, Kirchhoff experimented with electric circuits and made the important discovery that electricity travels at the **speed of light.** Upon graduation from the university, he was hired to teach at Breslau University.

It was at Breslau that Kirchhoff met Bunsen. It soon became apparent to the two men that they would make a formidable research team. Thus, four years later Kirchhoff transferred to the University of Heidelberg, where Bunsen taught, and the two started working together on the design of a new **spectroscope.** Their instrument was different from earlier models in that it directed the incoming light through a thin slit to produce a narrow beam of light, which produced a spectrum of greater detail and sharper focus.

Gustav Kirchhoff.

Kirchhoff and Bunsen also experimented with a new method of spectroscopy. They set a sample of a chemical substance on fire and directed its light toward the thin slit in one end of the spectroscope. The light then passed through a prism, producing an emission spectrum, a series of thin, colored, bright lines. The bright lines, called **emission lines,** represented colors (or wavelengths) at which a particular object gave off light. They found that an emission spectrum was like a fingerprint, in that it was different for each element they tested. They then began recording the emission **spectra** for all known elements.

Kirchhoff next pointed his spectroscope toward the sky, to study the emission spectra of stars. By comparing observed spectra to the recorded spectra of the elements, he was able to determine which elements were present in certain stars. He also discovered a relationship between emission and absorption (**absorption lines** indicate wavelengths at which the object absorbs radiation). Now known as Kirchhoff's Law, it states that any substance that produces a particular emission line when heated produces an absorption line at the same wavelength when cooled.

Modern spectroscopy is not limited to the production of spectra of visible light. To the contrary, spectra now can be produced from all types of radiation on the **electromagnetic spectrum,** from **radio wave**s to **gamma ray**s. Astronomers use these methods to learn about **comet**s, stars, and other celestial objects, gaining such information as their chemical composition, temperature, movement, pressure, and the presence of **magnetic field**s.

See also **Spectroscopy**

Kitt Peak National Observatory

If you ever find yourself in the southwestern United States, make a point of visiting Kitt Peak. This mountaintop observatory is located 56 miles (90 kilometers) southwest of Tucson, Arizona, on the Tohono O'Odham Indian Reservation. A major highway takes the traveler through the initial leg of the journey from Tucson to Kitt Peak. The last 11 miles (18 kilometers), however, consists of a winding road that twists and turns its way up 6,875 feet (2,100 meters) to the peak. Visitors can tour the grounds and museum any day between 10 A.M. and 4 P.M., but the real spectacle occurs at night. On designated evenings, usually once per week, forty lucky souls are bussed to Kitt Peak to watch the sun set through the **solar telescope,** hear a lecture from a visiting astronomer, and then observe the marvels of space through some of the world's finest equipment.

The Kitt Peak National Observatory (KPNO), which began operating in 1960, is one of three branches of the National Optical Astronomy Observatories (NOAO). The other two NOAO organizations are the National Solar Observatory (which has stations on Kitt Peak and on Sacramento Peak, California) and the Cerro Tololo Interamerican Observatory in Chile. Like Cerro Tololo (its counterpart in the Southern Hemisphere), the KPNO is operated by the Association of Universities for Research in Astronomy (AURA) and is funded by the National Science Foundation.

The KPNO is the site of the world's second largest concentration of optical telescopes after Mauna Kea Observatory in Hawaii. Its largest instrument is the Mayall Telescope, a **reflector** with a 158-inch-diameter (400-centimeter-diameter) mirror. Housed inside an eighteen-story glistening white dome, it is one of the ten largest optical telescopes in the world. The observatory also has six other reflector telescopes with mirrors ranging in size from 84 inches (213 centimeters) down to 16 inches (41 centimeters), plus a Burrell-Schmidt telescope which is used to survey stars over large areas of the sky. Two of the reflectors can observe infrared as well as visible light.

The process of selecting a site for the observatory began in 1955 and took three years. It involved a survey of 150 mountaintop locations. The

Kitt Peak National Observatory.

site selection team was looking for a place that had a large number of clear nights, that had a high altitude (to minimize atmospheric interference), and that was far from city lights, yet still in the vicinity of a university.

Kitt Peak, which is about two hours from the University of Arizona, had all those features. Yet one problem remained: the mountaintop was on Indian land. Thus, the final hurdle had to be cleared through carefully conducted negotiations with the Tohono O'Odham elders. Observatory officials agreed not to create noise (such as **rocket** blasts, which the Indians associated with the U.S. space program) and to allow the native peoples to sell their crafts at the observatory's visitor center. These negotiations led to the signing of an agreement that is valid as long as the agreed-upon conditions do not change.

Use of Kitt Peak's facilities is open to astronomers from around the world who are selected on the merits of their written proposals. Over three hundred astronomers (mostly university professors and graduate students) come to Kitt Peak every year for stays of three to five nights. Some areas of observation undertaken at Kitt Peak include the chemical and physical characteristics of **comet**s and **asteroid**s; evidence indicating the existence of **brown dwarf**s; and studies of distant **galaxies** and **quasar**s.

See also **Cerro Tololo Interamerican Observatory** and **National Solar Observatory**

Korolëv, Sergei (1906–1966)
Russian engineer

The Russian (formerly Soviet) space program owes its greatest accomplishments to one man, Sergei Korolëv. Korolëv was largely responsible for his country's being the first nation to put a satellite into orbit around the Earth, to send a man into space, and to land a spacecraft on the moon.

Born in what was then Russia and is now the Ukraine, Korolëv built his first glider at the age of eighteen. He then entered flying school, but dropped out in 1930 to devote all his time to rocketry.

In 1931, Korolëv became director of the **rocket** research group in Moscow, called the Group for the Study of Jet Propulsion (GIRD). At the group's headquarters, scientists and engineers designed and built rocket models, including the first Soviet liquid-**propellant** rockets and winged engines. Many of the individuals employed there later formed the core of the Soviet space program.

During World War II, Korolëv was imprisoned by the Soviet secret police. Along with several other scholars, Korolëv was forced to work in a scientific labor camp, where they designed aircraft and weapons in support of the war effort.

Korolëv Begins Space Research

When the war ended, Korolëv returned to rocket research. He was first assigned to incorporate the advances the Germans had made in rocketry into the Soviet program. In August 1957, Korolëv's work resulted in the construction of the first Soviet intercontinental ballistic missile (ICBM).

Less than two months later, a rocket based on the ICBM was used to launch *Sputnik 1,* the first man-made satellite to orbit the Earth. At a length of 100 feet (30 meters) and a weight of about 300 hundred tons (272 metric tons), it became the most widely used rocket in the world.

Korolëv was next involved in the launch of *Luna 3,* the **space probe** that in 1959 gave humans their first look at the far side of the moon. (Since the moon rotates at the same rate as it orbits the Earth, the same side always faces us.) This achievement boosted the Soviets to the position of world leaders in space exploration.

Sergei Korolëv.

Two years later, Korolëv led the team that designed *Vostok 1,* the world's first spacecraft to carry a human passenger, **cosmonaut** Yuri Gagarin. Korolëv was also responsible for putting Valentina Tereshkova, the first woman in space, into orbit 1963.

In 1966, Korolëv was in charge of the *Venera 3* mission, the first mission to land a spacecraft on another planet. *Venera 3* was destroyed by its crash-landing on Venus, so it was not able to transmit any pictures of that planet. On its way to the planet, however, it did send back a great deal of useful information about interplanetary space.

Also in 1966, Korolëv's *Luna 9* landed on the moon. The spacecraft provided television footage showing that lunar dust, which scientists had anticipated finding, did not exist. The fear of encountering thick layers of dust had previously discouraged both the **Soviet Union** and the United States from sending a man to the moon. Now the **space race** was on. The next victory belonged to the United States when, in 1969, Americans Neil Armstrong and Buzz Aldrin became the first humans to set foot on the moon.

Korolëv died at the age of sixty and was buried in the Kremlin Wall, an honor the Soviets reserved for only their most distinguished citizens. The Soviets had kept his identity concealed from the public through his whole life. The name of the man referred to as "Chief Designer of Launch Vehicles and Spacecraft" was revealed only after his death.

See also **Space race**

Kuiper Airborne Observatory

The Kuiper Airborne Observatory (KAO) combines the best of both worlds. Like a **space telescope,** it flies above the Earth's turbulent atmosphere. Yet, like astronomy stations on the ground, it is easily accessible for repairs and upgrades. The KAO is a modified C-141 Starlifter military cargo airplane with a 6,000-pound (2,720-kilogram) infrared telescope on board. Like ground-based observatories, the KAO is used by hundreds of guest astronomers.

The KAO is a project of the National Aeronautics and Space Administration (NASA) and is based at the Ames Research Center near San Francisco, California. The project has been in existence since 1974 and conducts about seventy research flights a year. Most of the time the flying observatory takes off from and lands at Ames. However, during two or three months a year, it uses bases in Hawaii, Australia, New Zealand, Chile, and other parts of the world where it can best view astronomical hot spots. Astronomical hot spots are areas of the sky where particular activities, such as a **comet** passing by, are occurring.

The KAO conducts research at an altitude of about 41,000 feet (12,500 meters), which is above 99 percent of the atmospheric water vapor. This fact is significant because water vapor absorbs incoming **infrared radiation,** making **infrared astronomy** very difficult to conduct

Crew members Carl
Gillespie (seated,
right) and Rick Doll
(seated, left) take
part in the flight of
the Kuiper Airborne
Observatory on May
8, 1995.

on the ground. At the cruising altitude of the KAO, however, infrared light reveals regions of the **galaxy** where stars are in formation, as well as aspects of planets, stars, and galaxies that would be undetectable through optical telescopes.

On a typical excursion, the KAO takes off at about 10 P.M. It carries four astronomers and a pilot on a loop to Arizona and back, covering a good portion of the western United States. Once it ascends to about 33,000 feet (10,060 meters), a door opens, revealing the 36-inch-diameter (91-centimeter-diameter) telescope. The instrument is carefully padded and controlled to remain level, even while the airplane bumps and jolts through the turbulent air. Inside the noisy, chilly cabin (the plane has no thermal or sound insulation since it's not meant to carry passengers), the crew trains the telescope on a particular patch of sky, watches images that appear on monitors, and records data. At about 6 A.M. the next morning, the plane returns to Ames, and the sleepy crew disembarks.

Kuiper astronomy teams have been responsible for the discovery of rings around Uranus, water vapor in Jupiter's atmosphere, the thin atmosphere surrounding Pluto, and various substances in the **interstellar medium.** The airplane has also gone on special assignments, such as studying Halley's comet when it was in our neighborhood in 1986.

The KAO is named for airborne astronomy pioneer Gerard P. Kuiper. It is not the first airborne observatory, nor will it be the last. Observational forays high into the atmosphere have been made by astronomers since 1957. Then in the late 1960s, a Convair 900 jet was converted into the first long-term airborne observatory. It was succeeded in the early 1970s by a Lear jet with a 12-inch-diameter (30-centimeter-diameter) telescope. The Kuiper is the latest in this series and, after more than two decades of service, is becoming obsolete.

The next airborne observatory, called Stratospheric Observatory for Infrared Astronomy (SOFIA), is now in the planning stages. SOFIA will consist of a 100-inch-diameter (254-centimeter-diameter) telescope installed in a Boeing 747 jet. Astronomers hope that SOFIA will be flying by the year 2000, but the project's 180 million dollar price tag, coupled with fiscal belt tightening at NASA, keeps SOFIA's future hanging in the balance.

See also **Infrared Astronomical Satellite**; **Infrared astronomy**; and **Infrared Space Observatory**

Kuiper belt

According to a theory proposed in 1950 by Dutch astronomer Jan Oort, **comet**s originate in the **Oort cloud,** a spherical region of space that envelopes our **solar system.** The Oort cloud is far beyond Pluto's orbit, about one to two **light-year**s from the sun and extends halfway to the next closest star, Proxima Centauri. The Oort cloud is believed to contain trillions of inactive comets, which periodically are jolted into orbit around the sun.

Most comets have random orbits, traveling at all degrees of inclination to the ecliptic. For instance, some comets have orbits nearly perpendicular to the orbits of the planets, while others cross the planetary orbits at a 45-degree angle. In addition, they may take hundreds or even thousands of years to complete a single journey around the sun. (By comparison, Pluto takes 247.69 years to orbit the sun). These facts lend support to the existence of a distant zone of comets, encasing the solar system on all sides.

The Oort cloud, however, cannot account for the comets that travel along the ecliptic and have relatively short orbits. In 1951, another Dutch astronomer, Gerard Kuiper, suggested that a second reservoir of comets exists just beyond the edge of our solar system, about one thousand times closer to the sun than the Oort cloud. This hypothetical **Kuiper belt** is located somewhere between 35 and 1,000 **astronomical unit**s (AU) from the sun. It contains an estimated ten million to one billion comets—far fewer than the Oort cloud.

The flat disk of the Kuiper belt rings the solar system, lying on the same plane as the planetary orbits. Kuiper theorized that the material in this region is actually **planetesimal**s, small chunks of matter that are the building blocks of planets. In this case, however, the planetesimals never coalesced into a planet because they were spread so thin that they rarely collided with one another.

Images recently collected by the Hubble Space Telescope (HST) support the existence of such a belt beyond the orbit of Neptune. It is even suspected that Pluto and its moon Charon, which are only about 750 and 375 miles (1,207 and 603 kilometers) across respectively, may be the belt's largest members.

In the period between 1983 and 1984, the international Infrared Astronomical Satellite (IRAS) found, for the first time, rings of material surrounding other stars. These rings, similar to the proposed Kuiper belt, did not extend all the way to the star's surface, but at the closest point were about ten to thirty AU away. It is possible that there was once material between the ring and the star, which formed into planets (like our own solar system) too faint to be seen by IRAS.

It stands to reason that if rings of material can surround other stars (and possibly other solar systems), then one could surround our sun as well. Yet only in the past few years have telescopes been developed that are powerful enough to discern small objects ringing the sun. The first discovery of an object believed to be a member of the Kuiper belt was made in 1992 by David C. Jewitt and Jane Luu at the Mauna Kea Observatory in Hawaii. They found an object beyond Pluto, about 120 miles (93 kilometers) across, orbiting the sun at a distance of 3.2 billion miles (5.2 billion kilometers) away. Since that time, over thirty small objects have been discovered in a similar region, some by Jewitt and Luu and some by others. This discovery raises the possibility that thousands (or more) of other objects may be out there, but are too small to be detected by Earth-based telescopes.

Following up on this hunch, astronomers Harold F. Levison, Anita L. Cochran, Martin J. Duncan, and F. Alan Stern pointed the HST at an area of the sky in the **constellation** Taurus that is relatively uncluttered by celestial objects. They captured faint images of about thirty comet-like objects (meaning they are small, dark, and icy) ranging from 7 to 12 miles (11 to 19 kilometers) across, in what they believe is the inner region of the Kuiper belt. Assuming that this small sample of the sky is typical, they estimate that a total of two hundred million to five billion small objects occupy the entire belt.

These Hubble astronomers believe that comets with relatively short orbits —two hundred years or less—that lie in the same plane as planetary orbits come from the Kuiper belt. Examples of such comets include the Shoemaker-Levy comet, parts of which smashed into Jupiter in 1994, and Halley's comet. In contrast, comets with longer orbits and those that travel at various angles of inclination to the ecliptic are more likely originate in the far-away Oort cloud.

One of the most fascinating aspects of the Kuiper belt is that it may contain material left over from the formation of the solar system. "This represents a wonderful laboratory for studying how planets formed," stated Levison in a 1995 article in *Scientific American*.

See also **Comet**; **Oort, Jan**; and **Planetesimals and protoplanets**

Lagrange, Joseph Louis (1736–1813)
Italian-born French mathematician

Joseph Louis Lagrange was born to French parents in the Italian kingdom of Piedmont. His father encouraged him to become a lawyer, but after reading an article by Edmond Halley on the use of algebra in optics (the study of light), the young Lagrange decided to study mathematics.

Lagrange had a brilliant mind for mathematics. By the age of eighteen, he was teaching geometry at the Royal Artillery School in his home town of Turin. Just four years later he founded a discussion group that later became the Turin Academy of Sciences.

Around this time, Lagrange published an article on the variation of the orbits of celestial objects, called "On the Calculus of Variations." He sent it to mathematician Leonhard Euler, who was studying the same topic. Euler was so impressed with the article that he arranged for Lagrange to be admitted to the Berlin Academy of Sciences.

Lagrange then undertook an analysis of the wobble of the moon about its axis. In 1764, this work won him an award from the Paris Academy of Sciences. Lagrange next began working on an overall description of the way

Joseph Louis Lagrange.

that various forces act on material objects, a project Galileo Galilei had begun years before. Lagrange eventually succeeded in devising several general equations, which he published in a 1788 book entitled *Méchanique Analytique (Analytical Mechanics)*.

Lagrange Studies the Many-Body Problem

In 1766, when Euler moved on, Lagrange took his place as director of the mathematics department at the Berlin Academy. Lagrange went on to explore the interactions between objects in the **solar system.** Isaac Newton's theory of universal gravitation addressed only the effects that two objects have on one another, but did not explain the relationships among multiple objects.

Lagrange worked out equations describing the interactions among a group of objects, such as the sun, Earth, and moon and of Jupiter and its four moons (the only four known at that time). He discovered that regions exist within the solar system in which a small object can act as a balance between two larger objects, if the three together form an equilateral triangle. These areas today are called Lagrange points. Over one hundred years later a stunning example of this discovery became apparent. A swarm of **asteroid**s was discovered along the orbit of Jupiter, held in place by the combined gravitational forces of Jupiter and the sun.

In 1787, Lagrange moved to Paris at the invitation of King Louis XVI. Six years later, he was appointed to a commission on weights and measures, and helped create the metric system. In 1797, Lagrange resumed teaching mathematics, this time at the École Normal.

Lagrange spent his final working years trying to develop a new system of calculus not based on Newton's limits. His attempts, although unsuccessful, inspired the work of a new generation of mathematicians.

In 1808, French ruler Napoleon Bonaparte recognized Lagrange's lifelong achievements by naming him to the Legion of Honor and making him a Count of the Empire. Lagrange died in Paris five years later.

Langley, Samuel (1834–1906)

American astronomer and physicist

While the Wright brothers received all the fame and glory for the invention of the airplane, fewer people recognize the name of the man who very nearly achieved that same feat—Samuel Langley.

Langley, born in Roxbury, Massachusetts, was fascinated by science and literature and read extensively from his youth. Although he had no formal schooling beyond high school, Langley went on to receive numerous honorary degrees and to become well respected in the scientific community.

From 1851 to 1864, he worked as a civil engineer and an architect. In 1866, he was hired as an assistant professor of mathematics at the U.S. Naval Academy in Washington, D.C. He was also made director of the observatory—a facility that had fallen into disrepair and that Langley had to restore. Then in 1867, Langley switched to the Western University of Pennsylvania (it was later renamed the University of Pittsburgh) where he was a professor of physics and astronomy and director of the Allegheny Observatory.

It was there that Langley made one of his most important contributions to the field of astronomy—the invention of the **bolometer.** This is an instrument that can detect **electromagnetic radiation** entering the Earth's atmosphere, especially **infrared radiation** and **microwave**s. Astronomers use bolometers to determine the energy output of the sun and stars.

Langley's next position, which he began in 1887, was secretary of the Smithsonian Institution. He requested and received a grant from the *Samuel Langley.*
U.S. War Department (now the Department of Defense) to study the possibility of piloted flight. Langley then began building large, steam-powered models of an aircraft he called Aerodrome. Beginning in 1891, he tested models by launching them from the roof of a houseboat. After several failed attempts, he found limited success in very short flights of two Aerodromes in 1896.

Langley was premature, however, in announcing his success. In 1903, after assembling a crowd that included members of the press, Langley attempted to launch his first full-size Aerodrome from a houseboat. The aircraft fell into the water upon launch. Langley blamed the failure on his launching equipment, but later attempts ended the same way. His funding ran out and the project ended.

A few years after Langley's death, engineers attached a stronger engine to the Aerodrome and managed to fly it. But by that time the credit for air flight belonged to the Wright brothers who had already flown the first powered airplane at Kitty Hawk, North Carolina, on December 17, 1903.

Today, Langley's name lives on in the Langley Air Force Base and the National Aeronautics and Space Administration's Langley Research Center, both in Virginia.

Laplace, Pierre-Simon (1749–1827)
French mathematician and astronomer

Little is known about the early life of Pierre-Simon Laplace other than that he was born at Beaumont-en-Auge in Normandy, France. Laplace went to Paris when he was eighteen years old and, based on a paper he had written on mechanics, was hired as a professor of mathematics.

Pierre-Simon LaPlace.

Together with chemist Antoine-Laurent Lavoisier, Laplace founded the science of thermochemistry, the science dealing with the interrelationship of heat and chemical interactions. Laplace and Lavoisier measured the specific heats of various substances and in 1780 showed that the amount of heat necessary to decompose a substance is equal to the heat given off when the object is originally formed.

In the field of astronomy, Laplace was primarily interested in the movements of the moon and the planets. In particular, he was puzzled by the variations in their orbits. For instance, he noticed that at times the moon traveled faster in its orbit around the Earth than at other times. Aided by the work of his friend and fellow astronomer Joseph Louis Lagrange, Laplace concluded that the moon's orbit is influenced by changes in the Earth's orbit and that the Earth, in turn, is influenced by changes in the orbits of Jupiter and Saturn. Laplace had discovered that the **solar**

system maintains its balance through the interactions of its members, each on their own orbit around the sun. For instance, planets do not veer off their orbits and crash into the sun or into one another.

Laplace published his results over a twenty-five-year period beginning in 1799 in a five-volume book called *Traité de Méchanique Céleste* (*Celestial Mechanics*). Since his work expanded on the gravitational theories of Englishman Isaac Newton, Laplace earned the nickname "French Newton."

Laplace went on to apply Newtonian calculus in his experiments with the forces acting between particles of ordinary matter, light, heat, and electricity. By examining their results, Laplace and his colleagues were able to determine equations explaining the refraction of light, the conduction of heat, the flexibility of solid objects, and the distribution of electricity on conductors.

Together with English geologist John Michell, Laplace introduced the concept of gravitationally collapsed objects, now known as **black hole**s. In 1783, Michell calculated the speed at which an object would have to travel in order to escape the **gravity** of the sun. In 1796, Laplace conducted a similar study. The two scientists agreed that if a star was big enough and dense enough, it would exhibit so much gravitational attraction that nothing could escape from its clutches.

Laplace also developed a theory explaining how the planets were formed. He suggested that the sun formed from a spinning **nebula** (cloud of gas and dust) and that as the nebula shrank, it gave off rings of gas. Material in these orbiting rings then condensed into the planets through collisions and gravitational attraction. To support his theory, Laplace pointed out that the planets continue to orbit the sun, all in roughly the same plane.

This nebular hypothesis, as it came to be known, was published in Laplace's 1796 book *Exposition du Système du Monde* (*The System of the World*). The theory has risen and fallen in popularity over the years. Since the late 1800s, it has been in competition with the particle accretion theory, the suggestion that the planets formed by the accumulation of particles.

Laplace died in Paris at the age of seventy-eight. His famous last words were: "That which we know is mere trifle, that we are ignorant of is immense."

See also **Black hole**

Large and Small Magellanic Clouds

The **Milky Way**'s two closest galactic neighbors, visible to naked-eye observers in the Southern Hemisphere, are the Large and Small Magellanic Clouds. They were named after explorer Ferdinand Magellan, who first recorded their existence in 1519.

These two **galaxies** are relatively small and irregular in shape. The Large Magellanic Cloud (LMC) is about 32,600 **light-year**s across and 163,000 light-years from Earth. The Small Magellanic Cloud (SMC) is about 19,560 light-years wide and 195,600 light-years away. Each Magellanic cloud contains only a few percent of the **mass** of the Milky Way, which is approximately 100,000 light-years in diameter. In comparison, the Andromeda, our closest major galaxy at 2.2 million light-years away, is about four times the size of our home galaxy.

The Large Magellanic Cloud, a companion galaxy to our own Milky Way.

Both Magellanic galaxies exist within a cloud of cool neutral hydrogen gas, which extends far out into space. The total gas stream contains as much mass as ten billion suns combined.

The Magellanic clouds are known for their large **stellar nurseries,** areas where stars are being formed. The nurseries also have sizeable concentrations of young stars. Some of these stars are very large and progress through their evolutionary stages relatively quickly, with the end result being a **supernova.**

One such event was observed in 1987, when the first supernova visible from the Earth in nearly three centuries appeared in the LMC. The supernova was bright enough to be seen by the naked eye. It was a particularly important astronomical event, since it was the first time astronomers were able to observe a supernova using modern equipment.

See also **Andromeda galaxy**; **Galaxy**; and **Milky Way galaxy**

Las Campanas Observatory

Las Campanas Observatory is one of three astronomical centers situated near the mountain town of La Serena in north-central Chile. The other two centers are the European Southern Observatory, run by a group of eight European nations based in Garching, Germany, and the Cerro Tololo Interamerican Observatory, a project of the National Optical Astronomy Observatories that is funded by the National Science Foundation. Unlike its counterparts, Las Campanas is a private observatory financed by the Washington D.C.-based Carnegie Institution.

Astronomers from North America and Europe travel to the Southern Hemisphere in order to view parts of the sky not visible from the Northern Hemisphere. For instance, our closest neighbor **galaxies,** the Large and Small Magellanic Clouds, as well as the center of own **Milky Way,** can be seen only from sites south of the equator.

The quality of viewing at Las Campanas is superb, as it is at the other Chilean observatories. Las Campanas sits above the Atacama Desert, the second driest place in the world after Antarctica. This setting makes for generally clear, dry, and cloudless nights. And at its elevation of 7,200 feet (2,195 meters), the atmosphere is thin. A thin atmosphere is important because molecules in the air tend to scatter light from celestial objects, distorting their image.

Las Campanas, which opened in 1971, is home to two main instruments, both **reflector telescope**s. The telescopes have mirrors of 98 inches (249 centimeters) and 39 inches (99 centimeters) in diameter. While these telescopes are certainly adequate, they pale in comparison to many other ground-based telescopes. For instance, the Hale Telescope at Palomar Observatory in California is 200 inches (508 centimeters) across, while the Keck Telescope at Mauna Kea Observatory in Hawaii (the largest optical telescope in the world) measures 393 inches (998 centimeters) across.

The big news today at Las Campanas is not its existing equipment, but the instruments that are soon to be built there. Construction began in 1994 on the first telescope of the Magellan Project, a planned two-telescope system, each with mirrors 255 inches (648 centimeters) across. And to paint an even more spectacular picture, discussions are being conducted about the possibility of linking the two telescopes at some point in the future. This arrangement would create the equivalent viewing power of a single telescope with a 300-foot-diameter (91-meter-diameter) mirror.

Bigger telescopes, by letting in more light, produce a clear view of even very distant, faint objects. A telescope with the power of the linked Magellans could see far-away objects fifty times more clearly than the Hubble Space Telescope. As an example of its potential, the Magellan system could be used to investigate areas of space where stars are in formation, search for **black hole**s, and study millions of galaxies in order to calculate the **mass** of the universe.

The twin Magellan I and II telescopes, estimated to cost 68 million dollars, are being jointly financed by the Carnegie Institution, the University of Michigan, Harvard University, and the Massachusetts Institute of Technology. The first telescope is scheduled for completion in 1998 and the second in 2001.

See also **Cerro Tololo Interamerican Observatory** and **European Southern Observatory**

Launch vehicle

The process of placing satellites and piloted spacecraft in space begins on the ground, with the **launch vehicle.** Once the countdown to liftoff begins, engines fire and clouds of exhaust appear. Tremendous, carefully controlled explosions power up the launch vehicle, which rises from the

*The Saturn V
launch vehicle
boosts Apollo 13
into space and
history.*

launch pad and accelerates to tremendous speeds, sending the spacecraft hurtling to the edge of the Earth's atmosphere and beyond.

A wide variety of launch vehicles have been used since 1957, the year the first satellite (the Soviet *Sputnik 1*) was propelled into space. Most of these launch vehicles have consisted of **rocket** systems designed to be used just once. Since the 1970s, however, **space shuttles,** which can be used over and over, have also joined the ranks of launch vehicles.

The quality of launch vehicles has improved markedly since the earliest days, when the failure rate was about 50 percent. Nonetheless, in the 1970s and early 1980s, it looked as if the United States was going to stop using rockets altogether, since rockets are wasteful compared to multi-use space shuttles. The *Challenger* disaster of 1986, however, plus the commercial success of the European Ariane rocket, led the National Aeronautics and Space Administration (NASA) to change this decision and not abandon the use of rockets altogether. Rather than resume building its own rockets, however, NASA turned this task over to private corporations. As a result, rocket production in the United States today is a highly competitive, "booming" industry.

The world's two largest producers of launch vehicles have historically been the leaders of space flight, the United States and former **Soviet Union.** Today, however, several other nations, including Japan, China, Israel, India, and the organization of European nations called the European Space Agency, possess their own launch vehicles, which they use to lift their communication and military satellites into orbit.

Such a wide array of launch vehicles exist, many of them consisting of various combinations of the same components, that it would be impractical to describe every one of them. What follows is a description of some of the most important American launch vehicles and a sampling of those from the former Soviet Union.

Important U.S. Launch Vehicles

The three longest-lived U.S. launch vehicles, all still in use today, are the Atlas, Delta, and Titan rockets. An Atlas rocket was first used to launch John Glenn's *Mercury 6* flight in 1962. Since then, Atlas has propelled numerous **space probe**s and military and communications satellites into space. Today four different versions of Atlas rockets are produced by the military supply company General Dynamics. The most powerful of these rockets can launch payloads of up to 19,050 pounds (8,640 kilograms).

The current Atlas is used in combination with a Centaur upper-stage missile, for additional thrust.

The Delta rocket began its career in 1960 with the launch of the first communications satellite, *Echo 1*. Since that time, it has sent several other satellites and interplanetary **probe**s into space. The original Delta was based on an intermediate range ballistic missile. Many modifications later, today's Delta is a much more powerful machine and is the Department of Defense's launch vehicle of choice for military satellites. Delta undertook its two hundredth launch in October 1990.

The Titan rocket, first used in 1959, is today NASA's most powerful launch vehicle. Like Delta, it was adapted from a military missile and converted by NASA for use in the space program. Titans sent up the Gemini piloted missions in the 1960s, and later, the interplanetary *Viking* and *Voyager* probes. Today's Titan IV, developed by military contractor Martin-Marietta, is used primarily to launch large military satellites and, secondarily, NASA's deep space missions.

Two of the most widely used Soviet launch vehicles are Vostok and Soyuz (also the names of Soviet piloted spacecraft). Vostok, which means "east," was designed in the late 1950s by the famous engineer Sergei Korolëv. It was used in 1961 to send the first man into space, Yuri Gagarin, as well as to launch other piloted missions and unpiloted satellites. Soyuz, which means "union," was used as early as 1957 to launch the first satellite, *Sputnik*. It is still used today to send crews up to the *Mir* **space station.**

See also **Saturn V rocket**; **Space shuttle**; and **Spacecraft voyage**

Leavitt, Henrietta Swan (1868–1921)
American astronomer

Henrietta Swan Leavitt was born in Lancaster, Massachusetts. After attending public schools in nearby Cambridge, she continued her education at the Society for Collegiate Instruction of Women (later renamed Radcliffe College). In 1892, during her senior year, Leavitt took a course on astronomy and found it fascinating. Three years later she began volunteering at the Harvard College Observatory, where she was made a permanent staff member in 1902.

Leavitt was appointed to head the observatory's **photographic photometry** department, which deals with measuring the brightness of stars. Her task was to search the southern skies for **variable star**s (stars that vary in brightness over time) and to capture their images on photographic plates. She discovered a total of about twenty-four hundred variable stars.

Leavitt's most important discovery was a special class of variables, blinking yellow **supergiant**s called **cepheid variable**s. Leavitt's study of cepheids led to a formula that astronomers now use to measure distances to objects in space.

Cepheid variables become brighter and dimmer on a regular cycle. In 1904, Leavitt realized that the longer it took one of these stars to complete a cycle, the brighter it was. This relationship between time and brightness, however, can not be observed in stars in our **galaxy.** The reason is that a star in our own galaxy may appear relatively bright or dim due to its nearness or farness from us, or our view of the star may be blocked by dust. A star's true brightness, or **absolute magnitude,** can be observed only in another galaxy so far away that all the stars are roughly the same distance from us.

Thus Leavitt traveled to Harvard's observatory in Peru and examined cepheids in a nearby galaxy called the Small Magellanic Cloud. She timed how long it took each cepheid to complete its bright-dim cycle and measured its absolute magnitude. Based on the relationship of these two variables, Leavitt was able to estimate their distance (and consequently, the distance of the entire galaxy) from Earth.

Leavitt then constructed a **period-luminosity curve.** This is a graph with absolute magnitude on the vertical axis and period (days to complete a cycle) on the horizontal axis. The relationship of the star's brightness to period can then be plugged in to a formula to determine distance from Earth.

Leavitt's cepheid variables, which have earned the nickname "astronomical yardsticks," are still the best indicator of distance in the skies. Originally their usefulness was limited to the thirty or so galaxies in which they could be detected. Now with the Hubble Space Telescope we are able to locate cepheids in galaxies up to sixteen million **light-year**s away.

See also **Cepheid variables**

Legendre, Adrien-Marie (1752–1833)
French mathematician

Adrien-Marie Legendre's greatest contribution to the field of astronomy was his painstaking development of elliptical functions, mathematical formulas that in part explain the oval-shaped pattern of the orbits of planets and **comet**s.

Legendre was born into a wealthy family and became interested in mathematics at an early age. Later, at the College Mazarin in Paris, Legendre studied mathematics and science. In 1775, he became a mathematics teacher at the École Militaire in Paris, and in 1780 left to pursue his own research.

Legendre first studied the speed, path, and flight dynamics of missiles. In 1782, he wrote a paper on this topic, which earned him both a prize from the Berlin Academy and a degree of fame. A year later he was elected to the French Academy of Sciences.

Over the next couple of years, Legendre published articles on a number of topics, but his main areas of study were celestial mechanics (the effect of various forces on objects in space) and abstract mathematics. His career at the Academy flourished, and in 1785 he was promoted to the position of associate professor. The next year he published *Memoires de l'Academie des Sciences (Memoirs of the Academy of Sciences),* a text on the branch of calculus dealing with elliptical functions.

Soon thereafter the French Revolution began and research at the Academy was brought to a standstill. Legendre had used up the fortune he inherited and had to take a temporary job as a mathematics instructor. One year later, in 1794, he was hired by the French government to work on the standardization of weights and measures, and the general advancement of science. In that same year he published an instructor's manual for elementary geometry that was widely used for the next century.

From 1799 until 1815, Legendre worked in the mathematics department of the École Polytechnique. There he continued his study of orbits and published his results in 1806, in a book called *Nouvelles méthodes pour la détermination des orbits des cometes (New Methods for the Determination of Orbits of Comets).*

Legendre's next move was to the Bureau of Longitudes in Paris, a position he kept until his death in 1833. During this time he published highly regarded, detailed papers on elliptical functions.

Lemaître, Georges-Henri (1894–1966)
Belgian astrophysicist

Georges-Henri Lemaître, known as the "Father of the Big Bang," was born in the Belgian town of Charleroi. He spent a considerable number of years at the University of Louvain in Belgium, first as a student and later as a professor.

Lemaître's studies in civil engineering were interrupted when World War I broke out in 1914. He left school to serve as an artillery officer, but returned to school after the war and earned his Ph.D. In 1923, Lemaître was ordained a Jesuit priest. He then moved to London to study **astrophysics** at Cambridge University. He later transferred to the Massachusetts Institute of Technology (MIT), where he completed a second Ph.D. in 1927. After that Lemaître returned to the University of Louvain to teach.

Lemaître studied Albert Einstein's equations involving **gravity** and came to the conclusion that they described an expanding universe. Einstein himself disagreed with this theory. He was convinced that the universe was unchanging. In 1929, however, American astronomer Edwin Hubble found proof that all matter in space is moving away from all other matter.

Georges-Henri Lemaître.

Shortly thereafter, Lemaître deduced that if the universe were expanding, then by going back in time one would find that the universe must have originated from one point. He suggested that the universe had started out as a great primitive atom or "cosmic egg," which exploded and expanded, scattering matter outward at great distances.

Thus Lemaître became one of the pioneers of the **big bang theory,** the most commonly accepted theory today as to how the universe began. The big bang theory states that fifteen to twenty billion years ago, a huge explosion occurred, after which the universe expanded rapidly. It became flooded with subatomic particles that slammed into one another, forming the building blocks of stars, planets, and other celestial objects.

Lemaître published his findings in a book called *The Primeval Atom.* In a note to the reader he wrote, "I shall certainly not pretend that this hypothesis of the primeval atom is yet proved, and I would be very happy if it has not appeared to you to be either absurd or unlikely." He described the beginning of the universe as follows: "The evolution of the world could be compared to a display of fireworks just ended—some few red wisps, ashes, and smoke. Standing on a well-cooled cinder we see the slow fading of the suns and we try to recall the vanished brilliance of the origin of the worlds."

Lemaître was "a man of robust vigor," according to English astronomer Sir William McCrae. "He appeared to be the complete extrovert; he had a stentorian [extremely loud] laugh, which was readily provoked. To some extent, however, I think all that appearance was a protection for a sensitive personality. He was a man of courage."

See also **Big bang theory**

Leonov, Alexei (1934–)

Soviet cosmonaut

Alexei Leonov was the first person to travel in outer space outside of a spacecraft. On March 18, 1965, he floated for twelve minutes outside his vessel, *Voskhod 2.* This "first" represented yet another aeronautics victory for his country, the former **Soviet Union.** Since the early 1950s, both the Soviet Union and the United States had been frantically developing space programs. The **space race,** as it was called, had become an important element of the **cold war** between the two rival superpowers.

Leonov's historic flight was the tenth piloted space mission of all time and the sixth for the Soviet Union. On *Voskhod*'s second orbit around the Earth, Leonov put on a white spacesuit and a backpack containing an oxygen tank, and entered the spacecraft's airlock. When the entrance to the vessel was sealed off, Leonov opened the outer hatch and climbed out. He floated 17.5 feet (5.3 meters) away from the spacecraft, the total length of his safety line. He landed on top of the craft, where he remained a few minutes before pulling himself back to the hatch. Leonov then found that his spacesuit had ballooned out in places, making it impossible for him to

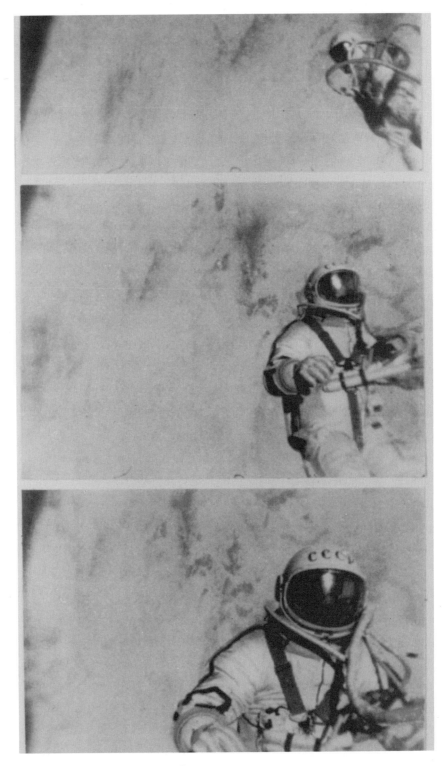

*Cosmonaut Alexei
Leonov floats away
from* Voskhod 2
*above the curvature
of the Earth—the
first man ever to be
in outer space
outside of a
spacecraft.*

fit back inside the hatch. He quickly solved the problem by releasing air from the suit.

Later in the flight, as Leonov and his crewmate Pavel Belyayev were preparing to return to Earth, they noticed their ship was pointed in the wrong direction. It took them another orbit to turn it around, making it necessary for them to alter their landing site. The two **cosmonaut**s parachuted to Earth in a remote region of the Ural mountains and spent two cold days in the woods before rescue teams reached them.

Alexei Arkhipovich Leonov was born in Listvyanka, Siberia. He had many siblings, including an older brother, a mechanic in the air force who inspired Leonov to become a pilot. Leonov also exhibited artistic talent as a youngster, leading his parents to expect he would become a professional artist.

After high school, Leonov began training at the Riga Academy of Arts, and at the same time, at a prep school for pilots. Once he decided on his career choice, he left art school and went to an air force school in the Ukraine. After graduation from that school in 1957, he continued his training as a jet pilot in the former East Germany and at the Zhukovsky Air Force Engineering Academy.

Leonov's Career As a Cosmonaut

In late 1959, Leonov was chosen to be among the first twenty cosmonauts. Upon completion of training, Leonov was considered a strong candidate to take the first ride into space. Unfortunately, he was too tall to fit comfortably into the small *Vostok* cabin and the honor for the first flight was given instead to a shorter cosmonaut, Yuri Gagarin. Leonov's big chance came two years later. In the summer of 1963, he began training for the mission that would make him the first man to walk in space.

Surprisingly, Leonov's closest brush with death came not in space, but on the ground. Two years after his **space walk,** Leonov was in a limousine on the way to a government reception at the Kremlin. A gunman approached and fired two bullets, each of which grazed Leonov's coat, and a third, which whizzed by Leonov's face. It turned out that the gunman had mistaken Leonov for President Leonid Brezhnev, whom he intended to assassinate.

At that time, Leonov was finishing his studies at the Zhukovsky. He had also been assigned to train the next team of cosmonauts to undertake a space walk, on the *Soyuz 1* mission. That mission was plagued with problems throughout and ended in tragedy when it crashed to Earth, killing cosmonaut Vladimir Komarov.

Leonov then participated for two years in the Soviet effort to land a cosmonaut on the moon, a goal that was never attained. After that, in 1969, Leonov began preparing for a long-term mission aboard the *Salyut* **space station.** But a series of setbacks made sure Leonov never made it. In spring of 1971, Leonov's crewmate, Valerly Kubasov, contracted a lung ailment, and the crew had to be replaced. The replacement crew, unfortunately, was from *Soyuz II,* launched on June 6, 1971. During their descent to Earth a valve opened unexpectedly, allowing the oxygen in the cabin to escape. The crew suffocated.

The string of disappointments ended in 1973. In May of that year, Leonov joined the team of the *Apollo-Soyuz* Test Project. This project was the first U.S.-Soviet joint venture in space and came to symbolize a new era of cooperation between the two nations. In preparation for the link-up between the two vessels in space, Leonov had to visit the United States several times and to play host to American visitors in the Soviet Union.

On July 15, 1975, Leonov and crewmate Valerly Kubasov launched into space aboard *Soyuz 19.* Seven hours later, the U.S. *Apollo 18* took off. That evening, the two spacecraft rendezvoused for the historic "handshake in space." The spacecraft remained docked for two days, during which time the crew members carried out joint astronomical experiments. After separating, *Soyuz* returned directly to Earth, landing six days after it had launched.

Leonov's next post was deputy director of the Gagarin Cosmonaut Center, where he was in charge of training cosmonauts. He remained there until his retirement in 1992.

Leonov never completely gave up his artistic endeavors. He has continued to paint, and his work has been exhibited at galleries around the world, including in the Smithsonian National Air and Space Museum in Washington, D.C. Leonov is also an accomplished author. He has published three art books, together with artist Andrei Sokolov, and has co-authored a screenplay. He is also the editor of the cosmonaut newspaper *Apogee* (formerly called *Neptune*).

Leonov and his wife, Svetlana, a teacher, live in Star Citya town near Moscow. They have two daughters. Leonov continues to travel the world, giving lectures on the importance of space flight.

See also **Apollo-Soyuz** **Test Project**; **Space race**; and **Vostok program**

Leverrier, Urbain (1811–1877)

French astronomer

Urbain Jean Joseph Leverrier is best known for his 1846 co-discovery of the planet Neptune. His name grew even more famous during the ensuing controversy over who really deserved credit for the find. Leverrier and English astronomer John Couch Adams had each independently predicted the same location of this new planet. That prediction was later confirmed by scientists at the Cambridge Observatory and the Berlin Observatory. The discovery was initially attributed to Leverrier. After much debate within the scientific community, however, Adams was named co-discoverer. It seemed as though the only two who avoided the bickering were Adams and Leverrier, who through it all became lifelong friends.

Leverrier was born in St Lô, in Normandy, into a family of modest means. His father was so dedicated to the young Leverrier's education that he sold his house to finance his son's schooling in Paris. Leverrier was admitted to the École Polytechnique (Technical School) in 1831, where he studied chemistry and mathematics.

Upon graduation, Leverrier went to work first for the state tobacco company, then for a chemical research firm. At the age of twenty-six, however, he switched fields to astronomy. A few years earlier, Leverrier had published a paper on shooting stars, which led to his being hired to teach astronomy at the École Polytechnique.

Urbain Leverrier.

Leverrier's Research On Celestial Mechanics

Leverrier chose as his specialty celestial mechanics, the movement of planets and other objects in the universe. Specifically, he investigated the mutual attractions of planets to one another. It was this study that led to his discovery of Neptune, which he suspected was causing irregularities in the orbit of neighboring planet Uranus.

All of Leverrier's planetary quests were not as fruitful. For instance, he also noticed unexplained irregularities in the orbit of Mercury

and in 1859 predicted they were caused by a planet even closer to the sun. He even gave this planet the name of Vulcan. Although numerous sightings of this supposed planet were reported, none was ever confirmed.

In 1847, Leverrier started on the massive task of compiling tables of the **mass**es and movements of all the planets, as well as devising theories to explain his findings. In the words of Leverrier, it was a way "of embracing in a single work the whole of the planetary system." This four thousand-page work was completed only a month before his death.

Leverrier was also a pioneer in the field of modern meteorology (the study of weather). He studied hurricane patterns and learned how to predict their paths. Then, in 1863, he devised a network to alert sailors all across continental Europe about the arrival of dangerous storms.

In 1854, at age forty-three, Leverrier became director of the Paris Observatory. It was there that his authoritarian nature began to cause problems for him. Leverrier became so unbearable that staff members, one by one, refused to work for him until they had all quit. The mass resignations led to Leverrier's replacement in 1870 by his rival Charles-Eugene Delaunay.

Three years later, after Delaunay's death, Leverrier was given a second chance at the position. Leverrier made good on this opportunity, and his second tenure was more positive than his first. For the first time in his career he trained a student, J. B. Gaillot, who continued Leverrier's research after Leverrier had passed away.

Beginning in 1848, Leverrier was also active in politics. He was elected as a representative from La Mancha to the government of the French Empire. His campaign stressed his Catholic and conservative values. He was subsequently appointed to the Imperial Senate.

Leverrier died at the age of sixty-six from a liver ailment, from which he suffered for the last five years of his life.

See also **Adams, John Couch** and **Neptune**

Lick Observatory

Lick Observatory has the dubious distinction of serving not only as an astronomical research center, but as a tomb for its founder, James Lick. Lick was the eccentric millionaire who made his fortune through land speculation during the California gold rush. He is buried beneath the observatory's oldest telescope, the 36-inch-diameter (91-centimeter-diameter) **refractor** Lick Telescope. At its base is a bronze plaque that reads simply: "Here lies the body of James Lick."

Founded in 1888 at Mount Hamilton in California, Lick Observatory was the first U.S. observatory to be placed on a mountaintop. James Lick wrote that his purpose in funding the venture was to construct ". . . a powerful telescope, superior to and more powerful than any telescope ever yet made . . . and also a suitable observatory." He had both of his wishes fulfilled. At the time it became operational, the Lick Telescope was the world's largest, and the Mount Hamilton observatory has proven "suitable" for a wide range of astronomical endeavors.

James Lick personally scouted out the site for his observatory. He first considered Lake Tahoe and then Mount St. Helens before deciding on Mount Hamilton, which is located near San Jose, California. The obser-

The Lick Observatory, home of the 120-inch (305-centimeter) Shane Telescope.

vatory occupies a 3,762-acre (1,522-hectare) parcel of land, about 4,200 feet (1,280 meters) above sea level.

There is now a small town on the mountain, populated primarily by the permanent observatory staff members and their families. The town includes a one-room schoolhouse for students in kindergarten through eighth grade, a post office, and recreational facilities.

Lick had instructed that the observatory be turned over to the University of California (U-Cal) on completion. This event occurred in 1888, twelve years after his death. The observatory headquarters—which consists of offices, a library, a computing center, and laboratories—is located on the U-Cal campus in Santa Cruz. The facilities provide support for astronomy faculty members and graduate students who come to the observatory from U-Cal branches in Berkeley, Los Angeles, and San Diego.

Today there are six telescopes on Mount Hamilton in addition to the original Lick Telescope. The most prominent is the C. Donald Shane Telescope, a 120-inch (305-centimeter) **reflector** that also functions as a **spectrograph.** Constructed in 1959, the Shane reflector remains one of the twenty largest telescopes in the world today. It also enabled astronomers, for the first time, to view a star's **spectrum** while it was being recorded. The observatory also includes a 20-inch (51-centimeter) **refractor telescope;** reflector telescopes of 40 inches (102 centimeters), 36 inches (91 centimeters), and 30 inches (76 centimeters); and a 24-inch (61-centimeter) **Coudé telescope.** A Coudé telescope is a modified reflector that has the eyepiece angled so that it keeps the image of an object in view, even as that object moves across the sky.

Over the years, the Lick Observatory has been the site of much pioneering work in astronomy. Four of Jupiter's moons were discovered there, as well as over five thousand pairs of **binary star**s. Recently, Lick astronomers have been studying **galaxies, quasar**s, **black hole**s, and the structure of stars and star clusters.

Lick Observatory is a now a partner in the joint-venture Keck Telescope, the largest telescope in the world, located at the Mauna Kea Observatory in Hawaii. Thus, staff astronomers from Lick and the U-Cal system regularly use this state-of-the-art instrument to supplement their ongoing research at Mount Hamilton.

See also **Spectroscopy**

Lovell, James (1928–)

American astronaut

Jim Lovell is a veteran of four space flights and very nearly became the fifth man to walk on the moon. On April 13, 1970, his *Apollo 13* spacecraft was over halfway to the moon when a serious accident took place. An explosion occurred, leaving the three-person crew without oxygen, water, and power. The only thing that saved the Lovell and his crewmates was their decision to return to Earth in the **lunar module,** which still had a basic life support system. The lunar module was far from comfortable, however. The temperature was just above freezing and there was very little water to last three-and-a-half days.

This "successful failure," as it has been called, would probably have ended in tragedy if not for the cool-headedness of the crew and the ground controllers in Houston and their ability to improvise new methods of spacecraft operation. *Apollo 13* appears to have provided Lovell with a lifetime of adventure. It was his final space flight.

James Arthur Lovell, Jr. was born in 1928 in Cleveland, Ohio. Ever since he was a youngster, he was fascinated by **rocket**s. In high school, Lovell, aided by his chemistry teacher, built a rocket that soared 80 feet (24 meters) in the air before crashing back down.

Lovell spent his first two years of college at the University of Wisconsin, where he also took flying lessons. He then transferred to the Naval Academy at Annapolis, Maryland. After writing his senior thesis on liquid-fuel rocketry, Lovell graduated in 1952. Three-and-a-half hours after the graduation ceremony Lovell married his high school sweetheart, Marilyn Gerlach. They eventually had four children: Barbara, James, Susan, and Jeffrey.

Lovell next underwent training in naval aviation. This job took him to various navy bases before he was assigned to the U.S. Naval Test Pilot School at Patuxent River, Maryland, in 1958. Two years later, Lovell was invited by the National Aeronautics and Space Administration (NASA) to apply to be among the first group of astronauts. He was ultimately excluded, however, because of a minor medical problem.

Lovell Becomes an Astronaut

In 1962, while working as a safety engineer for a fighter squadron at the Naval Air Station in Oceana, Virginia, Lovell applied for an astronaut position again. This time he was accepted. He spent the next year learning the basics of space flight.

Lovell became an astronaut during the Gemini program, which was intended to resolve some of the early problems of piloted space flight. Gemini flights were basically a dress rehearsal for the upcoming Apollo program, whose objective it was to land men on the moon.

In December 1965, Lovell piloted his first flight, *Gemini 7*. That fourteen-day flight had two objectives: to study the effects of long stays in space on humans and to rendezvous with *Gemini 6*, which had been launched eleven days after *Gemini 7*.

The following November, Lovell commanded the final mission of the series, *Gemini 12*, with Buzz Aldrin as pilot. The main goal of that flight was to perform a lengthy task outside the spacecraft, called an **ex-**

Apollo 13 commander James Lovell points to the lunar module that he and his crewmates were forced to travel back to Earth in after an explosion in the service module turned their moon landing mission into a mission of survival.

travehicular activity (EVA). Aldrin spent a total of five-and-a-half hours completing twenty simple spacecraft-maintenance tasks.

In December 1968, Lovell went into space on *Apollo 8* with crewmates Neil Armstrong and Aldrin. This flight, which lasted just over six days, was the first piloted flight around the moon. During one sixteen-hour period the spacecraft orbited the moon ten times. The crew of *Apollo 8* became the first humans to see the back side of the moon. None could have guessed at the time that Lovell would be the only man among them never to feel the lunar surface under his feet.

After the *Apollo 13* disaster, Lovell took a break from NASA to take classes at Harvard. He soon returned to assist in the mission control room for the *Apollo 14* flight on which Alan Shepard, the first man to fly in space, became the fifth man to walk on the moon. In May 1971, Lovell was named deputy director for science and applications at the Johnson Space Center in Houston, Texas, where he was assigned to the **space shuttle** program.

Lovell left NASA in 1973 to work in private industry. He started out with the Bay-Houston Towing Company, then became president of Fisk Telephone Systems. In January 1981, he took an executive position with Centel Corporation in Chicago. Lovell is now retired and lives in Texas.

See also **Apollo program**; *Apollo 13*; and **Gemini program**

Lowell, Percival (1855–1916)

American astronomer

Percival Lowell was a slightly eccentric astronomy buff remembered in different ways by different people. He is most often thought of as the famous "life-on-Mars enthusiast," and secondarily as the wealthy businessman/diplomat turned full-time amateur astronomer. Still others consider him the true discoverer of Pluto. Lowell's influence in the astronomical world continues to be felt today through the research carried out at the Flagstaff, Arizona, observatory which he founded and which bears his name.

Percival Lowell was born on March 13, 1855, into an affluent family in Brookline, Massachusetts. From a young age, Lowell was a superb student in all subjects, with a special gift for mathematics. He was drawn to astronomy early on and spent hours looking through a telescope on the roof of his family's house.

After high school, Lowell attended Harvard University, where he studied mathematics, physics, classical literature, and history. He continued his outstanding academic performance and graduated with high honors. One math teacher of Lowell's at the time referred to him as one of the most brilliant scholars he had ever seen.

The natural next step for Lowell was to join the family linen business, an occupation that took him to all corners of the globe. Lowell was quite a successful businessman and greatly increased the already large family fortune. His experience in Asia eventually earned him a diplomatic post with the first Korean embassy in the United States. Then, as Lowell approached his fortieth birthday, he made a career move. He abandoned his promising future as a diplomat and returned to his passion: astronomy.

*Percival Lowell
peers through one
of the the refractor
telescopes at the
Lowell Observatory.*

Lowell's Theories About Life on Mars

Lowell's decision to redirect his life was based in part on new discoveries about the surface features of Mars. Italian astronomer Giovanni Schiaparelli had reported observing a series of markings crossing the planet that he termed canali, or "channels." The term was mistranslated, however, and the rumor spread that Mars was covered with "canals," the products of an intelligent life form. In addition to providing fodder for science fiction writers, this information proved irresistible to many amateur astronomers like Lowell.

Lowell envisioned a dying Martian civilization, desperately trying to pump water from the poles to the desert-like populated areas near the equator. The dark color of the poles suggested that they might be covered with water. Based on information gathered by a series of **space probe**s launched by the United States and former **Soviet Union** in the 1960s and 1970s, scientists now know that Mars is a barren, desolate, crater-covered world incapable of supporting life. But in Lowell's time, before the turn of the century, the existence of life on Mars seemed a distinct possibility, and Lowell was determined to be the one to find it.

To this end, Lowell decided to build his own observatory. The first step was to find a suitable site. Lowell and Harvard astronomer Andrew Douglass headed west and made an extensive survey of the region before settling on Flagstaff, Arizona. At the time, Arizona was still a territory and Flagstaff merely a blip on the map. At that location, 7,200 feet (2,195 meters) above sea level, the night sky came to life through the telescope.

Lowell then borrowed, and later returned, two telescopes from a Philadelphia telescope-maker and oversaw the construction of a temporary dome in which to house the instruments. In April 1894, he began observations at the Flagstaff site, which he named "Mars Hill." He soon purchased the observatory's first telescope, a 24-inch (61-centimeter) **refractor.**

Lowell observed the Martian surface in earnest. In his mind, every new feature he discovered supported the existence of intelligent life. Lowell publicized his findings through a series of lectures and magazine articles. He also authored three books on the subject. While the general public was receptive to Lowell's ideas, the scientific community was not. The criticism and skepticism of professional astronomers weighed heavily on Lowell, contributing to his nervous breakdown in 1897.

After a four-year break from his work, Lowell returned to his observations of Mars, as well as Venus, Mercury, and Saturn. He hired additional staff for the observatory and expanded its program to include a range of astronomical quests. One of his assistants, Vesto Melvin Slipher, made an important discovery about "spiral **nebulae**" moving away from the Earth. This was the first evidence that the universe was expanding.

Lowell also instigated the search for a Planet X beyond the orbit of Neptune. He painstakingly photographed the area of the sky where he believed it should exist, but came up empty-handed. We now know that Lowell did indeed capture the image of a planet—Pluto—on film, but its presence was overlooked by his assistants. The credit for the discovery of Pluto goes instead to Clyde Tombaugh, another Mars Hill staff member who finally spotted the elusive planet during a search in 1930.

When Lowell died in 1916, he had been mistaken on two counts: he believed that life existed on Mars and that he had not found the ninth planet in our **solar system.** He would certainly be surprised to learn that he was wrong about the second point.

Lowell's astronomical legacy lives on in the Lowell Observatory. He left a sizable endowment which funded the observatory's operation for decades. Now run on grants, the observatory features modernized equipment and a large staff of talented astronomers. The observatory is known for its innovative educational programs and cutting-edge research.

See also **Lowell Observatory**; **Mars**; and **Pluto**

Lowell Observatory

The Lowell Observatory was founded in 1894 by the wealthy amateur astronomer Percival Lowell. At the age of thirty-nine, Lowell gave up a promising career as a diplomat and set out for Flagstaff, Arizona, to pursue his lifelong passion—astronomy. The observatory, which recently celebrated its one hundredth birthday, began as a humble facility with one building, one telescope, and two staff members. It has since evolved into a world-class operation with several sophisticated instruments and a staff of more than thirty people plus visiting astronomers from all over the world.

Lowell Observatory occupies a tract of land dubbed "Mars Hill" by its founder. Mars Hill is in north-central Arizona, 7,200 feet (2,195 meters) above sea level. The observatory overlooks Flagstaff, which is today a medium-sized town and home to Northern Arizona University. As the population of Flagstaff increased and light pollution became a problem, the observatory acquired a second site at Anderson Mesa, 12 miles (19 kilometers) southeast of Flagstaff. Lowell Observatory also operates a telescope at the Perth Observatory in western Australia.

A number of prominent astronomers have made important discoveries at Lowell over the years. Perhaps the best known is Clyde Tombaugh's discovery of Pluto in 1930. Equally significant, however, was Vesto Melvin Slipher's 1912 finding that "spiral **nebula**e" are moving away from the Earth. Slipher's discovery provided the first evidence of an expanding universe.

The observatory has also been the site of pioneering work in the field of **infrared astronomy** by Carl Lampland and Arthur Adel, as well as the discovery of many **white dwarf** stars by Henry Giclas. After World War II, the U.S. Weather Bureau signed a contract to study the atmospheres of Mars, Saturn, and Jupiter at the observatory. The Air Force later made a similar arrangement to study the effects of sunlight on Uranus and Neptune.

Lowell Observatory Telescopes

The observatory's earliest instrument—a 24-inch-diameter (61-centimeter-diameter) **refractor telescope** made by famed telescope maker Alvan G. Clark—is still in use today. The second telescope, a 13-inch (33-centimeter) refractor was donated by Percival Lowell's brother, Lawrence Lowell, who was president of Harvard. The telescope was built specifically for the search for Pluto, and now remains on the site as a part of a historic display. Mars Hill also now contains an 18-inch (46-centimeter) refractor for tracking the positions of stars as well as a 21-inch (53-centimeter) **reflector telescope** for studies of the sun. Three more reflector telescopes are located at Anderson Mesa: a 31-inch (79-centimeter), a 42-inch (107-centimeter), and a 72-inch (183-centimeter) moved there in 1961 from the Perkins Observatory in Ohio. Most of these telescopes are equipped with electronic cameras, modern **spectrograph**s, and various computerized devices.

A wide range of research projects has been undertaken at Lowell in recent years. A sampling of these studies include: the mapping of Pluto, studying the rings around Uranus, and cataloguing the properties of **comet**s. There is also an ongoing investigation into the nature and orbits of **asteroid**s, as well as research on the star-forming regions known as "**stellar nurseries**" of the **Milky Way** and other **galaxies**.

The current staff of Lowell Observatory continues the tradition begun by Percival Lowell of welcoming the public and contributing to the education of young astronomers. Every summer the observatory hires student interns and hosts a three-week field camp for undergraduate students from the Massachusetts Institute of Technology. It also offers observing time on its 31-inch (79-centimeter) telescope to undergraduate students and faculty from a number of small colleges, as well as to graduate students conducting research on their doctoral theses.

The facility is open to the general public for guided tours and browsing, and in the evening guests can observe the skies through the original Clark Telescope. A newly constructed visitor center contains exhibits, a library, and a lecture room where slides are shown.

See also **Infrared astronomy**; **Lowell, Percival**; **Red-shift**; **Slipher, Vesto Melvin**; **Stellar evolution**; **Tombaugh, Clyde**; and **White dwarf star**

Lucid, Shannon (1943–)

American astronaut

Shannon Lucid was born a traveler. She started out life in Shanghai, China, where her parents were Baptist missionaries. In her early years, her family moved from China to Texas, back to China, and then to Oklahoma. As a child, Lucid longed to go back in time and be a pioneer, so she could explore the uncharted territory of the western United States. Since that kind of trip was not an option, she looked for another wide open place to visit and found it: space.

On March, 23, 1996, the fifty-three-year-old Lucid blasted off in the **space shuttle** *Atlantis,* bound for the Russian *Mir* **space station.** That was Lucid's fifth space flight, making her the first woman to undertake that number of missions. And that was not the only record set by Lucid. She remained for 188 days on the space station, the longest period of time ever spent by a U.S. astronaut in space.

Shannon Wells Lucid was born in China in 1943. At the age of six weeks, she and her parents were taken prisoner by Japanese forces. They were held in a concentration camp for a year before being released in a prisoner exchange. The family came to the United States to wait out the end of World War II, after which they returned to China. In 1949, the Chinese Communist revolution drove the Lucids back to the United States.

From that point on, the Lucid family considered Bethany, Oklahoma, their home. Shannon attended high school there, graduating in 1960. She next attended the University of Oklahoma, from which she earned a bachelor's degree in chemistry in 1963, a master's degree in biochemistry in 1970, and a Ph.D. in biochemistry in 1973.

During her college years, Lucid held a number of research jobs with medical organizations, such as the University Health Science Centers Department of Biochemistry and Molecular Biology and the Oklahoma Medical Research Foundation. After earning her Ph.D., Lucid continued to work as a research associate at the Foundation until joining the National Aeronautics and Space Administration (NASA) in 1978.

Lucid was selected by NASA to be among the first group of female astronauts, which also included Sally Ride and Judith Resnik. In August 1979, after a year of training, Lucid qualified to serve as a mission specialist (the person responsible for equipment and cargo) on space shuttle missions. In the six years before her first space flight, Lucid worked on equipment development and shuttle testing in Downey, California, and at the Kennedy Space Center (KSC) in Cape Canaveral, Florida.

Lucid's Space Shuttle Missions

Lucid's first space shuttle mission was on the *Discovery*. The eight-day mission, which was launched on June 17, 1985, transported into space three communications satellites: the Mexican *Morelos,* the Arab League *Arabsat,* and the American *Telstar.* The crew also set the SPARTAN (Shuttle Autonomous Research Tool for Astronomy) satellite outside of the cargo bay, leaving it to perform **X-ray** astronomy experiments for seventeen hours before retrieving it.

Not until October 1989, did Lucid fly in space again. This time she was a crew member of the space shuttle *Atlantis*. The purpose of the short flight was to send out the *Galileo* **probe** in the direction of Jupiter. On that mission, Lucid and her crewmates also performed a number of scientific experiments on subjects ranging from atmospheric ozone, to radiation, to lightning. They even carried along a student experiment on crystal growth in space.

Lucid again flew aboard *Atlantis* in August 1991. On that nine-day mission, which orbited the Earth 142 times, the crew transported into space a Tracking and Data Relay Satellite and conducted thirty-two science experiments. Two years later, Lucid participated in the longest shuttle mission up to that time, a fourteen-day trip on the *Columbia*. On that mission, Lucid and her crewmates performed numerous medical tests on themselves and on forty-eight rats.

Soon after her fourth flight, Lucid was selected to be one of four NASA astronauts to take turns living on the *Mir* space station over a two-year period. To prepare for her five-month stay, Lucid began a year-long training program in February 1995 at a city outside of Moscow, called Star City. There she learned basic Russian and information about the science experiments she would conduct on *Mir.*

Lucid has three grown children, two daughters and a son. She and her husband, Michael Lucid, live in Houston, Texas.

See also Mir **space station**

Luna program

Between the years 1959 and 1976, the **Soviet Union**'s Luna **space probe**s thoroughly explored the moon and the space around it. This series of twenty-four **probes** accomplished a number of "firsts" in unpiloted space exploration, including orbiting, photographing, and landing on the moon. Two Luna craft even deposited robotic moon cars that crossed the lunar surface, analyzing soil composition. Experts have speculated that the Soviets intended the Luna program to be a stepping stone for piloted lunar missions, a feat they were never able to achieve.

Luna 1, the first satellite to travel beyond the Earth's gravitational field, was launched toward the moon in January 1959. Although it missed its mark and was eventually pulled into orbit around the sun, it did fly within 3,400 miles (5,470 kilometers) of the moon. During this fly-by, *Luna 1* measured and reported valuable information on the moon's radiation and **magnetic field**s.

Luna 2, launched the following September, was right on target. It was so right on that it crashed, becoming the first human-made object to land on the moon. The next Luna, *Luna 3,* passed behind the moon and took pictures that provided humans with the first view of the far side of the moon (the side that never faces Earth).

The Luna program then was put on hold while Soviet engineers developed more sophisticated craft, capable of "soft landings" (as opposed to crashing) on the moon. As it turned out, a soft landing was not so easy. Beginning in 1963, the next seven moon probes launched by the Soviets (five of which bore the name *Luna*) either self-destructed during launch, missed their target, or crash-landed.

The Soviets finally scored a victory in February 1966 when *Luna 9* was dropped to the lunar surface and made history's first soft landing of a human-made object on the moon. The spherical probe contained a television camera, with which it transmitted footage of the moonscape all around it. People the world over were dazzled by this first detailed look at the moon.

The successful *Luna 9* was followed by a series of probes, launched over the next two years, that went into lunar orbit. These probes studied

Luna 9, *1966.*

the conditions in space around the moon, such as radiation and **gravity,** to determine how they might affect human travelers.

The Shift from a Piloted to an Unpiloted Program

Not long after these flights, however, the Soviet program changed direction. The 1966 death of their brilliant space program leader Sergei Korolëv, coupled with the U.S. victory in the race to put a man on the moon, prompted Soviet planners to give up their quest for piloted lunar landings. They shifted their emphasis instead to a program of robotic moon exploration.

In September 1970, after one unsuccessful attempt in the previous year, *Luna 16* landed on the moon. It collected a sample of lunar soil, placed it on a return capsule, and sent it back to Earth. Three successive Luna probes over the next few years landed on various parts of the moon and sent back samples.

Also between November 1971 and January 1973, two lunar roving cars were placed on the moon by Luna probes. The remote-controlled vehicles, called *Lunakhod 1* and *2,* were bathtub-shaped eight-wheelers. Each was 8 feet (2.4 meters) long by 5.25 feet (1.6 meters) wide and had a lid made of solar cells. The first car operated for nearly a year and the second for about two-and-a-half months. They cruised over the rocky terrain, taking photographs and measuring the chemical composition of the soil, before sending this information back to Earth.

The highly successful moon-exploration series ended with *Luna 24* in August 1976. The Soviets next turned their attention to the exploration of Venus and the development of the Salyut program of **space station**s.

See also **Lunar exploration** and **Pioneer program**

Lunar eclipse

A **lunar eclipse** occurs when the Earth passes between the sun and moon, casting a shadow on the moon. This event is different than a **solar eclipse,** which occurs when the moon passes between the sun and the Earth, preventing the sun's light from reaching our planet. One way to remember the difference is that one can only witness a lunar eclipse at night, when the moon is up, whereas a solar eclipse occurs during the day, when the sun is up.

The term "eclipse" means literally the complete or partial blocking of a celestial body by another. Eclipses happen only when the sun, moon, and Earth are all positioned in a straight line. This situation does not occur often because the plane of the Earth's orbit around the sun is at different angle from the plane of the moon's orbit around the Earth. Therefore, the moon is usually located just above or below the imaginary line connecting the sun and Earth. Only about every six months do the planes of the Earth, moon, and sun all intersect, creating the conditions needed for an eclipse.

A lunar eclipse can only occur during a full moon, when the moon lies behind the Earth, opposite the sun, and is fully illuminated. As the moon crosses into the Earth's **umbra** (the dark, core area of its shadow), it does not become totally hidden. The reason is that molecules of gas in the Earth's atmosphere cause the sun's light to bend around the surface of the planet. Some light still reaches the moon, giving it a reddish appearance.

Five phases of a lunar eclipse are pictured in multiple exposure over the skyline of Toronto, Ontario, Canada, on August 16, 1989.

If the entire moon falls within the umbra, the result is a total lunar eclipse. If only part of the moon passes through the umbra, or if it only passes through the **penumbra** (the lighter shadow region surrounding the umbra) a partial lunar eclipse occurs. A partial lunar eclipse may be difficult to detect because the moon dims only slightly.

A total lunar eclipse occurs in stages. As the moon moves first into the Earth's umbra, one edge of the moon begins to darken. Gradually, the umbra covers the whole moon and then recedes, leaving a full moon once again.

Lunar eclipses are more common than solar eclipses. With a solar eclipse, the sun, moon, and Earth have to be in nearly perfect alignment. The reason that perfect alignment is necessary is that the Earth, the sun and moon all appear to be about the same size in the sky. Thus, if the moon lies directly in the sun's path, it will block out the sunlight, and a total eclipse occurs. If the moon is even slightly above or below the line connecting the sun and Earth, no more than a partial eclipse will result. Lunar eclipses, however, are a different story. The Earth is relatively close to and large compared to the moon. Thus, any shadow cast by the Earth will at least partly cover the moon.

A lunar eclipse also lasts longer than its solar counterpart. When the sky is clear, a lunar eclipse can be viewed all night. A solar eclipse, on the hand, lasts only a few minutes. Also unlike a solar eclipse, which is only visible along a narrow strip of the Earth's surface, a lunar eclipse can be seen from everywhere on the planet where it's nighttime.

See also **Lunar phases** and **Solar eclipse**

Lunar exploration

As the Earth's closest neighbor, the moon has long represented a natural place to begin our exploration of the **solar system.** Since 1958, over five dozen space vehicles have been launched toward the moon, the vast majority of them unpiloted. This list includes vehicles that have flown past the moon for a quick glimpse; those that have gone into orbit around the moon, sending back information for years; and those that have missed their target altogether and ended up orbiting the sun. Some **space probe**s have crash-landed on the lunar surface or descended to a soft landing, taking pictures and collecting soil samples. The most celebrated of all lunar vehicles have been the piloted Apollo missions that transported the first humans to the moon. Outside of the Earth, the moon remains today the most throughly explored celestial body and the only one to have been visited by humans.

For over a decade, the moon was a major focus of the **space race,** the contest between the United States and former **Soviet Union** for superiority in space exploration. The Soviets gained the lead in the first leg of the race with victories in the categories of satellite launch, moon exploration, and piloted space flight. But the United States swept the final stages of the race, becoming the first and only nation to succeed in putting a man on the moon.

Early Years of Lunar Exploration

In 1957, the Soviets ushered in the **space age** with the launch of the first satellite, *Sputnik.* Early the next year, the United States sent off its

On the moon: Mount Hadley rises 14,765 feet (4,500 meters) above the lunar surface.

first satellite, *Explorer 1*, followed by three unsuccessful attempts to send Pioneer **probe**s into lunar orbit. In early 1959, the Soviets accomplished what the Americans could not with *Luna 1*, the first lunar fly-by (voyage past the moon).

Between the years 1959 and 1976, the Soviet Union's Luna space **probe**s thoroughly explored the moon and the space around it. This series of twenty-four probes accomplished a number of "firsts" in unpiloted space exploration, including orbiting, photographing, and landing on the moon. Two Luna craft even deposited robotic moon cars that crossed the lunar surface, analyzing soil composition.

Luna 2 was launched in September 1959 and crash-landed onto the lunar surface, becoming the first human-made object to reach the moon. A few months later, *Luna 3* took the first pictures of the far side of the moon (the side that never faces Earth).

In February 1966, *Luna 9* was dropped to the lunar surface, making the first soft-landing of a human-made object on the moon. The spherical probe contained a television camera that transmitted footage of the moonscape around it. In September 1970, *Luna 16* became the first of four probes to collect lunar soil samples and return them to Earth. Between November 1971 and January 1973, two lunar roving cars were placed on the moon by Luna probes. The remote-controlled vehicles, called *Lunakhod 1* and *2*, cruised over the rocky terrain, taking photographs and measuring the chemical composition of the soil.

The U.S. Lunar Exploration Program

The U.S. lunar exploration program saw its initial success in March 1959, two months after *Luna 1*, with the lunar fly-by of *Pioneer 4*. Two years later, the Ranger series of probes was inaugurated. After launch failures of *Ranger 1* and *2*, the third flew past the moon and entered a solar orbit. The fourth through sixth vessels in the series, launched between 1962 and 1964, either crashed into the moon or missed it altogether. In any case, they failed to return any information to Earth. The last members of the fleet—*Rangers 7, 8,* and *9*—made up for the shortcomings of the first six. Each of these missions, which took place in 1964 and 1965, transmitted detailed pictures of the lunar surface before crash landing.

Over the next three years, the United States deployed a dozen space probes to the surface of, and into orbit around, the moon. The purpose of the Surveyor and Lunar Orbiter vessels was to collect information that would assist in planning the route and landing sites of the upcoming piloted lunar landing missions of the Apollo program.

The Apollo program was the focus of U.S. efforts in space for the years 1967–1972. The initial successful piloted mission of the series, *Apollo 7*, was launched in October 1968. During that mission, three astronauts orbited the Earth for eleven days. Two months later, the crew of *Apollo 8* became the first humans to escape the Earth's gravitational field and orbit the moon.

Apollo 11, the most famous Apollo flight, was launched on July 16, 1969. Four days later astronauts Neil Armstrong and Buzz Aldrin climbed into the **lunar module** and landed on the moon. Over the next three years, five more Apollo missions landed twelve more Americans on the moon.

Since the days of the Apollo and Luna flights, lunar exploration has slowed considerably. In fact, not a single vehicle was sent to the moon between the years 1976 and 1989. Then in 1990, the Japanese twin *Muses-A* became the only probes not launched by the United States or Soviet Union to reach the moon. These vessels went into lunar orbit, but failed to transmit any data.

The most recent U.S. lunar probe was the *Clementine*, launched in 1994 by the Department of Defense. It orbited the moon for seventy days, making a detailed map of the lunar surface. Three more moon probes are scheduled for launch between 1997 and 2002, two from the United States and one from Japan. The purpose of these probes is to learn more about the moon's interior structure, **magnetic field**s, and gravitational field.

See also **Apollo program**; **Luna program**; **Moon**; and **Pioneer program**

Lunar module

The **lunar module** (LM) is the detachable portion of the Apollo spacecraft in which U.S. astronauts descended to the moon. The LM was used in all six lunar landing missions (*Apollo 11* through *17*, not counting the aborted *Apollo 13*) during the years 1969–1972. The other components of an Apollo spacecraft were the **command module** (CM), where the astronauts and control center were situated, and the **service module** (SM), which contained supplies and equipment.

At launch, the LM was sandwiched in a short section of the spacecraft between the top portion of the **rocket** and the SM. The cone-shaped CM perched at the top of the vessel. After launch, the rocket fell away from the three modules one stage at a time. Once the vessel left its Earth orbit and began heading toward the moon, the command and service modules (together called the CSM) separated from the LM, turned around, and docked so that the LM was attached to the front of the CM. When the spacecraft was positioned above the moon, the LM again separated, this time with astronauts inside. Two astronauts used the LM as a shuttle to and from the lunar surface, while the third astronaut waited in the CSM, which orbited the moon.

The LM was an odd-shaped, very un-aerodynamic-looking structure. With its landing gear extended, this 16.5-ton (15-metric ton) vessel stood 23 feet (7 meters) high and 31 feet (9.4 meters) across. It had a bulky body set atop four spindly landing legs, which earned it the nickname "the bug."

Lunar module.

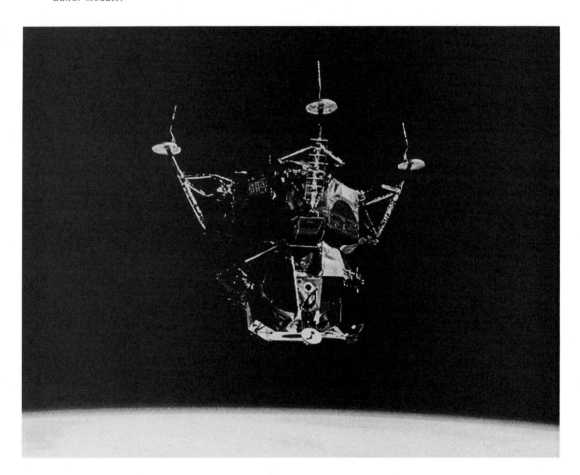

The LM was divided into two sections, the ascent (upper) stage and the descent (lower) stage. The ascent stage consisted of a pressurized cabin with computer, navigation, and propulsion systems. The cabin was 92 inches (234 centimeters) in diameter, just large enough for two astronauts to stand side-by-side. The cabin had two forward-facing, triangular windows set in one wall and a square-shaped entry hatch set in another. While on the lunar surface, the astronauts were able to repressurize the LM cabin four times, meaning they could make only four journeys out of the craft and back.

The descent stage contained the landing gear, main engines, and water and fuel tanks. It also held self-contained scientific experiments that recorded data on the moon's **magnetic field** and the effects of the **solar wind** as well as a seismometer which measured "moonquakes." The descent stage remained on the lunar surface when the ascent stage lifted off. Once the astronauts were back inside the CSM, the ascent stage fell back to the surface as well.

In the final three lunar landing missions (*Apollo 15, 16,* and *17*) the LM's descent stage also carried a lunar roving vehicle, better known as a "moon buggy." This vehicle looked like a golf cart, except it was larger (10 feet, or 3 meters, long by 6 feet, or 1.8 meters, wide), with wider tires and various antennae sticking out. The moon buggy was able to travel at a speed of no more than 9 miles (14 kilometers) per hour, yet it gave the astronauts a greater range in which to collect rocks and soil.

See also **Apollo program**; **Command module**; **Lunar exploration**; and **Spacecraft design**

Lunar phases

A lunar phase is defined by the shape of the illuminated portion of moon, as it appears to observers on Earth. At successive points on the moon's path around the Earth, we can see various portions of the moon's sunlit surface. How the moon looks to us depends on the relative positions of the sun, Earth, and moon. For example, when the moon passes in front of the Earth (between the Earth and sun) it is not visible at all. But when it passes behind the Earth, it appears full. As the moon moves between these two extremes, we can see various amounts of its surface.

It takes the moon about one month (twenty-nine and one-half days) to complete a cycle of phases, the equivalent of one lunar orbit around the

Earth. The lunar cycle begins with a new moon, one that is not visible. A new moon occurs when the moon lies in the same direction as the sun (positioned between the Earth and the sun). Since sunlight strikes the side of the moon facing away from us, we cannot see the moon at all.

Each day thereafter, as the moon moves along its orbit around the Earth, a larger slice of the sunlit side of the moon faces us. For the first week of its cycle, the moon is said to be in the waxing crescent phase. The term "waxing" means an increasing amount of surface is visible. By the end of the week the moon is about one quarter of the way through its orbit. The phase at this point is referred to as a first quarter moon. In this position, the moon forms a right angle with the Earth and sun and about half of the moon's illuminated side is visible from Earth.

During the second week, as the moon travels to a point behind the Earth (where the moon and sun are opposite one another with the Earth in between), it's said to be in the waxing gibbous phase. Gibbous refers to the shape of the moon when more than half, but not all, of it is illuminated. During this leg of the moon's journey, our view of the lighted part of the moon continues to increase daily. This phase peaks when the moon is about fourteen days through its cycle, assuming a position directly across from the sun with the Earth in between the two bodies. At that point, the entire lighted side of the moon is facing the Earth, and we see a full moon, one which appears as a complete circle in the sky.

Occasionally during a full moon the sun, moon, and Earth are all positioned in a straight line and a **lunar eclipse** results. A lunar eclipse does not occur very often because the plane of the Earth's orbit around the sun is at a different angle from that of the plane of the moon's orbit around the Earth. Therefore, the moon is usually located just above or below the imaginary line connecting the sun and Earth. Only twice a year, about every six months, do the planes of the Earth, moon, and sun all intersect.

After the full moon, the second half of the lunar orbit begins, and the phases repeat in the reverse order. In the third week the moon enters the waning gibbous phase. As it moves to the side of the Earth opposite where it was in the first quarter, we see less and less of it. About twenty-two days into the cycle, the moon again appears as a semi-circle, or a third quarter moon. The fourth and final quarter of the moon's revolution is called the waning crescent phase. Each day, leading up to day twenty-nine, the moon appears as a thinner and thinner slice until it disappears altogether. Then it is once again a new moon and the process starts over again.

See also **Lunar eclipse**; **Moon**; and **Tides**

Magellan

On May 4, 1989, the **space probe** *Magellan* was launched from the **space shuttle** *Atlantis,* making it the first planetary explorer to be launched from a shuttle. The **probe** circled the sun one-and-a-half times before reaching Venus fifteen months later on August 10, 1990.

For the next four years, *Magellan* used sophisticated radar equipment to survey 99 percent of the planet's surface. In this way, it created the most highly detailed map of Venus to date and produced images of such high quality that for the first time scientists could study the planet's geological history. *Magellan* also measured the Venusian gravitational field. It eventually entered the planet's atmosphere and burned up on October 12, 1994.

The forerunner to the *Magellan* was the Venus Orbiting Imaging Radar, proposed by the National Aeronautics and Space Administration (NASA) in the early 1980s and rejected because of its cost. In response to this rejection, NASA officials designed the more economical Venus Radar Mapper (VRM), which would incorporate spare parts left over from *Voyager, Galileo,* and *Ulysses* spacecraft. In 1984, VRM was approved by Congress and two years later was renamed *Magellan.*

The *Magellan* spacecraft weighed 3.3 tons (3 metric tons) and measured nearly 20 feet (6 meters) tall by 14.75 feet (4.5 meters) wide. Protruding from the top was an 11.5-foot-diameter (3.5-meter-diameter) antenna dish used for radar and communications with Earth, salvaged from the Voyager program. *Magellan* contained radar electronics, control systems, star trackers, maneuvering thrusters, and energy-generating solar panels.

Magellan

Image of the space probe Magellan being launched from the Atlantis space shuttle.

Beginning in 1961, a long string of space probes from the United States and the former **Soviet Union** have examined the Venusian atmosphere and peered beneath its dense cloud cover. They have found that Venus is an extremely hot, dry planet, with no signs of life. Its atmosphere is made primarily of carbon dioxide with some nitrogen and trace amounts of water vapor, acids, and heavy metals, and its clouds are laced with sulfur dioxide. The surface is rocky and covered with volcanoes, lava plains, mountains, and craters.

Magellan discovered that, from a geological viewpoint, the planet's surface is relatively young. Astronomers analyzing *Magellan*'s data have concluded that about three hundred to five hundred years ago lava surfaced and covered the entire planet, giving it a fresh, new face.

Magellan collected enough information to keep scientists busy with analyses for years to come. Even so, there is discussion of sending a joint U.S.-Russian space probe-laboratory back to Venus to learn more as early as 1997.

See also **Mariner program**; **Vega program**; **Venera program**; and **Venus**

Mariner program

Between the years 1962 and 1975, the United States launched or attempted to launch ten Mariner **space probe**s. The goal of this series of unpiloted spacecraft was to explore Mercury, Venus, and Mars. The Mariner program was one of the first projects undertaken by the National Aeronautics and Space Administration (NASA), following its creation in 1958.

The Mariner program was conceived near the start of the **space race** in which planetary investigation was an important category. It was in this competitive spirit that NASA rushed to get the first Mariner **probe** into space. On July 22, 1962, as *Mariner 1* began to lift off the launch pad, problems were discovered with the **launch vehicle.** The launch **rocket** misfired, causing the spacecraft to veer off course. Engineers at the control station had to destroy *Mariner 1* over the Pacific Ocean so that it would not crash into a populated area.

Almost one month later another launch was attempted. This time all went well and *Mariner 2,* the backup to *Mariner 1,* became the first successful interplanetary spacecraft. As it orbited the sun for nearly a year, *Mariner 2* transmitted data on **magnetic field**s, **cosmic dust,** and the **solar wind.** In December 1962, the probe flew past Venus and reported that the planet had a much hotter surface temperature than expected, an incredible 900 degrees Fahrenheit (482 degrees Celsius).

The next probe, launched in 1964, did not reach its intended destination, Mars. After attaining an Earth orbit, the probe's systems failed. First, it did not achieve the velocity it needed to escape Earth's orbit and head for Mars. Next, its solar panels did not unfold properly, meaning that it was unable to generate electricity. Ground control finally lost communication with the vessel, and it drifted out into orbit around the sun.

Mariner Studies of Mars and Venus

Once again, NASA had created a backup—*Mariner 4*. In 1965, after a seven-and-a-half-month journey, it became the first vessel to fly past

July 13, 1965. Mariner 4 prepares for its historic voyage to Mars.

Mars. In addition to providing the first pictures of the cratered Martian surface, it found that Mars has a thin atmosphere made mostly of carbon dioxide. Much to the disappointment of science fiction enthusiasts, the probe found no sign of life on the planet.

Mariner 5, a spacecraft similar to *Mariner 4,* set out in 1967 to explore Venus. In October 1967, four months after launch, the probe flew within 2,480 miles (3,990 kilometers) of the planet. It studied the Venusian magnetic field and atmosphere before entering into a solar orbit.

At about the same time the *Apollo 11* astronauts were taking their historic moonwalk in 1969, *Mariner 6* and *7* again flew by Mars. These two probes carried two television cameras each and produced over two hundred images of Mars, many close-up and quite spectacular. They also obtained detailed measurements of the structure and composition of the Martian atmosphere and surface. Their findings confirmed earlier suspicions that Mars is a lifeless world.

Mariner 8, intended as the first spacecraft to orbit Mars, was launched in May 1971. It experienced a launch failure, however, and tumbled into the Atlantic Ocean.

Six months later, *Mariner 9* was launched successfully and became the first vessel to orbit any planet besides Earth. Over the course of a year, its two television cameras sent back footage of an intense Martian dust storm, as well as images of 90 percent of the planet's surface and the two Martian moons.

Mariner 10, the first and only probe to visit Mercury, was launched in 1973. That vessel, the final in the Mariner series, first approached Venus in February 1974, then used that planet's gravitational field to send it like a slingshot around the sun in the direction of Mercury. After another seven-week journey it came within 470 miles (756 kilometers) of Mercury and photographed about 40 percent of the planet's surface. The probe then went into orbit around the sun. It flew past Mercury twice more in the next year before the remaining control gas ran out and contact with *Mariner 10* was lost.

See also **Mars**; **Mercury**; and **Venus**

Mars

The planet Mars was named for the Roman god of war. It was long believed to hold life, perhaps even intelligent, human-like life. Early astronomers peered through telescopes and saw dark areas on the planet, connected by lines. Some imaginative scientists theorized that the dark spots were seas and that the lines were channels dug by Martian engineers to bring water to populated areas. However, a series of **space probe**s launched by the United States and the former **Soviet Union** in the 1960s and 1970s put an end to such speculation.

Spacecraft sent to Mars revealed a barren, desolate, crater-covered world prone to frequent, violent dust storms. They found little oxygen, no liquid water, and **ultraviolet radiation** at levels that would kill any known life form. The high temperature on Mars was measured at -20 degrees Fahrenheit (-29 degrees Celsius) in the afternoon, and the low was -120 degrees Fahrenheit (-84 degrees Celsius) at night.

The two most distinguishing features of the northern hemisphere of Mars are a 15-mile-high (24-kilometer-high) volcano called Olympus Mons, larger than any other in the **solar system,** and a 2,000-mile-long

Mars, the red planet.

(3,220-kilometer-long) canyon called Valle Marineris, twenty-six times as long and three times as deep as the Grand Canyon. The southern hemisphere is noteworthy for Hellas, an ancient canyon that was long ago filled with lava and is now a large, light area covered with dust.

Mars is also marked by what appear to be dried riverbeds and flash-flood channels. These features could mean that ice below the surface melts and is brought above ground by occasional volcanic activity. The water may temporarily flood the landscape before boiling away in the low atmospheric pressure. Another theory is that these eroded areas could be left over from a warmer, wetter period in Martian history.

Mars is about half the size of Earth and has a rotation period just slightly longer than one Earth day. Since it takes Mars 687 days to orbit the sun, its seasons are about twice as long as ours. Mars has two polar caps. The northern one is larger and colder than the southern. Two small moons, Phobos and Deimos, orbit the planet.

Exploration of Mars

The Soviet Union was the first nation to send an unpiloted mission to Mars. After a number of unsuccessful attempts, they launched the *Mars 1* spacecraft in late 1962, but lost radio contact with it after a few months. In 1971, they succeeded in putting *Mars 2* and *Mars 3* in orbit around Mars. Both of these craft carried landing vehicles which successfully dropped to the planet's surface. But in each case, radio contact was lost after about twenty seconds. Two years later the Soviets sent out four more spacecraft from the Mars series, only one of which successfully transmitted data about the planet.

In 1988, the Soviets renewed their interest in Mars with the Phobos program. They launched two identical spacecraft, *Phobos 1* and *Phobos 2,* both headed for the Martian moon Phobos. Contact with both probes was lost before either reached its destination.

In the meantime, the U.S. space program was busy with its own study of Mars. The first U.S. probe, *Mariner 4,* flew past Mars in 1965. It sent back twenty-two pictures of the planet and gave us our first glimpse of its cratered surface. It also revealed that Mars has a thin atmosphere made mostly of carbon dioxide and that the atmospheric pressure at the surface of Mars is less than 1 percent of that on Earth.

The 1969 fly-by flights of *Mariner 6* and *Mariner 7* produced 201 new images of Mars, as well as more detailed measurements of the structure and composition of its atmosphere and surface. They determined that the polar ice caps are made of haze, dry ice, and clouds.

Two years later, *Mariner 9* became the first spacecraft to orbit Mars. During its year in orbit, *Mariner 9*'s two television cameras sent back pictures of an intense Martian dust storm, as well as images of 90 percent of the planet's surface and the two Martian moons. It observed an older, cratered surface on Mars' southern hemisphere and younger surface features on the northern hemisphere.

The most recent and most direct encounters with Mars were made in 1976 by the U.S. probes *Viking 1* and *Viking 2*. Each *Viking* spacecraft consisted of both an orbiter and a lander. *Viking 1* made the first successful soft landing on Mars on July 20, 1976. A soft landing is one in which the spacecraft is intact and functional on landing. Soon after, *Viking 2* landed on the other side of the planet. Cameras from both landers showed rust-colored rocks and boulders with a reddish sky above. The rust color is due to the presence of iron oxide in the Martian soil.

The *Viking* orbiters sent back weather reports and pictures of almost the entire surface of the planet. They found that, although the Martian atmosphere contains low levels of nitrogen, oxygen, carbon, and argon, it is made principally of carbon dioxide and thus could not support human life. The soil samples collected by the landers show no sign of past or present life on the planet.

Life-on-Mars News Flash!

In early August 1996, a team of nine NASA-led researchers detected what *Viking 1* and *2* did not on their visit to Mars—possible evidence of ancient Martian life. In 1984, American scientists in Antarctica discovered the 4.5-billion-year-old chunk of rock (named ALH 84001) and identified it as a fragment of the **asteroid** Vesta. Ten years later, scientists re-analyzed the rock and found that its chemical composition matched that of the surface of Mars.

Since that time, scientists around the world have been studying samples of ALH 84001. The NASA-led research team was the first to announce the discovery of tiny, sausage-shaped markings that resemble the fossilized bacteria found in rocks on Earth. They believe these particles, which only occupy a space the size of a billionth of a pinhead, may well be traces of a primitive Martian life form.

Some astronomers, such as Cornell University professor Carl Sagan, met the news with excitement and optimism. In news reports immediately following the NASA team's announcement, he called the findings "the most provocative and evocative piece of evidence for life beyond Earth," and added that "it could be a turning point in human history." Others, such as John F. Kerridge, a planetary scientist at the University of California, San Diego, were far more skeptical. "The conclusion is at best premature and more probably wrong," said Kerridge.

Even NASA director Daniel Goldin called the evidence "exciting, even compelling, but not conclusive." Nonetheless, the possibility that life once existed on Mars led Goldin to declare a "robust program of exploration" of the red planet. He promised that, in addition to the two spacecraft scheduled to launch toward Mars in the fall of 1996, there will be a total of eight more spacecraft (two every other year) sent to Mars within a decade.

See also **Mariner program**; **Mars program**; and **Viking program**

Mars program

Before the first **space probe**s were sent to Mars, many people believed that our neighboring planet may support life, perhaps even intelligent, human-like life. In 1877, Italian astronomer Giovanni Schiaparelli reported observing a series of markings crossing the planet, which he termed canali, or "channels." The translation of the original Italian word became skewed, however, and the rumor spread that Mars was covered with "canals" which had been dug by Martian engineers to bring water to populated areas.

The Mars series of space **probe**s, launched by the **Soviet Union** in the 1960s and 1970s, was the first to put an end to such speculation. They revealed Mars as a barren, desolate, crater-covered world prone to frequent, violent dust storms. They found little oxygen, no liquid water, and **ultraviolet radiation** at levels lethal to any form of life as we know it. The maximum temperature on Mars was measured at -20 degrees Fahrenheit (-29 degrees Celsius) in the afternoon, and the low was -120 degrees Fahrenheit (-84 degrees Celsius) at night.

The Soviets initiated their Mars program at the height of the **space race,** the contest with their rival superpower, the United States, to achieve a variety of "firsts" in space exploration. The Soviets had been the first to send an unpiloted spacecraft to the moon and also wanted to be the first to undertake an interplanetary mission. In 1960, they made their first attempts to reach their chosen targets, Mars and Venus.

The Mars program got off to a shaky, even tragic, start. For political reasons, Soviet leader Nikita Krushchev was intent on having a Mars-bound spacecraft launched during his 1960 visit to the United States. Two launches were attempted in September 1960. Because of **rocket** failures, both probes went up a short way and fell back to Earth. An embarrassed Kruschev ordered another attempt the following month. This time, however, the rocket exploded during the final check, killing everyone in the vicinity.

The Mars program was then put on hold for two years. In October 1962, the Soviets finally launched the *Mars 1* space probe toward Mars. This probe weighed nearly a ton. Its central component was an 11-foot-long (3.4-meter-long) cylinder, attached to which was an umbrella-shaped radio antenna and solar panels. It also contained cameras, **meteoroid** detectors, and instruments to measure radiation. Five months after launch, when the probe was over half way to Mars, radio contact with it was lost.

The First Successful Missions

In 1971, the Soviets succeeded in putting *Mars 2* and *Mars 3* into orbit around Mars. In May of that year, they launched three space probes, each of which consisted of an orbiter (a vessel designed to remain in orbit, once reaching Mars) and a lander (a capsule designed to land on the Martian surface). The plan was for each spacecraft to drop its lander to the planet's surface, take photographs, and analyze the composition of the ground. Meanwhile, the orbiter was to remain above the planet collecting atmospheric data.

Unfortunately, the spacecraft reached Mars while the planet was in the midst of a dust storm. The storm was probably the reason for the failure of the landers. *Mars 2*'s lander descended first and vanished, never to be heard from again. The outcome of *Mars 3*'s lander initially seemed more promising. It reached the surface and began beaming back the first television pictures of the Martian surface. Twenty seconds later, however, the transmission ended, and communications were never re-established.

All was not lost from those missions, however. The orbiters continued functioning for the next year and relayed data on the temperature of Mars and the composition of its atmosphere, as well as taking numerous photographs.

Two years later, in July and August 1973, the Soviets sent out four more spacecraft from the Mars series. Two of these were orbiters and the other two, landers. They could not simply repeat the *Mars 2* and *3* missions because the distance between Earth and Mars had increased since 1971 (due to their orbits around the sun). The combined orbiter-landers would have been too heavy to be launched to a height necessary for such a long journey.

Early on, when all four vessels were on track for Mars, this mission looked hopeful. One at a time, however, three of the vessels met with failure. First *Mars 4,* an orbiter, never adjusted its course to enter into orbit and shot past Mars and into deep space. Next, *Mars 5,* the only success story of the group, went into orbit around Mars and was prepared to receive signals from the landers. Both landers failed, however. *Mars 6* crash-landed into the planet and was destroyed. And *Mars 7's* aim was off. It missed the planet completely.

Pictures of the planet taken by *Mars 5* were later combined with those taken by the U.S. probe *Mariner 9* to produce a complete map of the Martian surface. Despite the limited achievements of *Mars 5,* the Mars program overall was considered a failure by Soviet authorities and was discontinued.

Currently, however, plans are underway to resurrect the series with one more mission. *Mars 96* was originally scheduled for launch in 1992 and then in 1994 before being delayed once more. This mission is being touted as the centerpiece program of the Russian Space Agency for the next ten to fifteen years.

Mars 96 will consist of an orbiter, two small **space station**s that will land on the Martian surface, and two penetrators that will bore into the surface to examine underground layers of the planet. The spacecraft will carry over twenty scientific instruments for the study of Martian surface, atmosphere, and surrounding **plasma** layer. *Mars 96* is expected to reach Mars in October 1997.

See also **Mars** and **Mariner program**

Mauna Kea Observatory

The Mauna Kea Observatory (MKO) is widely considered to be the world's best ground-based astronomical observatory. The summit of

Mauna Kea Observatory

Mauna Kea stands nearly 13,800 feet (4,205 meters) above sea level, which is above 40 percent of the Earth's atmosphere. The altitude at MKO is so high that astronomers and construction workers coming to the mountain must first spend time at a station about two-thirds the way up the mountain in order to get used to the lower levels of oxygen. Even then, many people experience headaches and dizziness at the mountaintop.

Mauna Kea (which means "White Mountain") is an extinct volcano and the largest island-mountain on Earth. It is located on the island of Hawaii, the southernmost and largest in the string of islands that make up the state of Hawaii. The observatory is situated above a semi-permanent layer of clouds that act as a barrier between the moist, sea air below and the dry, crisp air above.

Dryness is a particularly important quality for an observatory because water vapor tends to scatter radiation, particularly **infrared radiation,** thus blurring the view of space. **Infrared astronomy**—the study of infrared ra-

The UK Infrared telescope (left) being installed at Mauna Kea Observatory in Hawaii, 1980.

diation produced by celestial objects—is very difficult to conduct on the ground. Generally, to get a picture of the infrared sky, astronomers turn to space-based telescopes. MKO is an exception. From the mountaintop, infrared telescopes reveal such objects as distant **galaxies,** regions of the **Milky Way** where stars are in formation, and planetary atmospheres.

Another reason that MKO is ideal for astronomical viewing is the lack of artificial light. The site is far from population centers, and the state of Hawaii has enacted strict legislation ensuring that artificial light does not become a problem in the future. In short, almost every night at Mauna Kea is clear, dark, and dry—a stargazer's paradise.

As early as the late 1950s, astronomers recognized the potential of Mauna Kea for an observatory. Ground was broken in 1962 for the first building, and, with the installation of a small telescope, the observatory was dedicated two years later.

Mauna Kea Telescopes

Today, MKO houses the largest concentration of optical telescopes in the world. Among them is the world's largest telescope, the California Institute of Technology's Keck 1. This 394-inch-diameter (1,000-centimeter-diameter) instrument has been operational since November 1991. It can observe light in both visible and infrared wavelengths. Its counterpart, Keck 2, will be placed 279 feet (85 meters) away from Keck 1 when completed.

Future plans call for linking the two telescopes, in a process called **interferometry.** This process will create the equivalent viewing power of a single telescope with a 279-foot-diameter (85-meter-diameter) mirror. While radio interferometry has been in use since the 1950s, optical interferometry is much more complicated, and the technology for it is still being developed. A handful of small **optical interferometer**s are now operational, but the Keck 2, if installed as planned, will become the world's first large optical interferometer.

Mauna Kea currently has seven functional telescopes and an antenna of the Very Long Baseline Array (VLB) **radio interferometer** besides the Kecks. Four other instruments are also under construction. The smallest and oldest telescope in use at the observatory today (dating back to 1968) is the University of Hawaii's 24-inch (61-centimeter) optical telescope. The next smallest is an 88-inch (224-centimeter) optical/infrared telescope, constructed by the University of Hawaii in 1970. In 1979, an optical/infrared telescope measuring 144 inches (366 centimeters) across was erected jointly by Canada, France, and the University of Hawaii. Also in 1979, two infrared telescopes were placed on the mountaintop: the UK Infrared Telescope at 150 inches (381 centimeters), and the NASA Infrared Telescope Facility at 120 inches (305 centimeters).

Radio astronomers also consider Mauna Kea a superb research site. The James Clerk Maxwell Telescope, the world's largest telescope for the study of submillimeter **radio wave**s (the smallest radio wavelength), was set up in 1987. The Maxwell Telescope is owned jointly by the United Kingdom, Canada, and the Netherlands. Another state-of-the-art radio instrument, the CalTech Submillimeter Observatory, was placed on the site that year as well.

The largest instrument on the mountaintop is an 82-foot-diameter (25-meter-diameter) radio antenna dish, the Hawaiian component of the VLB. The VLB is a series of ten identical **radio telescope**s strung across the United States from the Virgin Islands to Hawaii. They are linked by powerful computers that combine their information to create detailed pictures of objects in space.

Between 1997 and 2000, another radio telescope and three more optical/infrared telescopes are scheduled to become operational at MKO. The first, the Smithsonian Submillimeter Array, will be an interferometer of six radio dishes, each nearly 20 feet (6 meters) in diameter. The three optical/infrared telescopes to be constructed are the 327-inch (831-centimeter) Subaru-Japan National Large Telescope and the twin 315-inch (800-centimeter) international Gemini Project telescopes.

See also **Infrared astronomy; Interferometry**; and **Radio astronomy**

Maxwell, James Clerk (1831–1879)
Scottish mathematician and physicist

Throughout his relatively brief lifetime, James Clerk Maxwell made important scientific contributions in a number of different areas, including **astrophysics,** thermodynamics, color vision, and most importantly, electromagnetism. In short, Maxwell accomplished in each of several fields more than most scientists would hope to achieve in just one field.

With his electromagnetic theory, Maxwell made sense of the relationship between electricity and magnetism that had intrigued scientists for years. In the 1830s, English physicist Michael Faraday had determined that the two forces were linked. It was not until the late 1860s, however, that Maxwell showed that an oscillating (changing) electric charge creates an electromagnetic field that radiates outward at a constant speed, the **speed of light.** Maxwell found that light itself is a form of **electromagnetic radiation,** and that visible light waves represent just one small part of the **electromagnetic spectrum.** The electromagnetic spectrum is the range of electromagnetic radiation that includes, besides visible light, **radio waves**, **infrared radiation, ultraviolet radiation, X-ray**s, and **gamma ray**s.

Maxwell's discovery significantly advanced the field of astronomy because electromagnetic radiation occurs naturally not just on Earth, but throughout the universe. For example, the radiation put out by the sun and other stars is electromagnetic in nature. Astronomers have found that many celestial objects that appear dim or are invisible to the eye are powerful emitters of other forms of electromagnetic radiation. For example, there are X-ray stars and entire infrared **galaxies** of which we would never know if we were searching only for sources of visible light.

Maxwell's aptitude for science and mathematics was evident at an early age. He was born to a wealthy family in Edinburgh, Scotland, in 1831, and attended the prestigious Edinburgh Academy. When Maxwell was just fourteen, a paper he had written on geometry was presented at the University of Edinburgh. While this made him unpopular with his classmates (they nicknamed him "Daftie"), it set in motion a lifelong career.

Maxwell's Academic Career

Two years later, Maxwell was back at the university, taking classes. In 1849, he had two papers published in the *Transactions of the Royal Society of Edinburgh,* one on geometry and the other on physics. The next year, he transferred to St. Peter's College at Cambridge University in England. There he studied physics (then called "natural philosophy"), mathematics, chemistry, and philosophy.

In 1855, when Maxwell was just twenty-four years old, he was elected a Fellow of the

*James Clerk
Maxwell.*

Royal Society of Edinburgh, an exclusive scientific club. He was elected to the Royal Society of London five years after that. In 1856, Maxwell returned to Scotland and assumed the chairmanship of the physics department at Marischal College in Aberdeen.

One of Maxwell's earliest claims to fame was producing the first color photograph in 1861. Since 1849, Maxwell had been exploring colors, particularly the way the eye processes red, yellow, and blue, the three primary colors. Maxwell found that any color of the rainbow could be made from combinations of the three primaries, knowledge that he then applied to photography.

During the same period, Maxwell conducted a study into the nature of Saturn's rings. Previously, scientists (including the discoverer of the rings, Christiaan Huygens) had suggested that the rings were solid or liquid. Maxwell believed that they were gaseous in nature. He took this concept one step farther, analyzing the motion of a gas, and concluded that molecules within any given gas move at random speeds. This research led to the development of his kinetic theory of gases, which describes the relationship between the motion of gas molecules and heat.

In 1860, following a merger of area colleges into Aberdeen University, Maxwell left for a teaching post at King's College in London. He remained there for five years, then took an extended leave of absence. Maxwell returned to academic life in 1871 as a professor of experimental physics at Cambridge University.

Maxwell remained on faculty at Cambridge until his untimely death from cancer in 1879, just eight days before his forty-eighth birthday.

See also **Electromagnetic waves**

McDonald Observatory

The McDonald Observatory in western Texas will soon be home to the largest optical telescope in the world. Slated for completion in 1997, the Hobby-Eberly Telescope (HET) will have a primary mirror made up of ninety-one separate hexagonal pieces arranged like a honeycomb, totaling 433 inches (1,100 centimeters) in diameter. That makes the HET 39 inches (99 centimeters) larger than the largest telescope in operation today, the Keck Telescope at the Mauna Kea Observatory in Hawaii.

The HET will be dedicated to spectroscopic research. **Spectroscopy** is the process of analyzing light by breaking it down into its component colors, its **spectrum.** From this spectrum, one can gather information about an object, such as its temperature and chemical composition. The HET will be used primarily to explore faint sources, such as **dark matter** and newborn stars, uncovering information that may provide additional clues about the origin of the universe.

The McDonald Observatory was founded in 1932 with funds provided by William Johnson McDonald, a millionaire banker and amateur astronomer from Paris, Texas. He bequeathed most of his estate to the University of Texas (UT), with the stipulation that the money be used to build an observatory. UT had only a modest astronomy program at the time, so university administrators enlisted the help of the University of Chicago (which had considerably more experience in this area) in building the observatory. The partnership lasted until 1962. Since that time, UT has been the sole operator of the observatory.

Selecting a Location for the Telescope

The site chosen for the observatory was at the summit of Mount Locke, a very isolated location. Mount Locke is 186 miles (298 kilometers) from El Paso and 496 miles (798 kilometers) from Austin, the campus of UT. The site's great distance from population centers means the skies are exceptionally dark, a key requirement for high-quality astronomical observations. Another advantage of this site is its **latitude.** At just 30 degrees north of the equator, the location is far enough south for observing parts of the sky that are below the horizon and therefore out of viewing range for observatories farther north.

Two other factors that led to the selection of Mount Locke are its altitude and low humidity. The peak of Mount Locke stands 7,000 feet (2,135 meters) above sea level, which is above a good portion of the Earth's atmosphere. Altitude is an important factor because molecules in the atmosphere tend to scatter light, distorting images of celestial objects. And the Davis Mountains, the range to which Mount Locke belongs, gets relatively little rainfall. The observatory averages two clear nights out of every three.

In 1939, the first big astronomical instrument was erected at the observatory, the 82-inch (208-centimeter) Otto Struve Telescope. Named for the first director of the observatory, this telescope was the second largest in the world at the time of its dedication. It is still used regularly today.

In 1969, the observatory purchased the 107-inch (272-centimeter) Harlan Smith Telescope, which was then the third largest in the world. Astronomers from the National Aeronautics and Space Administration (NASA) conducted research with this telescope in preparation for the Voyager missions to Jupiter, Saturn, Uranus, and Neptune in the late 1970s.

One of the observatory's most interesting features is the McDonald Lunar Laser Ranging Station. This instrument consists of a 30-inch (76-centimeter) telescope that fires a laser beam to the moon. The beam strikes reflectors on the lunar surface, placed there by U.S. astronauts, and returns to Earth. By timing the laser beam's round-trip, astronomers can track the movement of the moon, as well as artificial satellites in orbit around the Earth.

Public education has been an important aspect of McDonald Observatory since day one. In fact, William McDonald stressed in his will that one of the purposes of the observatory was to be the "promotion of astronomy" to the public. The earliest public programs were conducted on a 12-inch (30-centimeter) telescope. Now, in addition to daily tours, daily solar viewing, and every-other-night stargazing parties, the Harlan Smith Telescope is available once a month for public viewing nights.

See also **Spectroscopy**

Mercury

Mercury is a small, bleak planet, and the closest object to the sun. Because of the sun's intense glare, it is difficult to observe Mercury from Earth. Mercury is visible only periodically, just above the horizon, for about one hour before sunrise and one hour after sunset. For these reasons, many people have never seen Mercury.

Mercury is named for the Roman messenger god with winged sandals. The planet was given its name because it orbits the sun so quickly, in just eighty-eight days. In contrast to its short year, Mercury has an extremely long day. It takes the planet the equivalent of fifty-nine Earth days to complete one rotation.

Mercury is the second smallest planet in the **solar system.** Only Pluto is smaller. Mercury's diameter is a little over one-third the Earth's, yet it has just 5.5 percent of Earth's **mass.** On average, Mercury is 36 mil-

Mariner 10 *captured this photo of Mercury and its many craters from about 591,945 miles (952,600 kilometers) away.*

lion miles (58 million kilometers) from the sun. One effect of the sun's intense gravitational field is to tilt Mercury's orbit and to stretch it into a long ellipse (oval).

Little else was known about Mercury until the **space probe** *Mariner 10* photographed the planet in 1975. *Mariner* first approached the planet Venus in February 1974, then used that planet's gravitational field to send it around like a slingshot in the direction of Mercury. The second leg of the journey to Mercury took seven weeks.

On its first flight past Mercury, *Mariner 10* came within 470 miles (756 kilometers) of the planet and photographed about 40 percent of the its surface. The **probe** then went into orbit around the sun and flew past Mercury twice more in the next year before running out of fuel.

Mariner 10 collected much valuable information about Mercury. It found that the planet's surface is covered with deep craters, separated by plains and huge banks of cliffs. Mercury's most notable feature is an ancient crater called the Caloris Basin, which is about the size of Texas.

Astronomers believe that Mercury, like the moon, was originally made of liquid rock, and that the rock solidified as the planet cooled. Some **meteorite**s hit the planet during the cooling stage and formed craters. Other meteorites, however, were able to break through the cooling crust. The impact caused lava to flow up to the surface and cover over older craters, forming the plains.

Mercury's very thin atmosphere is made of sodium, potassium, helium, and hydrogen. Temperatures on Mercury reach 800 degrees Fahrenheit (427 degrees Celsius) during its long day and -280 degrees Fahrenheit (-173 degrees Celsius) during its long night, when heat escapes through the negligible atmosphere.

Mariner 10 also gathered information about Mercury's core, which is nearly solid metal and is composed primarily of iron and nickel. This core, the densest of any in the solar system, accounts for about four-fifths of Mercury's diameter. It may also be responsible for creating the **magnetic field** that protects Mercury from the sun's harsh particle wind.

At this point, no further space missions are scheduled to visit Mercury.

See also **Mariner program**

Mercury program

The Mercury program ushered in the era of Americans flying in space. It was begun in 1959 by the newly formed National Aeronautics and Space Administration (NASA) and included a series of test flights, followed by six piloted missions between the years 1961 and 1963. The short Mercury flights of the early 1960s gave way to the longer, more complex Gemini flights of the mid 1960s; and finally to the Apollo lunar landings at the end of the decade.

The Mercury program marked the U.S. entry into the **space race,** the contest between the United States and the former **Soviet Union** for superiority in space exploration. In 1961, cosmonaut Yuri Gagarin scored a victory for the Soviet Union by making the first piloted space flight. In response, President John F. Kennedy vowed that not only would the United States match the Soviet accomplishment, but that by the end of the decade the United States would put a man on the moon. The Mercury program, at that time in its early stages, suddenly shifted into high gear.

The Mercury space capsule was bell-shaped and a little less than 9 feet (2.7 meters) tall and 6 feet wide (1.8 meters). It was so small that it could accommodate only one astronaut at a time. The astronaut entered through a square hatch in the side of the capsule and sat on a chair that had been specially shaped to fit his body. Directly in front of him was the control panel.

The base of the capsule was enclosed in a heat shield, designed to withstand the scorching ride back into the Earth's atmosphere. Just before landing, the heat shield gave way to an inflated cushion, and parachutes sprang from the top of the capsule. Early Mercury vessels were launched into space by Redstone **rocket**s; later ones were launched by Atlas rockets.

The first stage of the Mercury program consisted of seven suborbital test flights, flights that did not reach the height necessary to go into orbit, Five of these were successful. The two other tests either veered off course or exploded. Next came four orbital test flights, two of which went as planned. The final test flight, in January 1961, carried a chimpanzee named Ham. Ham returned unharmed, and Mercury was deemed ready for a human pilot.

The original seven astronauts, also known as the Mercury Seven, were chosen from the top U.S. military pilots. They included M. Scott Carpenter, L. Gordon Cooper, Jr., John Glenn, Jr., Virgil "Gus" Grissom, Walter Schirra, Jr., Alan Shepard, Jr., and Donald "Deke" Slayton. All but Slayton, who was discovered to have an irregular heartbeat, flew Mercury missions. Slayton was assigned instead to work in the Astronaut Office until he was able to convince NASA officials to let him participate in the *Apollo-Soyuz* Test Project in 1975.

The Crewed Mercury Flights

The first Mercury piloted flight was made on May 5, 1961, by Alan Shepard. Shepard's suborbital flight in the *Freedom* capsule lasted fifteen minutes. It reached an altitude of 116 miles (186 kilometers) and traveled a distance of 303 miles (485 kilometers), at a maximum speed of 5,146 miles (8,234 kilometers) per hour. It then parachuted safely into the Atlantic Ocean.

The next suborbital flight was made two months later by Gus Grissom in the *Liberty Bell* capsule. His flight was similar to Shepard's until

The Mercury Seven: (front row, left to right) Walter M. Schirra, Jr., Donald K. Slayton, John H. Glenn, Jr., and M. Scott Carpenter; (back row, left to right) Alan B. Shepard, Jr., Virgil "Gus" Grissom, and L. Gordon Cooper, Jr.

The Right Stuff (1983)

This is a dramatization of the early days of the U.S. piloted space program. Adapted from a book by Tom Wolfe, it begins with the breaking of the sound barrier by pilot Chuck Yeager, continues with the selection and training of the first group of U.S. astronauts, and ends with the final Mercury mission. It delves deeply into the personal lives of those who were—and weren't—chosen to be among the first class of astronauts, and examines the rigors of being an astronaut.

the end. On splashdown, the *Liberty Bell* took in water and sank, becoming the only Mercury capsule not recovered. Grissom, however, was pulled from the ocean unharmed.

Mercury's first orbital mission was made by John Glenn in February 1962. Glenn traveled inside a capsule called *Friendship* for five hours on a journey that took him around the Earth three times. Glenn's flight was not entirely smooth, however. During his second orbit, NASA officials at the command center received signals that *Friendship*'s heat shield was loose. Glenn made some adjustments to release the retro-rocket, slowing the spacecraft, and hoped for the best. He had a frightening descent during which he watched pieces of flaming metal fly past the window in his capsule. But the heat shield held together, and the capsule plunged into the ocean as planned.

In May 1962, Scott Carpenter was the next to pilot a Mercury mission. Carpenter orbited the Earth three times, during which he took his spacecraft through a series of maneuvers. The only tense part of the mission came after splashdown. Carpenter's *Aurora* capsule landed 250 miles (400 kilometers) off-target, and it took NASA search crews three hours of combing the waters to find Carpenter, who was unharmed.

The next capsule to fly was *Sigma,* which was launched up in October 1962 with Walter Schirra on board. During his six orbits around Earth, Schirra produced the first-ever telecast from space.

The end of the Mercury series came in May of the following year. Gordon Cooper took his *Faith* capsule on the longest mission to date, twenty-two orbits around Earth in thirty-four hours and nineteen minutes. While in orbit, Cooper released a sphere with flashing lights, the first satellite deployed from a spacecraft.

Next on NASA's agenda was the Gemini program, in which twelve spacecraft were launched between April 1964 and November 1966. On those missions the crews mastered new skills, such as docking with other vessels and conducting activities outside the spacecraft, as well as setting new records for endurance and altitude. Those flights solved a number of space flight problems and paved the way for the Apollo lunar landing missions.

See also **Apollo program**; **Gemini program**; **Glenn, John**; **Shepard, Alan**; and **Space race**

Messier, Charles (1730–1817)

French astronomer

Charles Messier was an astronomer fascinated with viewing and recording celestial objects. He entered the field at a time when the telescope was still relatively new, and space suddenly seemed to be filled with objects just waiting to be discovered. Messier is famous for his catalogue of over one hundred non-star objects, such as **nebula**e and star clusters, which he published in the French journal *Connaissance des Temps* (*Knowledge of the Times*).

Messier was born in Badouvillier, in the French state of Lorraine. He became an orphan at an early age. In 1751, when Messier was twenty-one years old, he came to Paris to seek his fortune. His first job was as a draftsman for astronomer Joseph Nicolas Delisle, who assigned him to the task of copying a map of the Great Wall of China. Messier's work space was a long, chilly hallway in the College of France. This environment turned out to be a proper initiation into a future of long, cold nights studying the skies.

Delisle also taught Messier how to operate astronomical instruments. Within three years, Messier had become a competent astronomical observer and was hired to work as a clerk at the Marine Observatory in Paris. There Messier carefully watched the sky for the predicted return of Halley's **comet,** which he finally spotted in January 1759. Messier soon found out, however, that it had been discovered by a farmer in the French countryside a month earlier. News traveled slowly in those days and word of the comet's sighting had not yet reached Paris.

Shortly after that, Messier began working in the tower observatory at the Hotel de Cluny in Paris. From that post he discovered at least fifteen comets and recorded numerous eclipses, **transit**s, and **sunspot**s.

Messier Receives International Recognition

By 1762, Messier was considered the leading French astronomer by those outside of France, but his fellow countrymen looked down upon his work as being merely observational. For instance, he was criticized for not plotting the orbits of the comets he had discovered. It was not until 1770 that the French Academie Royale admitted him. By that time, he had already been made a member of elite science associations in three other countries.

Around that time, Messier produced the first section of his famous catalogue. The first object listed is the Crab nebula in the **constellation** Taurus. Messier described the nebula as "a whitish light, extended in the form of the light of a candle, and which contained no stars."

"This light was a little like that of a comet I had observed before," he continued. "However, it was a little too bright, too white, and too elongated to be a comet, which had always appeared to me before almost round, without the appearance either of a tail or a barb."

Messier labeled his objects according to the order in which they were discovered. Each number was preceded by the letter "M," for Messier. Thus, the Crab nebula is called M1, and the Andromeda **galaxy,** which was the thirty-first object discovered, is called M31. Many celestial objects are still referred to today by their Messier designations.

Messier originally included in the catalogue only those objects he had personally discovered. He eventually widened the catalogue to include objects discovered by other astronomers of the day and that he was able to confirm independently. His initial list of forty-five objects was ultimately expanded to over twice that number. For each entry, he included a description of the object, the date on which it was discovered, and the position at which it was observed.

Throughout his career, Messier used over a dozen telescopes. The largest one was a **reflector** which relied on a primary mirror only 7.5 inches (19 centimeters) in diameter to bring light rays into focus. This is very small compared to today's telescopes, such as the Keck Telescope at Mauna Kea Observatory in Hawaii. It has a primary mirror 394 inches

(1,000 centimeters) in diameter. Considering the limitations of his instruments, Messier's discoveries are even more impressive.

Messier's final addition to his catalogue was made in 1781. Following that he had a serious accident, falling 25 feet (7.5 meters) and breaking several bones. A year later, Messier returned to the observation tower and resumed his earlier study of comets and **solar eclipse**s. Within a few years, the French Revolution was underway. The observatory was closed down, and Messier stopped receiving a salary.

After the war's end Messier spent a few years at the Paris Observatory. He then suffered a stroke, after which he was cared for at home by his niece. Messier died in 1817 at the age of eighty-six.

Meteors and meteorites

Millions of objects from space come racing toward Earth every year. Fortunately, most of these burn up in the atmosphere and never reach the Earth's surface. Some of the larger objects, however, arrive intact, announcing their presence with anything from a barely noticeable "plink" to a literally earth-shattering thud.

These objects come in two different classes: **meteor**s and **meteorite**s. Meteors, also known as "shooting stars," are small particles of dust left behind by a **comet**'s tail. We encounter meteors every time our planet crosses the path of a comet or the debris left behind by a comet. Meteors appear as sparks that vaporize and fizzle in the sky, never reaching the ground.

Meteorites are larger chunks of rock, metal, or both that break off an **asteroid** or a comet and come crashing through the Earth's atmosphere, right down to the ground. They come in a variety of sizes—from a pebble to a 3-ton chunk. Every so often a meteorite causes damage. One killed a dog in Egypt in 1911; another struck the arm of, and rudely awakened, a sleeping woman in Alabama in 1954; and in 1992 a meteorite destroyed a Chevy Malibu.

Until the end of the eighteenth century, people believed that meteors and meteorites were atmospheric occurrences, like rain. Other theories held that they were debris spewed into the air by exploding volcanoes, or supernatural phenomena, like signs from angry gods.

Early Discoveries About Meteors and Meteorites

The first breakthrough in determining the true origins of meteors and meteorites came in 1714, when English astronomer Edmond Halley carefully reviewed reports of their sightings. After calculating the height and speed of the objects, he concluded that they must have come from space. He found that other scientists were hesitant to believe this notion. For nearly the next century they continued to believe that the phenomena were Earth-based.

In 1790, a group of stone-like objects showered France. German physicist G. F. Lichtenberg assigned his assistant E. F. F. Chladni to investigate the event. Chladni examined reports of those falling stones, as well as records from the previous two centuries. He, like Halley, con-

Host a Shooting Star Party

Meteors, also known as "shooting stars" (the streaks we see cross the sky on clear summer nights), are small particles of dust left behind by a comet's tail. While there are some meteors that streak through the sky every day and night, six times during the year meteor activity greatly intensifies, causing "meteor showers." These showers occur when the Earth passes through the orbit of a comet or the debris left behind by a comet.

The six periods when meteor showers occur are: January 1–4; April 19–23; August 10–14; October 18–23; November 14–20; and December 10–15. During a dark, clear night during the next meteor shower period, invite your friends over to watch the sky. Have a contest to see who can spot the greatest number of shooting stars.

cluded that the chunks of matter came from outside the Earth's atmosphere, and theorized that they were the remains of a disintegrated planet. His colleagues still were not convinced.

The conclusive evidence came in 1803 when another fireball, accompanied by loud explosions, rained down two to three thousand stones on France. French Academy of Science member Jean-Baptiste Biot collected some of the fallen stones, as well as reports from witnesses. After measuring the area covered by the debris and analyzing the stones' composition, he proved that they could not have originated in the Earth's atmosphere. His colleagues then guessed that meteorites came from volcanic eruptions on the moon.

In subsequent years, through radioactive dating techniques, scientists have determined that meteorites are about four and one-half billion years old—roughly the same age as the **solar system.** Some are composed of iron and nickel, two elements found in the Earth's core. This piece of evidence suggests that they may be fragments left over from the formation of the solar system. Further studies showed that the composition of meteorites matched that of asteroids.

Also in the early 1800s, German scientists Johann Benzenberg and Heinrich Brandes learned more about the origin and nature of meteors. They found that shooting stars travel at a speed of several miles per second, close to the speed at which planets move. Thus they concluded that the objects were approaching Earth from space and that the trail of light we see is a result of a meteor burning upon entering the Earth's atmosphere.

This study was taken a step further during a **meteor shower** in November 1833. The meteors seemed to originate from a single point in the sky, where the **constellation** Leo appeared (hence the name Leonid meteor shower). A look at the records showed that there was a meteor shower around that same time every year, although the intensity of the showers varied greatly. A similar pattern was detected with the Perseid meteor shower (named for the constellation Perseus) which occurred every August.

Italian scientist Giovanni Schiaparelli did more research on the origin of meteors in the mid-1800s and came up with the answer: meteors were the remnants of comets. Schiaparelli first plotted the path of the Perseid meteors and learned that they circled the sun. He then looked through records of comets and their orbits and found that the path of the Perseids was identical to that of a known comet. He found the same to be true of the Leonid meteors.

Most annual meteor showers can now be traced to the intersection of a comet's orbit and the Earth's orbit.

See also **Asteroids** and **Comets**

Michelson, Albert (1852–1931)
Polish-born American physicist

Albert Abraham Michelson was born in Strelno, Prussia, which is now part of Poland. When he was two years old, his family moved to the United States, attracted by the California gold rush. Michelson attended high school in San Francisco while his father worked as a supplier for miners. Upon graduation, Michelson competed for a government scholarship to attend the U.S. Naval Academy in Annapolis, Maryland. He scored among the highest, but the scholarship went to another boy. He appealed his case right up to President Ulysses S. Grant and was finally admitted.

At the Naval Academy, Michelson learned how to use precision instruments with great skill. After completing his training in 1873, he was offered a position teaching physics and chemistry at the academy.

Michelson was most interested in the speed and nature of light. French mathematician Jean Bernard Léon Foucault, in the mid-1800s, had calculated the **speed of light** using a series of mirrors in a laboratory. Michelson was determined to arrive at a more exact measurement through an experiment of his own. Funded with $2,000 of his father-in-law's money, he improved on Foucault's equipment and accomplished his goal. Michelson published his results in 1879, which gained him recognition in the scientific community.

Michelson next jumped into the centuries-long debate on the nature of light. One theory had it that light was made up of particles, and another said it was made up of waves. The latter theory claimed that these waves traveled through an invisible substance called ether (not the anaesthetic), similar to waves that travel through water. We know today that light can behave either as a wave or a particle, and, thanks largely to Michelson's experiments, that ether does not exist.

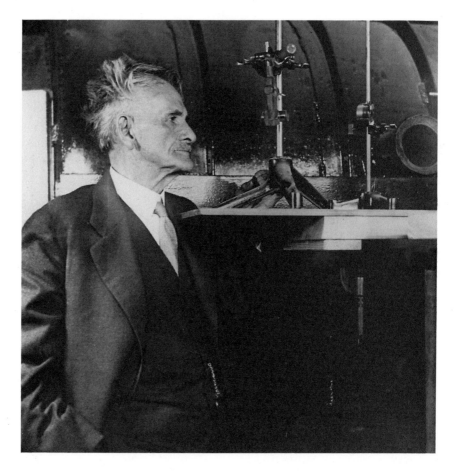

*June 23, 1930.
Albert Michelson
prepares to conduct
a series of tests on
the speed of light.*

Looking for Ether

Michelson, a proponent of the theory that light waves travel through ether, set out to prove ether's existence. He felt he could accomplish this by comparing the speed of two beams of light traveling in different directions, one with the ether current and the other against it. He thought that light traveling against the ether would move more slowly than light traveling with it. To conduct his experiment Michelson built an interferential refractometer, an instrument that splits light into two perpendicular beams and then brings them back together, forming a pattern. He measured the speeds of the two beams and found no difference between them, and thus no proof of the existence of ether.

Michelson didn't give up. In 1887, he went to teach at the Case School of Applied Science in Cleveland, Ohio. Working with fellow scientist Edward Morley of the nearby Western Reserve College, Michelson improved the design of his original instrument, producing an even more precise interferometer. An interferometer works by splitting a beam of light in two, each of which bounce off a series of mirrors. They then create an interference pattern when they come back together. An interference pattern consists of fringes, which represent the sum of the waves at the point where the light rays intersect. If the waves are in synch, meaning that a peak of one intersects with the peak of the other, then they reinforce each other and a bright fringe results. However, if a peak intersects with a valley, then the beams cancel each other out and a dark fringe results. Over the course of five days the two scientists conducted the now-famous Michelson-Morley experiment. At the conclusion they still were unable to detect ether.

Although Michelson had failed to accomplish his original goal, his exhaustive search for ether advanced science in two important ways. First, he virtually ruled out the existence of ether. Second, he gave birth to the science of **interferometry,** the study of wavelengths and astronomical distances.

Beginning in 1889, Michelson held two faculty posts: the first was teaching physics at Clark University in Worcester, Massachusetts, and the second was chairing the physics department at the University of Chicago. In 1914, when World War I broke out, Michelson returned to the Navy as a sixty-five-year-old officer. In that capacity he developed and perfected optical range finders.

In the early 1920s, while still maintaining his University of Chicago post, Michelson began spending more time in southern California. There he taught at the California Institute of Technology and conducted research at the Mount Wilson Observatory. Using his interferometer, Michelson tested the effect that the Earth's rotation has on the speed of light, helped design the optics for the 100-inch (254-centimeter) Hooker Telescope (then the world's largest), and attempted to measure the size and shape of the Earth.

Between 1924 and 1926, Michelson devised an elaborate system to measure the speed of light yet one more time. He set up two stations—one atop Mount Wilson, near Pasadena, California, and the other atop Mount San Antonio, which was 22 miles (35 kilometers) away. The distance between the two points was determined with an accuracy to the nearest centimeter, by the most precise land survey ever undertaken to that time. Michelson reflected light from a rotating, eight-sided mirror at the first site to a stationary mirror at the second. The light came back to the first mirror and was reflected off to another point. By computing the angles of the mirrors and the distance the light had traveled, Michelson found the speed of light to be 186,271 miles (299,710 kilometers) per second. He was only off the currently accepted value by 11 miles per second, a near-perfect measurement.

Michelson's next goal was to measure the speed of light in a vacuum, for which he began construction of a mile-long vacuum tube. Unfortunately he died in Pasadena on May 9, 1931, before the experiment was completed.

See also **Interferometry** and **Speed of light**

Milky Way galaxy

The **Milky Way** is our home **galaxy.** It contains the sun and billions of other stars. From Earth, we can see only the part of the galaxy that surrounds us, because so much of the galaxy (particularly near the center) is blocked from view by interstellar dust and gas. It is visible on clear, summer nights, in places far from the glare of city lights. The Milky Way appears as a starry expanse of light stretching across the sky. In ancient times, people felt this glowing band of light resembled a river of milk, which is how it got its name.

In addition to over one hundred billion stars and possible **black holes**, the Milky Way is comprised of star clusters, planets, glowing nebulae (gas clouds), dust, and empty space. It is approximately one hundred thousand **light-year**s in diameter and two thousand light-years thick from top to bottom. Older stars and denser clusters lie near the center of the galaxy while younger stars and **open cluster**s reside near the edges.

Before 1918, astronomers believed that our **solar system** was at the center of the Milky Way. Then, after studying the distribution of star clusters in the galaxy, American astronomer Harlow Shapley determined that this was not the case. Our sun, which is a relatively young star, lies about thirty thousand light-years from the center.

The Milky Way is a spiral-shaped galaxy, meaning it is shaped like a pinwheel. It has a group of objects at the center (mostly older stars and maybe a black hole), surrounded by a **halo** (a band of star clusters) and an invisible cloud of **dark matter,** with four arms spiraling out. The spiral shape is formed because the entire galaxy is rotating, with the stars at the

The Milky Way as photographed from the Lowell Observatory in Flagstaff, Arizona.

outer edges forming the arms. Our solar system is located in one of the arms, called the Orion arm.

Just as the Earth revolves around the sun, the sun revolves around the nucleus of the galaxy. The sun travels at a speed of about 130 miles (209 kilometers) per second and it takes about two hundred million years to complete a single orbit around the galactic center.

Galaxies are as plentiful in the universe as grains of sand on the beach. The Milky Way is part of a cluster of galaxies known as the Local Group, and the Local Group is part of a local supercluster that includes many clusters. Superclusters are separated by extremely large voids of space, with very few galaxies in between.

In the late 1500s, Galileo Galilei first examined the Milky Way through a telescope and saw that the glowing band was made up of countless stars. As early as 1755, German philosopher Immanuel Kant suggested that the Milky Way was a lens-shaped group of stars, and that many other such groups existed in the universe.

In 1924, American astronomer Edwin Hubble first proved the existence of other galaxies. He used a very powerful 100-inch (254-centimeter) telescope at Mount Wilson Observatory to discover that a group of stars long thought to be part of the Milky Way was actually a separate galaxy, now known as the Andromeda galaxy. He then discovered many other **spiral galaxies.**

Astronomers today use a number of sophisticated methods to examine the Milky Way and other galaxies. Until recently we did not have a picture of our galactic core. The reason is that dense clouds and dust block the visible light. It turns out, however, that **radio wave**s and infrared light shine through these obstacles, and objects can be distinguished by radio and infrared telescopes. Using these specialized instruments we have come closer to answering many questions about our own galaxy and others, including how stars are born and how galaxies are formed.

See also **Galaxy**; **Shapley, Harlow**; and **Spiral galaxy**

Mir space station

The Russian *Mir* is the only **space station** currently in operation. Now in its eleventh year, *Mir* has continuously hosted a series of Russian **cosmo-**

nauts and international space travelers. The space station's name comes from the Russian word for "peace" or "community living in harmony." Among the international visitors have been two American astronauts, Norm Thagard and Shannon Lucid, and a Japanese journalist, Toyohiro Akiyama.

When launched in February 1986, *Mir* had the benefit of fifteen years worth of Russian experience with space stations. In 1971, the Russians launched their first station, *Salyut 1,* which remained in operation for six months. Over the next twenty years, they operated six more Salyut space stations. Despite some failures and tragedies, the program was very successful overall. Now *Mir* is being used as a model for the upcoming International Space Station, slated for completion by the year 2002.

Mir is 43 feet (13 meters) long and 14 feet (4.3 meters) wide, with 98-foot-long (30-meter-long) energy-generating solar panels. It can accommodate six astronauts at a time for short stays, but only three com-

Space station Mir *in orbit around Earth.*

fortably for longer periods. In anticipation that crew members would come for long stays, *Mir* was designed with their comfort and privacy in mind. The longest period a cosmonaut has remained on board so far has been fifteen months.

One of *Mir*'s most outstanding features is that it has six docking ports. Thus, in addition to facilitating the arrival of piloted spacecraft (U.S. **space shuttle**s and Russian Soyuz vessels) and unpiloted resupply spacecraft, room is available for various scientific modules. These interchangeable modules enable *Mir* inhabitants to carry out a wide range of experiments.

Components of the *Mir* Space Station

The main body of *Mir* consists of four areas: a docking compartment, living quarters, a work area, and a propulsion chamber. The docking compartment lies at one end of the station. It contains television equipment and the electric power supply system, as well as five of the vessel's six ports. These ports the sites at which piloted spacecraft land, crew members are transferred, and scientific modules are attached.

The crew spends most of its time in the living and work areas. The living space consists of two small sleeping cabins and a common area with dining facilities and exercise equipment. The space also contains a toilet, sink, and water recycling system. The work compartment is the station's nerve center. It holds the main navigational, communications, and power controls. Attached to the sides of the compartment are two solar panels that provide *Mir*'s electricity.

At the other end of the station is the propulsion compartment. This area is not pressurized, meaning that crew members cannot enter it without wearing a spacesuit. The compartment contains the station's **rocket** motors, fuel supply, heating system, and the sixth docking port, which receives unpiloted refueling missions. Secured to the outside of that compartment, as well as to the docking compartment, are antennae used for communications with Earth.

Thus far, five scientific modules have been attached to *Mir*. The first, added in 1987, is an observatory with ultraviolet, **X-ray**, and **gamma ray** telescopes. The second, which arrived two years later, contains two solar panel arrays and an airlock for conducting repairs and other activities outside the station. In 1990, the third module was installed. It contains a variety of scientific equipment and a docking port for very heavy spacecraft.

Two more modules, with more equipment, solar arrays, and ports, were added in 1995.

On March, 23, 1996, fifty-three-year-old astronaut Shannon Lucid was transported to *Mir* on the space shuttle *Atlantis*. She was scheduled to remain for five months on the space station, the longest time ever spent by a U.S. astronaut in space. Lucid is one of four Americans to take turns living on *Mir* continuously over a two-year period.

The joint Russian/American crew of *Mir* is conducting research into the ways in which humans, animals, and plants function in space, as well as testing equipment that will be used on the upcoming International Space Station. Most important, perhaps, is the spirit of international cooperation their mission represents. The words of then-Senator (and later President) Lyndon B. Johnson, in a speech to the United Nations in 1958, still hold true: "Men who have worked together to reach the stars are not likely to descend together into the depths of war and desolation."

See also **International Space Station**; **Lucid, Shannon**; and **Salyut program**

Mitchell, Maria

(1818–1889)

American astronomer

Maria Mitchell.

Maria Mitchell was a teacher, astronomer, and advocate of women's rights. She was the first female member of the American Academy of Arts and Sciences and a founding member of the Association for the Advancement of Women. In an age when women were expected to stay at home, Mitchell made advances in the field of astronomy and encouraged a generation of young women to pursue careers in mathematics and the sciences.

Mitchell was born on August 1, 1818, on Nantucket Island, Massachusetts. Her mother, who worked in libraries, encouraged her to read, and her father, an astronomy buff, taught her about the stars. Her formal schooling ended at the age of sixteen, but Mitchell continued studying on her own.

When she was seventeen, Mitchell opened her own school. Her teaching style was very personalized and unconventional. Sometimes school would start before dawn with a bird watching session and other times it would continue into the night for astronomical observations.

Mitchell next worked as a librarian. She worked only afternoons and Saturday evenings and spent much of her spare time with a telescope. On October 1, 1847, she made the first discovery of a **comet** not visible to the naked eye. For this she received a gold medal from the King of Denmark.

In 1848, Mitchell's election to the American Academy of Arts and Sciences brought her a great deal of attention. Several magazines and newspapers ran stories about the first woman in the academy.

The next year Mitchell was hired by the *American Ephemeris and Nautical Almanac* to assist with the United States Coast survey. The survey was charged with establishing more accurate measures of time, **latitude,** and **longitude.**

In 1865, Mitchell moved to New York to join the faculty of the newly founded Vassar College for women. As an astronomy professor and director of the observatory, Mitchell became an outspoken advocate of women's rights. She also continued to stress individual attention, small class sizes, and other unconventional teaching methods just as she did in her earlier teaching experience. Mitchell remained at Vassar for twenty-three years. She retired at the age of seventy, one year before her death.

Throughout her life Mitchell made extensive observations of the sun, stars, and planets, and developed a number of theories based on what she saw. For instance, she correctly identified Jupiter's cloud layers as being part of the planet itself, and not just hovering in the atmosphere, as clouds on Earth do. She was also right in speculating that Saturn's rings were of a different composition than the body of the planet.

Molecular cloud

A **molecular cloud** is a cool area in the **interstellar medium** in which molecules are formed. While the substance formed in the greatest abundance is molecular hydrogen (H2). There have been about sixty different molecules detected in the largest clouds. Other examples of such molecules are those of carbon monoxide, water, and ammonia.

Within molecular clouds the concentration of interstellar matter is hundreds to thousands of times greater than in the surrounding interstellar medium. Interstellar matter is made up of both gas atoms and solid particles. The gas, which accounts for about 99 percent of interstellar matter, is about three-quarters hydrogen and nearly one-quarter helium, plus trace amounts of nitrogen, oxygen, carbon, sulfur, and possibly other elements. The solid particles, also called **cosmic dust,** consist primarily of carbon and silicate material (silicon, oxygen, and metallic ions), possibly with frozen water and ammonia, and solid carbon dioxide.

Molecules in space exist primarily in clouds (also called "dark **nebula**e") because there they are protected by cosmic dust. Without this protection, the molecules would be broken down by the ultraviolet light from stars. Less than 1 percent of the **mass** of a dark nebula is cosmic dust, yet this amount is enough to reflect away or absorb much of the starlight.

Molecular clouds can be enormous. The largest ones, called "giant molecular clouds," stretch across several **light-year**s and are one thousand to one million times as massive as the sun. Giant molecular clouds may contain several dense core regions, each one with a mass equal to one hundred to one thousand solar masses.

A few thousand giant molecular clouds are to be formed in our **galaxy.** The dark nebula crossing the **Milky Way** called the "dark rift," is actually a series of overlapping giant molecular clouds.

A molecular cloud lasts only ten million to one hundred million years, after which it condenses to form stars. Depending on the size of the cloud, it may produce a single star, a **binary star,** or a star cluster. The cloud increases in density and heat until it begins fusing hydrogen into helium, producing starlight.

See also **Interstellar medium** and **Stellar evolution**

Moon

Earthlings have been studying the moon for thousands of years, yet it has remained largely a mystery until recent years. Only in 1959 did we get our first glimpse of the half of the moon that always faces away from us. And it wasn't until the following decade that we learned that the moon has no water and supports no life.

The moon, on average, is 238,900 miles (384,390 kilometers) from Earth. It measures about 2,160 miles (3,475 kilometers) across, a little over one-quarter of the Earth's diameter. The Earth and moon are the closest in size of any known planet and satellite, with the possible exception of Pluto and its moon Charon.

The moon is covered with rocks, boulders, craters, and a layer of charcoal-colored soil from 5 to 20 feet (1.5 to 6.1 meters) deep. The soil consists of rock fragments, pulverized rock, and tiny pieces of glass. Two types of rocks are found on the moon: basalt, which is hardened lava; and breccia, which is soil and rock fragments that have melted together.

Elements found in moon rocks include aluminum, calcium, iron,

Earth's moon.

magnesium, titanium, potassium, and phosphorus. In contrast with the Earth, which has a core rich in iron and other metals, the moon appears to contain very little metal. And the total lack of water or organic compounds rules out the possibility that there is, or ever was, life on the moon.

The moon has no weather, no wind or rain, and no air. As a result, it has no protection from the sun's rays or **meteorite**s and no ability to retain heat. Temperatures on the moon have been recorded in the range of 280 degrees Fahrenheit (138 degrees Celsius) to -148 degrees Fahrenheit (-100 degrees Celsius).

How the Moon Was Formed

Both the Earth and the moon are about 4.6 billion years old, a fact which has led to many theories about their common origin. The most commonly accepted theory today is the collision theory. This theory states that when the Earth was newly formed, it was struck by an **asteroid** or **comet,** which created a huge crater and spewed a ring of matter into space. That ring gradually condensed to form the moon.

Another theory, called simultaneous creation, claims that the moon and the Earth formed at the same time, from the same planetary building blocks that were floating in space billions of years ago. This explanation is unlikely however, because the Earth and moon have very different compositions.

Yet another possibility is the capture theory. This theory states that the moon was created somewhere else in the **solar system** and was pulled from its original orbit by the Earth's gravitational field. The problem with this theory is that the Earth and moon are relatively close in size. Capture is a lot more likely to occur when one object is several times larger than the other.

However it occurred, the evolution of Earth and the moon has been completely different. For about the first seven hundred million years of the moon's existence it was struck by great numbers of meteorites. They blasted out craters of all sizes. The sheer impact of so many meteorites caused the moon's crust to melt. Eventually, as the crust cooled, lava from the interior surfaced and filled in cracks and some crater basins. These filled-in craters are the dark spots we see when we look at the moon.

To early astronomers, these dark spots appeared to be bodies of liquid. Italian astronomer Galileo Galilei in 1609 was the first to observe the

Create a Moonscape

The moon is covered with countless craters, both large and small. These are the result of meteorites that have struck the moon, mainly during the early years of the solar system when interplanetary matter was more plentiful. Since there is no wind or water to erode the lunar surface, the marks made by even the earliest meteorites remain, giving the moon its characteristic pockmarked face.

To make your own moonscape, you need a container (such as an old baking pan) filled with wet sand or dirt or a combination of the two, possibly mixed with flour—you can experiment with a variety of surface types. Drop objects of various sizes, from pebbles and marbles to larger rocks, from up to 4 feet (1.2 meters) above the pan, to see the variety of craters they form upon impact.

To form a "permanent" moonscape, drop objects into a pan of partially hardened plaster of Paris. Pull each object straight out, leaving only the craters to harden.

moon through a telescope and named the dark patches "maria," Latin for "seas."

In 1645, Polish astronomer Johannes Hevelius, known as the founder of lunar topography, charted 250 craters and other formations on the moon. Many of these were later named for philosophers and scientists, such as Tycho Brahe, Nicholas Copernicus, Johannes Kepler, and Plato.

Humans Land On the Moon

All Earth-based study of the moon, however, has been strictly limited by one factor: only one side of the moon ever faces us. This reason is that the moon's rotational period is the same as the time it takes to complete one orbit around the Earth. Thus, it wasn't until 1959, when the former **Soviet Union**'s **space probe** *Luna 3* traveled to the far side of the moon, that scientists were able to see the other half.

Then in 1966, the Soviet *Luna 9* became the first object from Earth to land on the moon. It took television footage showing that lunar dust, which scientists had anticipated finding, did not exist. The fear of encountering thick layers of dust was one reason both the Soviet Union and the United States feared sending a man to the moon.

Just three years later, U.S. astronauts Neil Armstrong and Buzz Aldrin on the *Apollo 11* became the first humans to walk on the moon. They collected rock and soil samples, from which scientists learned the moon's elemental composition. To this day, the moon remains the only celestial body to be visited by humans.

See also **Aldrin, Buzz**; **Armstrong, Neil**; **Lunar exploration**; **Lunar module**; and **Lunar phases**

Mount Wilson Observatory

The Mount Wilson Observatory is widely considered the premier major astronomical observatory in the United States. It is perhaps best known as the place where Edwin Hubble discovered the existence of **galaxies** beyond our own. He also found that these galaxies are moving away from one another, leading to the conclusion that the universe is expanding.

The observatory is located outside of Pasadena, California, in the San Gabriel Mountains, at a height of 5,700 feet (1,732 meters). One of that site's most important features is that observers can expect to have about three hundred clear nights a year. This turn-of-the-century observatory remains a center for cutting-edge research, although its operation in recent years has been hampered by light pollution from the neighboring metropolis, Los Angeles.

Previously owned by the Carnegie Institution, Mount Wilson Observatory was turned over to the nonprofit Mount Wilson Institute (MWI) in 1985. The board of trustees of MWI is made up of representatives from the business, legal, educational, and scientific communities. It also has members from the Los Angeles County government and the Carnegie Institution.

The observatory was initiated in 1902 with a ten thousand dollar grant from the private, Washington, D.C.-based Carnegie Institution. The money had been solicited by pioneer astronomer George Hale for the construction of a solar observatory, a research center designed specifically for the study of the sun.

Two years later, after Hale had made countless trips taking parts up the mountain on mule-back, the Snow Solar Telescope was erected. **Solar** telescopes are large, specialized instruments that break down sunlight into its component wavelengths and then photograph the resulting image. The Snow's mirror was 24 inches (61 centimeters) in diameter, three times as large as any existing solar telescope at the time. The sunlight entered the structure through a 29-foot-tall (8-meter-tall) tower and traveled through a wood-and-canvas tube to reach the subterranean mirror. The Snow was used for extensive studies of **sunspot**s (magnetic storms that create dark areas on the sun's surface)—the observatory's first claim to fame.

Later Telescopes At Mount Wilson

In 1908, an optical telescope was installed. The telescope was a **reflector** with a 60-inch-diameter (152-centimeter-diameter) mirror. A reflector telescope is one that uses a mirror to bring light rays into focus. The success of this project led to the planning of an even bigger telescope, one

Mount Wilson Observatory.

originally designed to have an 84-inch (213-centimeter) mirror. A grant from John D. Hooker, philanthropist and founder of the California Academy of Science, however, allowed for the construction of an instrument with a 100-inch (254-centimeter) mirror. The Hooker Telescope, subjected to building delays due to World War I, was completed in 1917. At that time it was the world's largest optical telescope, and it remained so for the next thirty years.

In the meantime, two additional solar tower telescopes had been completed at the observatory. The first had a 60-foot (18-meter) tower. In order to overcome some of the difficulties Hale had experienced with the Snow Telescope, no underground component was included. Instead, all of the instrumentation was located in the tower. Hale continued his exploration of sunspots on this telescope. He discovered by studying their **spectra** that magnetic forces were embedded in the spots. Prior to this discovery, there was no indication that **magnetic field**s existed anywhere other than on Earth.

Given this success, Hale immediately ordered a third solar telescope. Believing that "bigger is better," he designed an instrument with a 150-foot (46-meter) tower. This instrument produced a **spectrum** 70 feet (21 meters) across, with thousands of lines. The telescope was used mainly to learn more about the nature of the sun's magnetic field.

Mount Wilson's primary instrument remains the 100-inch-diameter (254-centimeter-diameter) Hooker Telescope. It has been in use continuously except for the period from 1985 to 1995, when it was being refurbished. Both it and the 60-inch (152-centimeter) reflector were recently equipped with advanced technology known as **adaptive optics.** Adaptive optics is a system that makes minute adjustments to the shape of the mirror within hundredths of a second of an arc, to correct distortions that result from disturbances in the atmosphere.

Two interferometers (systems that use multiple connected instruments that have a combined greater resolution than any single instrument) are also on site. One is the Infrared Spatial Interferometer, which examines **infrared radiation** emitted by space objects. This interferometer is operated by the University of California of Berkeley. The other instrument is a small **optical interferometer.** Finally, the observatory has a 24-inch (61-centimeter) telescope belonging to the Telescopes in Education Project, a program of the Mount Wilson Institute that introduces school children to astronomy.

The 60-inch (152-centimeter) reflector telescope is currently used for two main projects: the H-K Project, which studies the **chromosphere** of stars; and the Atmospheric Compensation Experiment, which tests the capabilities of the newly installed adaptive optics system.

All three solar telescopes are used in research today as well. The 60-foot (18-meter) tower is operated by the University of Southern California and the 150-foot (46-meter) tower by the University of California at Los Angeles. The Snow Telescope is reserved for use by the Telescopes in Education Project.

See also **Hale, George**; **Hooker Telescope**; **Interferometry**; **Palomar Observatory**; and **Solar telescope**

Musgrave, Storey (1935–)

American astronaut

Astronaut Storey Musgrave in 1972.

When Storey Musgrave flew on the **space shuttle** *Columbia* in November 1996, he became the oldest person to venture into space. With this flight, his sixth, the sixty-one-year-old Musgrave also set a record for the number of times in space. Age does not seem to hinder this frequent space flier. In addition to being a scientist-astronaut by day, Musgrave continues his schooling by night. He currently has two bachelor's degrees, three master's degrees, and a medical degree.

Musgrave applied to be an astronaut in 1967, the first year that the National Aeronautics and Space Administration (NASA) began seeking scientists to become astronauts. Before that time, most astronauts had been test pilots. During his first, flightless sixteen years at NASA, Musgrave helped design the *Skylab* **space station,** spacesuits, and equipment needed for **space walk**s. He also participated in designing the space shuttle.

In 1983, at age forty-seven, Musgrave finally flew on the maiden journey of the space shuttle *Columbia*. He and crewmate Donald Peterson made the first space walk from a shuttle. Two years later he was again aboard *Challenger,* this time to operate the Spacelab 2 scientific experiments. In 1989 and 1991, Musgrave flew space shuttle missions for the Department of Defense, the first on *Discovery* and the second on *Atlantis.*

Musgrave's most famous mission came in 1993, when he was part of the space shuttle *Endeavour* crew that repaired the Hubble Space Telescope. At age fifty-eight, Musgrave was then the oldest person to walk in space.

The November 1996 *Columbia* mission was Musgrave's last. While Musgrave feels that he is capable of more flights, he supports NASA's decision. "Space flight is an incredible privilege and needs to spread around among as many humans as you can," Musgrave said in a May 1996 published report.

Musgrave's Personal History

Musgrave's life has been a series of accomplishments. He was born in Boston, Massachusetts. After graduating from high school in 1953, he joined the U.S. Marine Corps. There he served as an electrician and aircraft crew chief in the Far East.

When his service in the Marines was over, Musgrave began his collegiate career. He first earned a bachelor's degree in mathematics and statistics from Syracuse University in 1958, then, a year later, a master's of business administration from the University of California at Los Angeles. The next year he completed a bachelor's degree in chemistry from Marietta College in Ohio and, in 1964, earned his medical degree from Columbia University. In 1966, Musgrave completed a master's degree in physiology and biophysics from the University of Kentucky. He finished his most recent degree, a master's in literature from the University of Houston, in 1987. In the years since, he has been taking classes in a variety of subjects, accumulating a total of two hundred credit hours.

Since becoming an astronaut, Musgrave has also worked part time as a surgeon at Denver General Hospital and as a professor of physiology and biophysics at the University of Kentucky Medical Center. Musgrave is divorced and is the father of six children.

See also **Hubble Space Telescope**; *Skylab* **space station**; and **Space shuttle**

National Aeronautics and Space Administration

The National Aeronautics and Space Administration (NASA) was created as an arm of the U.S. government by President Dwight D. Eisenhower in 1958. Its stated purpose was to lead "the expansion of human knowledge of phenomena in the atmosphere and space," as well as to explore commercial uses of space, such as the placement of communication satellites. NASA is the successor to the National Advisory Committee for Aeronautics (NACA), which was formed in 1915 when aviation was still brand new. The U.S. Congress created NACA to "supervise and direct the scientific study of the problems of flight, with a view to their practical solutions."

Both air flight and space flight have made tremendous gains under the guidance of NACA and NASA. "The journey begun in 1915 has taken American aviators, astronauts and robotic spacecraft from the dunes of Kitty Hawk to the edge of the atmosphere and to the surface of the moon," reads a NASA fact sheet. "American spacecraft have explored more than sixty worlds in our **solar system,** while methodically peering back in space and time to reveal many of the secrets of the Universe."

NASA is a sprawling bureaucracy, headquartered in Washington D.C. In 1995, NASA operated on a budget of 14.4 billion dollars. In addition to the twenty-one thousand people employed directly by NASA, thousands more work for private companies contracted to supply NASA with components for spacecraft and other equipment.

NASA is divided into several departments that operate out of ten different centers across the United States. These space centers are responsible for programs involving aircraft and **space shuttle** flight research; scientific satellite development; piloted space flight research; rocketry; spacecraft development; spacecraft launch; and space exploration. The primary centers are as follows:

Kennedy Space Center (KSC): Located in Cape Canaveral, on Florida's Atlantic Coast, KSC is NASA's main launch center. The site was selected because of its good weather and proximity to the ocean, into which used **rocket** fuel tanks and other components fall after launch. KSC is home to the 525-foot-tall (158-meter-tall) Vehicle Assembly Building, where rockets and space shuttles are put together, as well as launch pads and a 3-mile-long (5-kilometer-long) runway for space shuttle landings.

Johnson Space Center (JSC): Originally called the Manned Spacecraft Center, the Houston, Texas-based facility is the site of mission control for virtually all U.S. piloted space flights. JSC officials are responsible for selecting and training astronauts, planning and directing space mis-

Mission control's firing room at Kennedy Space Center's Launch Control Center.

sions, and determining the future course of NASA's piloted space flight program.

Ames Research Center (ARC): Situated next to the U.S. Naval Air Station at Moffat Field, California, ARC is devoted to scientific research and the advancement of space technology. It has been instrumental in developing the Pioneer series of deep **space probe**s, space-based telescopes, and the space shuttle. The center is named for the former president of NACA, Joseph Ames.

Jet Propulsion Laboratory (JPL): This branch of NASA is operated by the California Institute of Technology in Pasadena, California. Since 1960, it has been involved in solar system exploration through programs such as Ranger and Surveyor moon **probe**s. Today it serves at the command center for interplanetary missions, such as the Voyager program, *Magellan,* and *Galileo.* JPL also now participates in various Department of Defense projects.

Goddard Space Flight Center (GSFC): GSFC is located just outside of Washington D.C., in Greenbelt, Maryland. Its staff of scientists and engineers work solely on the development and operation of scientific satellites. Most of the space-based observatories studying the Earth, sun, and the stars are controlled by GSFC. The facility also houses the National Space Science Data Center, where data collected by dozens of satellites is stored.

Marshall Space Flight Center (MSFC): This center, which is dedicated primarily to rocketry, is located in the U.S. Army Redstone Arsenal in Huntsville, Alabama. Some of the United States' most powerful rockets, including the Jupiter-C, Saturn, and Redstone, have been developed there. MSFC has also been involved in the *Skylab* **space station,** Spacelab, and a number of unpiloted scientific missions.

Langley Research Center (LRC): LRC, located in Hampton, Virginia, is the oldest of NASA's space research centers. It was established in 1917, long before NASA and has been involved in aircraft development since the earliest days of aviation. The staff of LRC worked on military airplanes during World War II and conducted research leading to the first supersonic airplane. They were then put in charge of the initial stages of the Mercury program, which placed the first U.S. astronauts in space, and went on to play a support role in Gemini and Apollo manned space flight programs. After that, LRC staff turned to the development of communication and scientific satellites.

Dryden Flight Research Center (DFRC): Dryden has its roots in high-speed air flight missions. The facility, situated at Edwards Air Force Base in California, features long runways used by airplanes that first broke the sound barrier.

Lewis Research Center (LRC): LRC was founded in Cleveland, Ohio, in 1941 to conduct research into aeronautics and jet propulsion for NACA. Once it was taken over by NASA, LRC shifted its efforts to the development of medium-sized rockets, such as Agena and Centaur. Today, while LRC staff continue to develop new systems for propelling spacecraft, they also work on communication satellites.

Michoud Assembly Facility (MAF): This center, near New Orleans, Louisiana, is the site at which engineering, design, and manufacture of the external tank for the space shuttle takes place. It is operated by the Marshall Space Flight Center.

See also **Kennedy Space Center**

National Solar Observatory

The National Solar Observatory (NSO) oversees the operation of **solar telescope**s at two sites: the Kitt Peak National Observatory near Flagstaff, Arizona, and the Sacramento Peak Observatory in southern New Mexico. NSO is a branch of the National Optical Astronomy Observatories (NOAO), which was formed in 1984 by a consortium of university astronomy departments known as the Association of Universities for Research in Astronomy. In addition to Kitt Peak National Observatory and Sacramento Peak Observatory, NOAO runs the Cerro Tololo Interamerican Observatory in Chile.

Kitt Peak National Observatory

Kitt Peak has been in operation since 1960. Besides NSO's two solar telescopes it contains the world's second largest concentration of optical telescopes. Sacramento Peak was established in 1950. In contrast to Kitt Peak, it is dedicated solely to solar astronomy.

There are three major solar telescopes between the two facilities, two at Kitt Peak and one at Sacramento Peak. Solar telescopes differ in design from optical telescopes because solar telescopes must be constructed to take into account the sun's intense heat. Sunlight entering the telescope must be cooled or it will destroy the instruments. One way to do this is to direct the light to an underground chamber before it reaches the instruments. Another way is to create a vacuum around the telescope, because in a vacuum no air molecules are present to absorb the heat.

Located at 6,875 feet (2,096 meters) above sea level, Kitt Peak is home to the world's largest solar telescope, the McMath-Pierce Solar Telescope. It sits on the mountaintop like a giant upside-down "V" with one vertical side and one diagonal side. The vertical side is a 100-foot-tall (30-meter-tall) tower with a 79-inch-diameter (200-centimeter-diameter) flat, rotating mirror (called a **heliostat**) on top. Light strikes the heliostat first, then travels down the diagonal shaft to a depth of 164 feet (50 meters) underground. A 63-inch-diameter (160-centimeter-diameter) mirror then reflects the light back to an observation room, where it is passed through a **spectrograph.** This instrument breaks the light down into its component wavelengths and photographs the resulting image.

The primary use of this telescope is to analyze the **spectra** of various regions of the sun, as well as of stars, planets, and **comet**s. It addition to visible light, the McMath-Pierce Telescope can detect **infrared radiation** within a narrow band of wavelengths.

The second NSO instrument at Kitt Peak is called the Vacuum Solar Telescope. In this telescope, light enters at the top of a tower and is directed straight down to a 27.5-inch (69.9-centimeter) mirror. The main function of this telescope is to monitor activity such as temporary bright spots that explode on the sun's surface called **flare**s and **magnetic field**s on the sun.

Sacramento Peak Observatory

The 134-foot (41-meter) high Vacuum Tower Telescope sits on Sacramento Peak at an altitude of 9,184 feet (2,792 meters). It extends 219 feet (66.6 meters) underground, where light is reflected to a control room by a 27-inch (72-centimeter) mirror. The Vacuum Tower, which monitors activity on the sun, is the first solar telescope to be equipped with advanced technology known as **adaptive optics.** This system makes minute adjustments to the shape of the mirror within hundredths of a second of an arc to correct distortions that result from disturbances in the air.

In addition to the solar telescopes at Kitt Peak and Sacramento Peak, NSO is responsible for overseeing the Global Oscillation Network Group (GONG) Project. This ongoing study of solar internal structure and dynamics uses helioseismological methods, that is, it measures vibrations of sound waves within the sun. The instruments that measure the oscillations function in a way similar to seismographs (devices that detect earthquakes). Strong vibrations detected within the sun's core imply the presence of cavities. The frequency of oscillations is related to the temperature and chemical composition at specific regions within the sun.

The GONG project is conducted at six observatories around the world (Big Bear Solar Observatory, Learmonth Solar Observatory, Udaipur Solar Observatory, Observatorio del Teide, Cerro Tololo Interamerican Observatory, and Mauna Loa Observatory), spaced at approximately 60-degree intervals of **longitude.** Since it is always daytime in at least one of these places, the GONG project operates continuously.

See also **Big Bear Solar Observatory**; **Kitt Peak National Observatory**; and **Solar telescope**

Navigational satellite

Travelers throughout time have relied on the sun, moon, and stars to find their way. Early navigational instruments included the **astrolabe,** a star map engraved on a round sheet of metal; the **sextant,** a tool to measure the angle from the horizon to a celestial body; the seagoing chronometer, an accurate timepiece; and the compass, which aligns with the Earth's **magnetic field** and is still widely used today.

Next came the era of radio navigation which involves the transmission of radio signals from multiple sources. A ship's navigator with a radio receiver can roughly determine his location by the frequency of incoming signals. Although this method was made more precise by using high frequency signals, there was still the problem of the signals being blocked by mountains and not bending over the horizon.

Engineers realized that one way to overcome these obstacles was to send the radio signals from space. In the late 1960s and early 1970s, the U.S. Navy developed a system called *Transit,* an orbiting satellite that transmitted **radio wave**s. As the satellite moved closer to an object, the radio waves would increase in frequency and as the satellite moved away, the frequency of the waves would decrease. By measuring the shift in frequency of the waves, one could determine a position on Earth.

Transit was used originally for the navigation of nuclear submarines. In 1967, the Navy made it available commercially. Since then it has been used in geographic surveys, fishing, and offshore oil exploration.

The U.S. military in subsequent years developed an improved satellite, the Navigation Satellite for Time and Ranging Global Positioning System, called *Navstar*. Whereas *Transit* could give an object's position to within no more than 0.1 miles (0.16 kilometers), *Navstar* comes to within 33 feet (10 meters). The *Navstar* system has twenty-four satellites that each complete a 12,500-mile (20,115-kilometer) orbit of Earth every twelve hours. By using large receivers to pick up the satellites' signals, ships and airplanes can identify their position and their speed to within a fraction of a mile per hour. The military uses *Navstar* to locate objects ranging from airborne missiles to individual soldiers.

In 1979, an international effort by the United States, Canada, France, and the former **Soviet Union** led to the development of the *COSPAS-SARSAT* satellite system. This system is used for ground and sea search-and-rescue missions and has saved thousands of lives. It relies on four satellites in orbit above the Earth's poles, which pick up distress signals and send the location of those signals (to within 1.2 miles or 1.9 kilometers) to terminals around the world. From there they are transmitted to a mission control center which notifies rescue teams.

Argos is similar system, operated by the U.S. National Oceanic and Atmospheric Administration. It can locate objects on Earth to within 0.5 miles (0.8 kilometers), by picking up their signals and transmitting them to a ground station. *Argos*' primary function is to relay information necessary for environmental and atmospheric studies. For example, *Argos* is used by the U.S. Fish and Wildlife Service to track wildlife that have been fitted with miniaturized transmitters. It can also collect and send information about the weather, currents, winds, waves, and seismic (relating to earthquakes) and volcanic activity. In conjunction with balloons, *Argos* is used to study physical and chemical properties of the atmosphere.

Today, the general public enjoys widespread use of navigational satellites. Hand-held receivers, which pick up signals from the Global Positioning System (GPS), can be purchased for just a few hundred dollars. These have become very popular among back-country hikers. A GPS is particularly helpful in areas such as the desert, bush, or tundra, where the terrain looks the same for miles and maps are of little use.

To use a GPS, just stand in a clearing, pull out the antenna and turn on the unit. The GPS reads and combines the signals of whichever satellites are overhead (usually four are within range). Within minutes it gives readings of your position in terms of **latitude, longitude,** and in some GPS models, elevation—to an accuracy of 50 yards (46 meters) or less. You can then plot this reading on a map and see where you are and how far it is to your destination.

Nebula

Bright or dark clouds of gas and dust hovering in the **interstellar medium** are called **nebula**e. "Nebula," Latin for "cloud," is a visual classification rather than a scientific one. Objects called nebulae vary greatly in composition. Some are really **galaxies,** but to early astronomers they all appeared to be clouds.

Some categories of bright nebulae include spiral, planetary, emission, and reflection. Others are remnants of **supernova** explosions.

In 1923, American astronomer Edwin Hubble made a remarkable discovery about a spiral-shaped nebula: it was actually a gigantic **spiral galaxy.** Previously, astronomers had considered the Andromeda spiral nebula to be a cloud of gas within our galaxy, the **Milky Way.** Looking through the powerful Hooker Telescope at Mount Wilson Observatory in California, Hubble picked out several **cepheid variable**s, blinking stars used to measure distance in space. He determined that these stars were several thousand **light-year**s away, far beyond the bounds of the Milky Way. Since then many other spiral nebulae have been defined as galaxies.

Planetary nebulae truly are clouds of gas. They are called "planetary" because through a telescope, they look greenish and round, like planets. A planetary nebula is thought to be a star's detached outer atmosphere of hydrogen gas. This is a by-product of a star going through the later stages of its life cycle. As it evolves past the **red giant** stage, a star sheds its atmosphere, much as a snake sheds its skin. One of the most famous of these is the Ring nebula in the **constellation** Lyra.

An emission nebula is a glowing gas cloud with a hot bright star within or behind it. The star gives off high-energy **ultraviolet radiation,** which ionizes the gas. As the electrons recombine with the atoms of gas, the gas fluoresces, gives off light. A well-known example of this kind of nebula is the Orion nebula, a greenish, hydrogen-rich, star-filled cloud that is twenty light-years across. It is believed to be a **stellar nursery,** a place where new stars are formed.

Reflection nebulae are also bright gas clouds, but not as common as emission nebulae. A reflection nebula is a bluish cloud containing dust that reflects the light of a neighboring bright star. It is blue for a similar reason that the Earth's sky is blue. In the case of our sky, the blue component of sunlight is scattered by gas molecules in our atmosphere. In the same way, the nebula's dust scatters starlight only in the wavelengths of blue light.

The final type of bright nebula is that produced by a supernova explosion. Perhaps the most famous nebula of this type is the Crab nebula, an enormous patch of light in the Taurus constellation. At its center lies a **pulsar,** a rapidly spinning, incredibly dense star made of neutrons that remains after a supernova explosion.

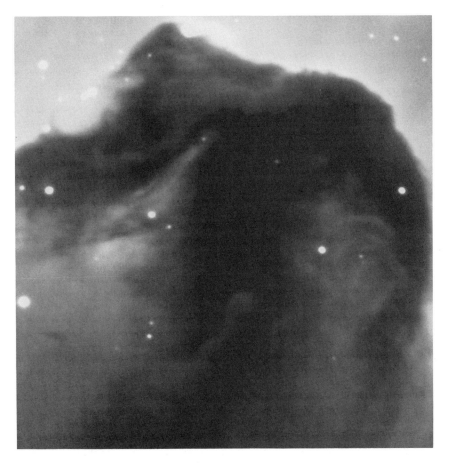

Close up of the Horsehead nebula.

Dark nebulae are also scattered throughout the interstellar medium. They are dark because they contain dust (composed of carbon, silicon, magnesium, aluminum, and other elements) that does not emit light and is of sufficient density to block the light of the stars beyond. These non-glowing clouds are not visible through an optical telescope, but do give off **infrared radiation.** Thus they can be identified either as dark patches on a background of starlight or through an infrared telescope. One example of a dark nebula is the cloud that blots out part of the Cygnus constellation in our home galaxy. Another example is the "Coal Sack" nebula, located in the Southern Cross constellation.

See also **Infrared astronomy** and **Interstellar medium**

Nemesis

About sixty-five million years ago, the Earth was engulfed in darkness. Many links in the food chain, from tiny plankton in the ocean all the way up to the dinosaurs, became extinct. There are many theories as to what caused this to occur, but the most popular is that the Earth was struck by a giant **asteroid** or **comet** which created a blast equal to the detonation of millions of tons of dynamite. So much dust was kicked up into the atmosphere that it blocked out the sunlight, possibly for over a month. This caused cold temperatures, killed off many species of plants, and caused large animals to freeze or starve.

This period of mass extinction may not have been a random occurrence. By digging down into layers of dirt and rock, scientists have found that most layers contain abundant fossils while others contain very few. These gaps in the fossil record, which tell us that during certain times many species suffered extinction, are found at roughly twenty-six-million-year intervals. In addition, the layer of Earth above the one from the age of dinosaurs, is rich in metals like iridium and gold, which are rare on Earth but abundant in asteroids.

What is it that would cause these relatively small members of the **solar system** to stray from their path and collide with Earth every twenty-six million years? Some astronomers believe that it is Nemesis, the hypothetical companion star to the sun, named for the Greek goddess who was the enemy of good fortune.

According to the theory, Nemesis is a small **red dwarf** or **brown** dwarf star, about ten times the **mass** of Jupiter, that orbits the sun on a very elongated path every twenty-six million years. Nemesis' farthest point from the sun is 2.4 **light-year**s away, many times farther away then Pluto. Its closest point, still beyond Pluto, is about half a light-year away.

As Nemesis passes near the sun, it crosses the **Oort cloud** (the area surrounding the solar system in which comets are believed to originate), possibly triggering the release of comets into the solar system. In addition, Nemesis' gravitational field may tug at asteroids, causing them to veer off orbit and collide with planets or moons. The gravitational pull of Nemesis may also explain why some of the outer planets sometimes stray from their predicted orbits.

That the sun has a companion star is not impossible. Systems of two or more orbiting stars are common throughout the universe. However, despite many efforts, no one has ever been able to detect any evidence for the existence of Nemesis. For a variety of reasons, however, many stars (especially companion stars) are difficult to see. Therefore we cannot discount Nemesis' existence merely because it has never been observed.

Neptune

Neptune was discovered in 1841 independently by English astronomer John Couch Adams and French astronomer Urbain Leverrier. Its existence was suspected because something seemed to be tugging at neighboring planet Uranus, causing irregularities in its orbit. Because Neptune is so far away (about 2.8 billion miles [4.5 billion kilometers] from the sun, or 2.7 billion miles [4.3 billion kilometers] from Earth) and difficult to observe, very little was known about it until fairly recently. In 1989, *Voyager 2* flew by Neptune, finally providing some answers about this mysterious, beautiful globe.

Neptune is a large planet, seventeen times more massive than Earth and far more blue. Since it is the color of water, Neptune was named for the Roman god of the sea. But Neptune's blue-green color is not that of a sea. It is due to methane gas. Neptune has a cold (-352 degrees Fahrenheit, or -213 degrees Celsius) outer layer of hydrogen, helium, and methane. Within that lies a layer of ionized (electrically charged) water, ammonia, and methane ice, and deeper yet is a rocky, iron core.

Neptune is subject to the fiercest winds in the **solar system.** It has a layer of blue surface clouds that whip around with the wind and an upper layer of wispy white clouds of methane crystals that rotate with the planet. Three storm systems are evident on its surface. The most prominent is a dark blue area called the Great Dark Spot, which is about the size of the Earth. Another storm, about the size of our moon, is called the Small Dark Spot. Then there is Scooter, a small, fast-moving white storm system that seems to chase the other storms around the planet.

A **magnetic field** has been measured on Neptune, tilted from its axis at a 48 degree angle and just missing the center of the planet by thousands of miles. Given the planet's frigid exterior, it is surprising that this field is created by 4,000-degree-Fahrenheit (2,204-degree-Celsius) water beneath its surface, water so hot and under so much pressure that it generates an electrical field.

Picture of Neptune taken by Voyager 2.

Voyager 2 found that Neptune is encircled by at least five very faint rings, much less pronounced than the rings of Saturn, Jupiter, or Uranus. These rings are composed of particles, some of which are over a mile across and are considered "moonlets." These particles clump together in places, creating relatively bright arcs, which originally led astronomers to believe that only arcs—and not complete rings—were all that surrounded the planet.

The Moons of Neptune

Neptune has eight moons, six of which were discovered by *Voyager 2.* The largest, Triton, was named for the mythical son of Neptune. It was discovered shortly after Neptune was discovered. Triton is 1,681 miles (3,705 kilometers) in diameter and has a number of unusual qualities. First, this peach-colored moon orbits Neptune in the opposite direction of all other planets' satellites, and it rotates on its axis in the opposite direction that Neptune rotates. In addition, *Voyager* found that Triton, which is the coldest place in the solar system, has an atmosphere with layers of haze, clouds, and wind streaks. All of this information has led astronomers to conclude that Triton was captured by Neptune long ago from an independent orbit around the sun.

The second Neptunian moon, a faint small body called Nereid, was discovered in 1949 by Dutchman Gerard P. Kuiper. The other six moons range from 250 miles (402 kilometers) to 31 miles (50 kilometers) in diameter.

Neptune is the most remote of the large planets. It lies a billion miles beyond Uranus and almost that far from the last planet in the solar system, Pluto. Although Neptune's day is shorter than ours (just over sixteen hours) it orbits the sun only once every 165 years.

See also **Voyager program**

Neutrino

The **neutrino** is a subatomic particle that has no electrical charge and no **mass,** or such a small mass as to be undetectable. Yet it contains a substantial amount of energy and has a tremendous ability to penetrate any substance.

Neutrinos are thought to have been one of the most primitive building blocks in the newly created universe. Scientists theorize that neutrinos were created about one second after the **big bang** during which time they and electrons were produced by the decay of free neutrons.

Most of the neutrinos that reach Earth today are solar neutrinos, produced by **nuclear fusion** on the sun. Nuclear fusion is the pairing of two small particles to form one larger particle. In the process a positron (a positively charged electron) and a neutrino are often given off.

Neutrinos can pass through virtually any substance without interference. The chances of a neutrino interacting with an atom as it passes through Earth are only about one in two hundred million. Scientists believe that a stream of neutrinos travel through our planet every day.

The existence of neutrinos was first suggested in 1930 by Austrian-American physicist Wolfgang Pauli. He was theorizing about beta decay and found that the total energy given off by this process was of a greater range than predicted. Beta decay is a type of radioactive decay involving the breakdown of an atomic nucleus, accompanied by the release of energy including beta radiation. He felt there must be another particle present to account for some of this energy. His colleague Enrico Fermi named this particle "neutrino," meaning little neutral one.

The GALLEX experiment is looking for neutrinos emitted by the sun. The experiment takes place under 4,593 feet (1,400 meters) of rock in the Gran Sasso Laboratory in Italy.

Detecting Neutrinos

Not until 1956 did American physicist Clyde L. Cowan, Jr. and Frederick Reines detect this tiny, elusive particle. They built a special neutrino detector in a nuclear reactor at Savannah River, South Carolina. For five years they observed reactions between electrons and positrons and modified their equipment, until they finally succeeded in their goal.

A number of neutrino detectors are now available around the world, each basically consisting of a huge tank of water. When a neutrino enters the tank, it produces a tiny flash of blue light.

An underground experiment to detect solar neutrinos was set up in 1967 in the Homestake Gold Mine near Lead, South Dakota. There, in a 100,000-gallon (378,500-liter) pool of dry-cleaning fluid, neutrinos interact with chlorine-37 atoms to produce radioactive argon-37. Another experiment, begun nearly two decades later in the Kamiokande mine in Japan, uses a tank of ultrapure water to detect high-energy neutrinos.

In 1987, these and other detectors had a chance to prove their competence. In that year, the first **supernova** in almost four hundred years easily visible from Earth appeared in the sky. Scientists had predicted that any supernova explosion would be preceded by a surge of neutrinos. Indeed, on the day before the supernova, detectors in Japan and Ohio recorded nineteen neutrinos, a very large number for a single day.

Solar neutrinos are of relatively low energy and are not considered harmful to living organisms. Scientists, however, are concerned about the possible effect of neutrinos that would accompany a supernova in the vicinity of our **solar system.** Because of their sheer numbers, these cosmic neutrinos would have a greater chance of interacting with atoms. Any atom hit by a neutrino would receive the neutrino's energy and become a potentially deadly particle, capable of mutating cells and causing cancers in living beings. Such an occurrence could be as devastating to life on Earth as whatever caused the dinosaurs to perish.

This scenario, however, is merely hypothetical. And it would only be possible if a "silent" supernova (one with no visible explosion) occurred nearby, something scientists estimate happens about once every hundred million years. A full-fledged supernova explosion, which may occur in our part of the universe every few billion years, would have other, more significant consequences, that would dwarf neutrino damage in comparison.

Neutron star

A star reaches the end of its life when it uses up all of its nuclear fuel. Without fuel it cannot undergo **nuclear fusion,** the process that pushes matter outward from the star's core and provides a balance to its immense gravitational field. The fate of a dying star, however, depends on that star's **mass.**

A relatively small star, like the sun, will shrink and end up as a **white dwarf** star. The largest stars—those more than twice the size of the sun—undergo a gravitational collapse so complete that all that remains is a **black hole.** And an intermediate star—one with greater than 1.4 times, but less than 2 times, the mass of the sun—will also cave in on itself. Following that, the intermediate star will experience a **supernova** explosion, leaving behind only a densely packed **neutron star.**

A neutron star is formed in two stages. First, within a second after nuclear fusion on the star's surface ceases, **gravity** crushes the star's atoms. This forces protons and electrons together to form neutrons and expels high-energy subatomic particles called **neutrino**s. The star's core, which started out about the size of the Earth, is compacted into a sphere less than 60 miles (97 kilometers) across.

In the second stage, the star first undergoes a gravitational collapse and then, becoming energized by the neutrino burst, explodes in a brilliant supernova. All that's left is a super-dense neutron core, about 12 miles (19 kilometers) in diameter yet with a mass nearly equal to that of the sun.

A neutron star spins extremely fast. For example, a neutron star in the Crab **nebula** rotates about thirty times per second. The spinning generates a **magnetic field** and the star spews radiation out of its poles like a lighthouse beacon. Neutron stars give off radiation in a variety of wavelengths: **radio wave**s, visible light, **X-ray**s, and **gamma ray**s.

If the **magnetic axis** of the star is tilted in a certain way, the rotating star's on-and-off signal can be detected from Earth. This fact is what led to the discovery of the first neutron star by English astronomer Antony Hewish and his student Jocelyn Bell Burnell in 1967.

Hewish and Bell Burnell were conducting an experiment to track **quasar**s (extremely bright, distant objects) when they picked up a mysterious, extremely regular, pulsing signal. They found similar signals coming from other parts of the sky, including one where a supernova was known to have occurred. With the help of astronomer Thomas Gold, they learned that the signals matched the predicted pattern of neutron stars. They named these blinking neutron stars **pulsar**s (short for "pulsating radio source").

Over four hundred neutron stars have now been found. Yet only three are within nebulae of supernova explosions. The reason for this pattern is probably that the clouds of gas produced by a supernova dissipate relatively quickly, while the neutron star lasts about one hundred times longer.

See also **Neutrino**; **Nova and supernova**; **Pulsar**; and **Stellar evolution**

Newcomb, Simon (1835–1909)

American astronomer

As a young man, Simon Newcomb arrived penniless in the United States from his native Canada. He eventually earned a degree from Harvard, directed the U.S. Naval Observatory, and gained the reputation of being the greatest American scientist of his time. Newcomb's most significant contribution to the field of astronomy was revolutionizing the system of measuring and recording the motions of the stars, sun, moon, and planets.

Newcomb was born in the Canadian province of Nova Scotia, although his family's roots were in New England. His father was a schoolteacher who traveled between several rural communities throughout Nova Scotia and Prince Edward Island. As a result, the young Newcomb led a migratory lifestyle.

At the age of eighteen, Newcomb came to the United States to seek his fortune. He first walked most of the 120 miles (193 kilometers) from his home in Nova Scotia to Calais, Maine. Then he worked on board an ocean liner for his passage to Salem, Massachusetts. There he met his father and the two traveled together to Maryland.

Newcomb followed his father's example for the next few years, teaching in country schools. In the meantime, he taught himself mathematics and became a regular visitor to the Smithsonian Institution library in nearby Washington, D.C. Among the books he found particularly interesting were Isaac Newton's *Philosophiae Naturalis Principia Mathematica* (*Mathematical Principles of Natural Philosophy*) and Pierre-Simon Laplace's *Traité de Méchanique Céleste* (*Celestial Mechanics*)—both of which contain advanced mathematical and astronomical theory.

Newcomb was befriended by the secretary of the Smithsonian, Joseph Henry, who referred him to a job at the Coast Survey. He wasn't hired there, but was directed to the Nautical Almanac Office in Cambridge, Massachusetts. In 1857, when he was just twenty-two years old,

Simon Newcomb.

Newcomb began working as an "astronomical computer." In those days, astronomical computers were humans, not machines. They performed the tiresome task of computing large amounts of data. During his few years at that post, Newcomb also completed a bachelor's degree in mathematics at Harvard University.

At the Nautical Almanac, Office Newcomb carefully studied the orbits of some large **asteroid**s. He found that each one occupied a distinct orbit, which did not intersect with the orbits of other asteroids. By demonstrating that the asteroids were not on collision courses with one another, he cast doubt upon the predominant theory that asteroids had originated as planets that had exploded or had been smashed to pieces in collisions with other objects.

Newcomb's Research At the U.S. Naval Observatory

Newcomb was probably one of the few people in America to benefit from the 1861 outbreak of the Civil War. Many professors in the mathematics department at the U.S. Naval Observatory in Washington, D.C., were also officers in the Navy, and were called away to serve in the war. Newcomb was selected to fill one of the vacancies that resulted from their departure. His first research assignment was to observe the apparent motion of stars across the sky due to the Earth's rotation. In 1865, Newcomb initiated a new system of observation that involved plotting the positions of stars during the day, as well as at night. He accomplished this using a special telescope called a **transit** circle that continually tracks the positions of stars.

Shortly after beginning his tenure at the Naval Observatory, Newcomb started on a project that he would come back to time and again, for the rest of his life. He observed the motion of the moon and detected times when its position was at odds with the predicted positions. Eventually Newcomb's observations, combined with those recorded since 1672, led him to conclude that the fluctuations in the moon's orbit were due the unevenness in the Earth's rotation. That rotation, in turn, led to fluctuating gravitational pulls on the moon.

In 1877, after rejecting an offer to become director of the Harvard College Observatory, Newcomb accepted the directorship of the Nautical Almanac Office, which by then had been relocated to Washington, D.C. As such, he was responsible for providing data on the positions of the moon, sun, and planets for the annual catalogue called the *American*

Ephemeris. At the same time, he developed a formula to explain the effect each planet has on the orbit of other adjacent to it.

Newcomb also conducted an experiment, similar to that of Jean Bernard Léon Foucault, to calculate the **speed of light.** Like Foucault, Newcomb bounced light off mirrors and noted the angles and distance between the mirrors and the time it took light to travel between them. Unlike Foucault, who conducted his experiment in a laboratory using one moving mirror and one stationary mirror, Newcomb used three stationary mirrors. The mirrors were positioned far apart, one at the Naval Observatory, a second at the Washington Monument, and a third at Fort Myer, Virginia. Whereas Foucault had come within 1 percent of the value accepted today, Newcomb's result was even closer. His value was long used as the astronomical standard for the speed of light.

Through the course of his career, Newcomb accumulated an impressive list of accomplishments. He helped found the Lick Observatory near San Jose, California; he wrote a catalogue of the movements and positions of the brightest stars; and he published many scientific papers and a text book, *A Compendium of Spherical Astronomy.* Newcomb also wrote mathematical texts, articles on economics, and three novels. And when he was nearly fifty years old, he became a professor of astronomy at Johns Hopkins University in Baltimore, Maryland.

Newcomb eventually made the rank of captain in the Navy and, on his retirement, was promoted to rear admiral. He died in 1906 and was buried with full military honors in Arlington National Cemetery, with President William H. Taft in attendance.

See also **Foucault, Jean Bernard Léon**

Newton, Isaac (1642–1727)
English mathematician and astronomer

Isaac Newton was born in Woolsthorpe, Lincolnshire, England on Christmas Day of 1642, the same year that Galileo Galilei died. Considered to be one of the most intelligent people who ever lived, Newton came up with the law of universal gravitation, and wrote one of the most important books about science of all time.

Isaac Newton had a difficult childhood. Born prematurely, he was not even expected to live. His father, an illiterate farmer, died before Newton's birth. Newton's mother then married an ill-tempered man who sent him away to live with his grandmother. At age eleven, when his stepfather died, Newton went back to live with his mother.

Newton got off to a slow start in school, but eventually rose from the bottom of his class to the top. At age sixteen he dropped out of school to work on his mother's farm. He remained an enthusiastic reader, however, and returned to school the following year. It was during that year, history has it, that Newton had his one and only romantic relationship.

Then, at age nineteen, Newton went off to Trinity College at Cambridge. There he studied the works of Johannes Kepler, René Descartes, Nicholas Copernicus, and Galileo. He graduated in 1665, the year the university closed due to an outbreak of bubonic plague, and returned to the family farm.

Agricultural work left Newton plenty of time to think and to conduct experiments. He studied the rainbow created by light passed through a prism and realized that white light is really a combination of all the colors. He also invented calculus, a method of calculation by a system of algebraic notations, at the same time as, yet independent of, German philosopher Gottfried Leibniz. And it was in that period that Newton developed his famous universal theory of **gravity.**

Isaac Newton.

The Law of Gravitation

As Newton watched an apple fall from a tree he wondered if the force that caused that action—gravity—also kept the moon in its orbit around the Earth. He felt that there had to be some reason why the moon did not just pass by the Earth in a straight line and keep on going. Prior to this time, gravity had been thought to work only on Earth. To Newton, however, it was clear that gravity was also at work in the heavens.

Newton explained that the gravitational force between any two objects depends on the **mass** of each object and the distance between them. The greater each object's mass, the stronger the pull, but the greater the distance between them, the weaker the pull. The relationship described in Newton's law is that gravitational force depends on the mass of each object divided by the square of the distance separating them. At the time, however, Newton could not get his calculations to match his theories. The reason was that he had used an incorrect figure for the diameter of the Earth. He became frustrated and abandoned his theory.

Newton later returned to Cambridge to assume the Lucasian Professorship of Mathematics. It wasn't until 1687 (twenty years after his original research) that Newton, with the prodding and financial backing of astronomer Edmond Halley, published his universal law of gravitation and three laws of motion in the much-acclaimed *Philosophiae Naturalis Principia Mathematica* (*Mathematical Principles of Natural Philosophy*). With this book, Newton radically changed society's notion of the universe and the interconnectedness of its components, much in the same way that Copernicus had done with his model placing the sun at the center of the **solar system.**

Newton's book brought him great fame, which radically changed his personality. Once a recluse, he became a very ambitious man. He even entered politics and won a seat in the British Parliament. A skilled investor, he was later appointed to oversee his country's money-printing operation. He was also elected president of the Royal Society (an elite, English science organization) and in 1705 became Sir Isaac Newton, the first scientist to be knighted.

Newton the Man

Newton has been described in so many different ways, it is hard to know for sure what he was really like. There is no doubt that he was one of the world's greatest thinkers. Astronomer Subrahmanyan Chandrasekhar, who explained the theoretical limits of the formation of **black holes**, went so far as to claim that ". . . Einstein was indeed a giant. But compared with Newton, Einstein runs a very distant second."

It seems, however, that in Newton's case being a genius had its price. Newton was known for his petty, mean-spirited, even vicious behavior. In one instance he leveled false claims of plagiarism against his intellectual competitor Gottfried Leibniz. And as master of the mint, he found that the death penalty was appropriate punishment for counterfeiters.

"If we evolved a race of Isaac Newtons, that would not be progress," wrote novelist Aldous Huxley. "For the price Newton had to pay for being a supreme intellect was that he was incapable of friendship, love, fatherhood, and many other desirable things. As a man he was a failure; as a monster he was superb."

Newton himself wrote, "I do not know what I may appear to the world, but to myself I seem to have been only like a boy playing on the sea-shore, and diverting myself in now and then finding a smoother pebble or a prettier shell than ordinary, whilst the great ocean of truth lay all undiscovered before me."

See also **Gravity** and **Newton's laws of motion**

Newton's laws of motion

In 1687, English mathematician Isaac Newton published *Philosophiae Naturalis Principia Mathematica* (*Mathematical Principles of Natural Philosophy*), the book containing his three laws of motion and the law of universal gravitation. This treatise, which demonstrated similarities between actions on the Earth and in the **cosmos,** is widely considered one of the most important science books of all time.

Shortly after finishing college, while back on his family's farm, Newton watched an apple fall from a tree and wondered if the force that caused it to fall, **gravity,** also applied to orbiting bodies in space. Why did they not fall away, instead of remaining in an orbital path? Prior to this time, gravity had been thought of as a force that only functioned on Earth. Newton explained the movement of orbiting planets as the result of motion along a straight line combined with the gravitational pull of the sun.

Newton put aside his notes for seventeen years, until astronomer Edmond Halley convinced him to write up his results. Three years after that, with Halley's financial backing, Newton's book was published.

Newton's three laws of motion, which predict interactions between objects, are: 1) a body at rest tends to remain at rest and a body in motion tends to remain in motion at a constant speed in a straight line unless acted on by an outside force; 2) force is equal to **mass** times acceleration. This means that any change in the acceleration of an object is proportional to (directly related to the strength of), and in the same direction as, the force acting on it. In addition, the effects of that force will be inversely proportional to the mass of the object (a heavier object will move more slowly than a lighter object, when affected by the same force); 3) for every action there is an equal and opposite reaction, meaning that the total momentum of a system of bodies not acted on by an external force remains constant.

Newton combined these laws to come up with the law of universal gravitation. This law states that the gravitational force between any two objects depends on the mass of each object and the distance between them. The greater each object's mass, the stronger the pull, but the greater the distance between them, the weaker the pull. This relationship, known as an inverse square law, states that gravitational force is equal to a gravitational constant times the mass of each object, divided by the square of the distance separating them.

See also **Gravity** and **Newton, Isaac**

Nova and supernova

The word **nova,** Latin for "new," was assigned by ancient astronomers to any bright star suddenly appearing in the sky. An extremely bright star was called a **supernova.** These names, however, do not accurately describe these objects since neither a nova nor a supernova is a new star. And, it turns out, they are two very different phenomena with little in common besides their brightness relative to other stars.

A nova occurs when one member of a **binary star** system temporarily becomes brighter. Most often the brighter star is a shrunken **white dwarf** and its partner is a large star, such as a **red giant.**

From time to time (once every fifty years or more) matter is transferred from the larger to its smaller partner, initiating a nuclear chain reaction on the smaller star's surface. When the reaction ceases, the material blows off the star, causing it to glow brightly. Days or weeks later the star fades and the process begins again.

A supernova is the result of a much different process. It occurs only once per star, and only in relatively large stars (those possessing more than 1.5 times the **mass** of the sun). It occurs at the end of a star's life, when the star has used up all of its nuclear fuel. The star first collapses in on itself, and then explodes outward with great force. As a result of the explosion, it sheds its outer atmospheric layers and shines more brightly than the rest of the stars in the **galaxy** put together.

What happens next depends on the original mass of the star. In intermediate-sized stars, a tremendously dense **neutron star** will be left behind. For the most massive stars (more than twice the size of the sun), the gravitational collapse is so complete that all that is left is a **black hole,** an infinite abyss from which nothing can escape.

Novas and Supernovas Throughout History

Ancient astronomers carefully recorded the mysterious appearance of these bright stars, believing they were divine omens. Danish astronomer Tycho Brahe, who observed one such phenomena in 1572, first gave it the name nova. In the mid-1600s, using telescopes and newly developed star charts, astronomers learned that these bright spots were not really new stars, but existing stars that had gained a tremendous amount of brightness.

Not until centuries later did astronomers learn what causes novas and supernovas. The pioneering work in this area was done in the 1930s by

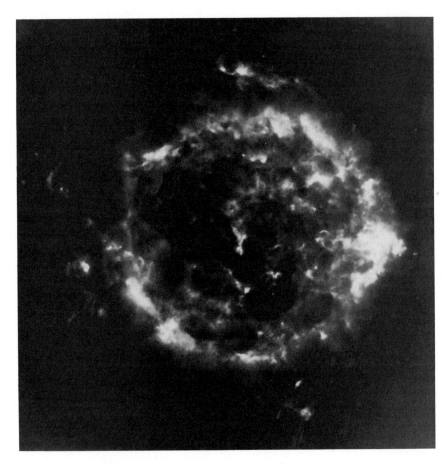

*January 1987.
Supernova
Cassiopeia A,
bursting into a
fireball the width of
ten thousand solar
systems, provided
new insights into
how stars explode.*

Fritz Zwicky and Walter Baade. They first measured the difference between novas and supernovas and suggested that neutron stars were the remains of supernovas. They also concluded that a supernova is a rare event, occurring only two or three times every one thousand years per galaxy. Recent studies, however, put that number at closer to one supernova every fifty years per galaxy. The new estimate is based on the assumption that supernovas are less visible because of interference by interstellar clouds.

Later in the 1930's, Indian-born American astronomer Subrahmanyan Chandrasekhar pieced together the sequence of events leading up to the formation of a supernova. He also calculated a figure for the mass (known as **Chandrasekhar's limit**) that would determine whether a star would end up as a black hole or a neutron star.

Various theories have been proposed to explain the reasons a star explodes outward while collapsing inward. One theory is that the results are caused by a final burst of uncontrolled **nuclear fusion.** Another, more recent, theory is that it's due to the expulsion of a wave of high-energy subatomic particles called **neutrino**s. The neutrino theory gained greater acceptance following the 1987 supernova in the Large Magellanic Cloud, our galaxy's closest extra-galactic companion. Just before the first supernova visible to the naked eye in nearly four hundred years came into view, a surge of neutrinos was detected in laboratories around the world.

See also **Black hole**; **Neutrino**; **Neutron star**; and **Stellar evolution**

Oberth, Hermann (1894–1989)
Austro-Hungarian German physicist

Hermann Oberth is considered one of the three founders of space flight, the other two being Russian engineer Konstantin Tsiolkovsky and American physicist Robert Goddard. Like Tsiolkovsky, Oberth was a theorist. That is, he conceptualized what it would take to launch a **rocket** into space. And like Goddard, Oberth was a hands-on builder and launcher of rockets.

Oberth's legacy rests on two primary accomplishments. The first was his development of mathematical theories of rocketry, which he applied to rocket design and the effects of space flight on humans. The second accomplishment, which he achieved through books he wrote, was to popularize the concept of space flight. Oberth was instrumental in moving space flight from the realm of science fiction to the realm of possibility.

Oberth was born in 1894 in Hermannstadt, Transylvania, which was then part of Austria-Hungary. The town is now known as Sibiu, Romania. His father, a surgeon, was the director of a hospital in Schässburg, Transylvania, where Oberth grew up. When Oberth was eleven, his mother gave him two books by Jules Verne—*From the Earth to the Moon* and *Travel to the Moon*—both of which left a lasting impression on Oberth. These books led him, even as a child, to attempt to calculate how space flight could be accomplished.

Oberth studied calculus in high school and in 1913 went on to study medicine at the University of Munich in Germany. Soon he had to leave school to serve in World War I. After being wounded in 1916, he spent the last two years of the war in a hospital. There he conducted research in

*Hermann Oberth is
interviewed by
journalists as he
arrives in
Frankfurt, West
Germany, on
November 4, 1958.
Oberth had just
returned from three
years' work with
the U.S. missile
program in
Huntsville,
Alabama.*

space medicine, using himself as a subject. He took doses of scopolamine, which is still given to victims of motion sickness.

After his discharge from the army, Oberth returned to his research on space flight. In 1918 he approached the German Ministry of Armament with a proposal to build "a long-range rocket powered by ethyl alcohol, water, and liquid air." The ministry rejected the idea. That same year, Oberth married Mathilde Hummel. They eventually had four children, two of whom died during World War II.

Oberth's Research On Space Flight

Oberth went back to school to study physics. He attended four different universities in Romania and Germany over the next few years, finishing his course work at the University of Heidelberg. Ultimately, however, his doctoral dissertation, on rockets and space-flight theory, proved to be too far outside of the mainstream and was rejected.

Shunned by academia, Oberth taught physics and mathematics at a series of high schools from 1922 to 1938. In 1928, he decided to publish his dissertation himself under the title "The Rocket into Planetary Space." This work, which sold many copies, explained the basic principles of space flight and rocket construction. It also addressed the possible effects of space flight on humans and introduced the concept of a **space station,** where spacecraft could be refueled.

The next year Oberth revised his book and published it as *Ways to Spaceflight.* He simplified the language so that it could be more easily understood by the general public.

From 1929 to 1930, Oberth presided over the German Rocket Society, which trained its members in rocketry and raised funds for Oberth's rocket experiments. One young member was Wernher von Braun, who later achieved fame on two counts: one for his development of destructive missiles for the Nazis during World War II and the other for his design of the first launch rockets for the new U.S. space program.

The Rocket Society attracted the attention of German film director Fritz Lang, who decided to make a film about the Society and hired Oberth as technical director. For his efforts, Oberth received funds to build a liquid-**propellant** rocket (one that uses liquid fuels, like gasoline and liquid oxygen), which he subjected to tests, but never launched.

In 1930, Oberth returned to Romania to teach and to continue experimenting with liquid-propellant rockets. By this time, however, he had become effectively isolated from the rocketry centers in Germany where true advances were taking place. One reason for Oberth's rejection was that his contemporaries were uncomfortable with his far-out ideas. As early as 1930, and through the 1950s, Oberth published writings on decidedly un-scientific topics such as UFO's carrying extraterrestrial beings and supernatural phenomena.

Oberth did try to reclaim a place in rocket-design centers during World War II, but found his efforts frustrated. First he was appointed to a position at the Technical Institute in Vienna, where the facilities were inadequate for rocket production. Two years later he was transferred to the Technical Institute of Dresden to work on the V-2, only to learn that the project was already essentially completed.

Oberth was then assigned to analyze technical information for possible use in rocket design. From 1943 until the war's end in 1945, Oberth worked on the development of a solid-propellant (using a solid fuel, like gunpowder) anti-aircraft rocket.

After World War II, Oberth worked as a technical writer in Switzerland. He then developed a solid-propellant rocket for the Italian Navy. In the mid-1950s, Oberth published two more books. The first, entitled *Man into Space,* was about electric spaceships and an electric moon-rover. He fleshed out the latter concept in his second book, *The Moon Car.*

In 1955, at the urging of von Braun, Oberth came to the United States to participate in the development of rockets for launching spacecraft. There Oberth worked on a number of rocket components and even was able to apply his theories for the design of a moon vehicle. Oberth returned to Germany in 1958 where he spent the rest of his life, with the exception of one trip back to the United States to witness the launch of the 1969 *Apollo 11* flight that landed the first men on the moon.

On December 29, 1989, at age ninety-five, Oberth died in Nuremberg, Germany.

See also **Braun, Wernher von** and **Rockets**

Olbers, Heinrich (1758–1840)
German astronomer and physician

Heinrich Wilhelm Matthäus Olbers was a man of amazing energy and intellect. He found time for two careers and a family, which he attributed to his unusually small sleep requirement of only four hours a night. Olbers was respected equally in both the medical and astronomical communities. As a physician, he was praised for his vaccination campaigns and for heroically treating people during several epidemics of cholera. As an astronomer, Olbers was best known for his discovery of five **comet**s and for devising a new method of calculating their orbits.

Olbers was born in 1758 in the German town of Arbergen, the eighth child of sixteen. His father, a Protestant minister, sent him to high school in the nearby city of Bremen. There they only taught humanities, no mathematics or science. So Olbers, who had developed an interest in astronomy, was left to study math and astronomy on his own.

In 1777, at the age of nineteen, Olbers entered the medical school in Göttingen, Germany. There he also attended lectures in physics, mathematics, and astronomy. It was during those years that he developed an interest in comets, an interest he retained for the rest of his life. He discovered his first comet in 1780.

In medical school Olbers specialized in the emerging field of ophthalmology (the study of the function and treatment of eyes) and wrote his dissertation on how the eye shifts its focus. Olbers was mistaken in his belief that the whole eyeball changes shape during this process. Scientists later learned that only the lens of the eye changes shape.

In 1781, Olbers established his medical practice in Bremen and quickly drew a large clientele. He also set up an observatory in the second floor of his house, where he pointed telescopes out of two large bay windows. He acquired a number of high-quality instruments and an extensive astronomical library. By the time of Olbers' death, his library held 4,361 items and was considered one of the best private collections in Europe.

In 1785, Olbers was wed to Dorothea Köhne, who died the following year during the birth of their daughter. He remarried in 1789. With his second wife, Anna Adelheid Lurssen, he had one son.

Olbers Research On Astronomy

Olbers published a work in 1797 that gained him a reputation as one of the leading astronomers of the time. This publication was based on a comet Olbers had discovered the previous year, for which he devised a new way of calculating its orbit. Olbers' method proved more accurate and easier to use than the cumbersome set of equations developed a few years earlier by French astronomer Pierre-Simon Laplace.

While the pursuit of comets remained Olbers' primary astronomical interest, he also was one of the first discoverers of **asteroid**s. His attention was drawn to these small, rocky objects by a young mathematician named Carl Gauss. Gauss had learned of the discovery of Ceres, the first asteroid, discovered on New Year's day 1801 by Italian monk Giuseppe Piazzi. Gauss, who had attempted to calculate its orbit, asked Olbers to look for Ceres one year after its discovery, in the location Gauss had predicted. Olbers spotted Ceres in the location predicted by Gauss, thus proving the mathematician correct. The event that initiated a lifelong friendship between the two men.

While following the path of Ceres, Olbers discovered a second asteroid, Pallas, in March 1802. He found a third asteroid, Vesta, in March 1807. After that Olbers returned to comet hunting. By the end of his life he had found four new comets and calculated the orbits of eighteen others. Olbers also hypothesized, correctly, that matter ejected by a comet's nucleus is swept back into a tail by the force of the sun.

After the death of his wife, Anna, in 1820, Olbers retired from his medical practice to become a full-time sky-watcher. A few years later he addressed a complex phenomenon that still bears his name, the "Olbers' paradox." Olber's paradox asks the question: "Why is the sky dark at night?" If one assumes that the universe is infinite and contains an infinite number of unchanging stars, then it stands to reason that the sky should be lit up continuously by stars too numerous to count. The paradox, however, is that this description does not match with what we observe.

Olbers attempted an explanation for this, one which we now know is only partially correct. He theorized that interstellar space is not transparent, but contains dust which absorbs energy from the stars, preventing some of their light from reaching us on Earth.

The rest of the answer comes in two parts. First, the number of stars is not infinite. There simply are not enough stars in the sky to keep it lit up day and night. It has been calculated that this would require roughly ten trillion times the number of stars that currently exist.

Second, we now know that the universe is not unchanging. To the contrary, the universe is expanding and **galaxies** are moving apart. The light **spectrum** of receding galaxies is **red-shift**ed. This means that these galaxies emit less radiation at optical wavelengths (they shine less brightly) than does our sun.

Olbers was well-liked and well-respected by his colleagues. He was known in particular for taking the time to instruct and encourage young astronomers. One example concerns twenty-year-old Friedrich Bessel, a merchant's apprentice who calculated the path of Halley's comet. Olbers was so impressed with this accomplishment that he helped Bessel obtain the directorship of the new Königsberg Observatory, something Olbers later claimed was his most significant contribution to astronomy.

See also **Asteroids**; **Bessel, Friedrich**; **Comets**; **Gauss, Carl**; and **Red-shift**

Oort, Jan (1900–)

Dutch astronomer

Jan Hendrick Oort is considered the leading Dutch astronomer of this century. His research has covered a great range of subjects, from the structure of **galaxies** to the way **comet**s are formed. He is also one of the pioneers of **radio astronomy,** an area of expertise in which the Netherlands is a world leader.

Oort was born in Frankener, Holland (the Netherlands), the son of a medical doctor and the grandson of a professor of Hebrew. He attended the University of Gröningen, from which he received his Ph.D. in 1926. Two years prior to that, he began working at the observatory at the University of Leiden, and became its director in 1945. He was jailed by the Nazis during their occupation of Holland in World War II, the one period in his life during which he was unable to continue his research.

In 1927, Oort came to an important realization about the **Milky Way:** it was rotating about its center. And by studying the motion of stars in our vicinity, Oort discovered that our **solar system** was not at the center of the galaxy, as was previously believed, but somewhere toward the outer edges.

Jan Oort.

A few years earlier, American astronomer Harlow Shapley had determined that the sun was about fifty thousand **light-year**s from the galactic center. This figure was re-calculated by Oort to be thirty thousand light-years, the value accepted today.

Oort then set out to map the structure of the Milky Way. This task was not easy because most of the stars in the galaxy are blocked from view by interstellar dust and clouds. **Radio wave**s, however, can penetrate the obstacles that visible light waves can not. Oort's colleague, Hendrik van de Hulst, determined the wavelength at which stars emit radio noise, paving the way for the star-charting project.

Oort found that the Milky Way is a spiral-shaped galaxy. It has a central core of stars, with four arms spiraling out like a pinwheel. The stars at the center rotate and the outer stars form the arms. He also learned that our solar system is located in one of the arms, called the Orion arm.

Oort next worked to determine the origin of comets. In 1950, he theorized that a great shell (now called the **Oort cloud**) containing trillions of inactive comets lies on the outskirts of the solar system, about one light-year from the sun. They remain there until a passing gas cloud or star jolts one of them into the inner solar system, and into orbit around the sun. This theory is currently the one most commonly accepted about the origin of comets.

See also **Comets**; **Milky Way galaxy**; and **Nemesis**

Oppolzer, Theodor (1841–1886)
Austrian astronomer

Theodor Ritter von Oppolzer was not the only astronomer who began his career in a different profession. For example, Edwin Hubble, who deduced that the universe is expanding, was initially a lawyer. And Percival Lowell, the life-on-Mars enthusiast and founder of the Lowell Observatory, was a well-established diplomat and businessman. Oppolzer, in order to please his father, trained to be a medical doctor. Yet, once he built an observatory just outside of Vienna, his fate as an astronomer was sealed.

Oppolzer was born in 1841 in Prague, then in Bohemia and now the capital of the Czech Republic. His father directed the school of medicine in Vienna, Austria, and also taught at the universities of Prague, Leipzig, and Vienna. Oppolzer excelled at mathematics at an early age and was encouraged by his first teacher to pursue the subject. Oppolzer went to school at the Piaristen-Gymnasium in Vienna from 1851 to 1859, where he studied, among other things, astronomy. After that he went on to medical school.

Oppolzer completed his medical degree in 1865, the same year he married Coelestine Mautner von Markhof. Together they had six children. Oppolzer named one of the **asteroid**s he discovered "Coelestine," for his wife, and two others "Hilda" and "Agatha," for two of his three daughters.

While in medical school, Oppolzer was also busy constructing his own observatory in the Vienna suburb of Josephstadt. He equipped it with what was then considered a very large telescope—perhaps the largest in all of Austria—a 7-inch (18-centimeter) **refractor.** He observed **comets** and asteroids, computed their orbits, and published some seventy astronomical papers by 1866.

Soon thereafter, in 1870, Oppolzer joined the astronomy faculty at the University of Vienna, where he also taught **geodesy.** Geodesy is the study of the Earth's external shape, internal construction, and gravitational field. In 1873, he became director of the Austrian geodetic survey and in 1886 was elected to the vice-presidency of the International Geodetic Association. That was the last position he held before his death, two months later.

Over the course of his lifetime, Oppolzer published over three hundred scientific articles, most of which were about the orbits of comets and asteroids. He also published a two-volume book explaining the new equations he had devised for computing those orbits. He also came up with an improved system for tracking the motions of the sun and the moon. But perhaps his most ambitious project was a compilation of data on every **lunar** and **solar eclipse** recorded between 1207 B.C. and A.D. 2163.

Oppolzer was also known for his devotion to social causes. He was particularly active in aiding an organization, begun by his father, to provide health care for sick students.

See also **Asteroids** and **Comets**

Optical telescope

An optical telescope is the type with which most people are familiar, the kind one looks through in the backyard. The only type of radiation it detects is visible light, meaning it sees what the human eye sees except magnified many times. Other types of telescopes are used to observe radiation from other regions of the **electromagnetic spectrum.** For example, there are infrared telescopes (that detect **infrared radiation**) and **radio telescopes** (that detect **radio waves**). There are also telescopes, placed on board satellites, that study **ultraviolet radiation, X-rays,** and **gamma rays** in space.

The two main types of optical telescopes are **refractors** and **reflectors.** A refractor was the first kind of telescope invented. It is also the simplest type. The refractor telescope gets its name from the word refract which means to bend. In a refractor, light enters through one end of a tube and passes through a lens, which bends the light rays and brings them into focus. The light then strikes an eyepiece, which acts as a magnifying glass.

Refracting Telescopes

The earliest refractor telescopes had a serious problem. The image of any bright object appeared with a ring of fuzzy colors around it, a condition known as chromatic aberration. Chromatic aberration occurs because each constituent color of the visible light spectrum bends at a slightly different angle as it passes through a lens. The various colors are scattered in a manner similar to that which occurs when light through a prism. This flaw could be corrected by placing a second lens, called an achromatic lens, just behind the first. The achromatic lens recombines the colors produced by the first lens. Eventually, telescope makers developed a single lens that is chemically altered to overcome the effects of chromatic aberration.

A reflector telescope is one that uses mirrors to bring light rays into focus. In a reflector telescope, light passes through an opening at one end of a tube to a mirror at the far end. The light is then reflected back to a smaller mirror, placed at an angle to the first mirror. The second mirror guides the light to an eyepiece on the side of the tube.

Over the years, telescopes have been continually improved to produce clearer images of ever-more distant objects. One principle that has guided their development is "bigger is better." The best images of celestial objects can be obtained through the largest instruments, since they let in the most light. Thus, we hear time and again about the construction of "the biggest telescope to date" at various observatories around the world.

Reflecting Telescopes

Today's giant optical telescopes are all reflectors. Reflectors are much better suited for large designs than refractors because mirrors, which reflect light from only one surface, can be supported from behind. Lenses, on the other hand can be supported only at the edges—their thinnest and most fragile part.

The world's largest refractor, with a lens diameter of 40 inches (102 centimeters), was built in 1897 at Yerkes Observatory in Wisconsin. This telescope, which is still in use today, is at the upper limit of size at which a refractor can be structurally stable. If its lens were any heavier, it could not be supported around its edges by technology currently available.

The Yerkes refractor pales in comparison to the world's largest reflector, the Keck Telescope at Mauna Kea Observatory in Hawaii. This telescope has 394-inch-diameter (1,000-centimeter-diameter) mirror, nearly ten times as large as the Yerkes refractor lens. Keck, which has been operational since November 1991, can observe light in both visible and infrared wavelengths.

The Schmidt Telescope

A third type of optical telescope also exists, a combined refractor-reflector called a **Schmidt telescope.** Named for its inventor, German optician Bernhard Schmidt, this telescope has a specially shaped thin glass lens at one end of a tube and a mirror at the other. This design results in sharper images than a reflector alone can provide, and a wider field of view than a refractor alone can provide. The eyepiece can be replaced with a photographic plate, making it ideal for wide-angle photography of slices of the sky (a practice called "astrophotography").

The largest Schmidt telescope, with a 48-inch-diameter (122-centimeter-diameter) mirror, is at the Palomar Observatory in California. This telescope was used between the years 1952 and 1959 to conduct the Palomar Sky Survey, an atlas of the northern sky and part of the southern sky. The survey consisted of 935 photographic prints, which formed a comprehensive panorama of cosmic objects, a resource that has been widely used by astronomers all over the world. The telescope has since been upgraded and is currently involved in a second survey of the northern sky.

The wave of the future in optical telescopes is **interferometry.** Similar to radio interferometry, this technique involves linking telescopes electronically to create a viewing power equal to that of a single telescope with a mirror the size of the distance among the telescopes. While radio interferometry has been in use since the 1950s, optical interferometry is much more complicated, and the technology for it is still being developed. At this point, only a handful of small optical interferometers around the world are in operation.

Construction is now underway on two giant interferometers, at Mauna Kea Observatory and at Las Campanas Observatory in Chile. At Mauna Kea, a second Keck telescope is being built 279 feet (85 meters) away from the first Keck. Linking these two telescopes will create an instrument with the equivalent viewing power of a single telescope with a mirror 279 feet (85 meters) in diameter. And at Las Campanas, work progresses on the Magellan Project, a two-telescope system, each one with a mirror 255 inches (648 centimeters) across. If the Magellan telescopes can be linked, the result will be an instrument with the equivalent viewing power of a single telescope with a 300-foot-diameter (90-meter-diameter) mirror. This instrument would provide views of far-away objects that are fifty times clearer than the images the Hubble Space Telescope can deliver.

See also **Hale, George**; **Hale Telescope**; **Hooker Telescope**; **Hubble Space Telescope**; **Las Campanas Observatory**; **Mauna Kea Observatory**; **Palomar Observatory**; and **Yerkes Observatory**

Palomar Observatory

Palomar Observatory is one of the two most famous historic observatories still operational in the United States today, the other being Mount Wilson Observatory. The two southern California astronomical research centers have an intertwined past, highlighted by legendary astronomers and landmark discoveries. Mount Wilson, with its 100-inch-diameter (254-centimeter-diameter) Hooker Telescope came first. Then, due to a tireless crusade by Mount Wilson astronomer George Hale, funding was secured for a telescope twice that size at a new site, Mount Palomar.

The casting of the mirror for the 200-inch (508-centimeter) **reflector** Hale Telescope was accomplished in 1934. That same year, Palomar Mountain was selected as the home for the mammoth instrument. The site had originally been considered for the Mount Wilson Observatory and rejected due to its inaccessibility. The main attractions of Palomar Mountain, which is located two hours northeast of San Diego and three hours southeast of Los Angeles, are its altitude of 6,000 feet (1,830 meters) and its dark skies. It is separated from both large cities by sets of hills, which block out the light. And in the early 1930s, the state of California agreed to use prison labor to build a road to the mountaintop.

Toward the end of 1947, the Hale's 20-ton (18-metric ton) mirror was brought to the mountain and erected inside the twelve-story, 1,000-ton (907-metric ton) rotating dome that had been built for that purpose. In 1948, scientific research finally began at what remained, for three decades, the world's largest optical telescope.

The studies conducted at this facility have led to important discoveries. For instance, in the observatory's early days, German-born American astronomer Walter Baade identified over three hundred **cepheid variable**s (pulsating stars that can be used to determine distance) in the Andromeda **galaxy.** And Swiss astronomer Fritz Zwicky, who worked at both Palomar and Mount Wilson observatories, made detailed studies of **supernova**s, **neutron star**s, and **dark matter.**

Telescopes In Use at Palomar

The 200-inch (508-centimeter) Hale Telescope at the Palomar Observatory. Polishing and grinding of the mirror began in 1936 and wasn't completed until 1947.

The Hale Telescope has been upgraded in recent years to include a **spectrograph**; an infrared filter, which detects **infrared radiation**; and high-speed computers that quickly process data. Observing time at the Hale is divided among the California Institute of Technology (CalTech),

which owns and operates Palomar Observatory; the National Aeronautics and Space Administration's Jet Propulsion Laboratory; and Cornell University.

Today, Palomar has a total of four telescopes. After the Hale Telescope, the most valuable instrument is the 48-inch (122-centimeter) Oschin Telescope. This instrument is a wide-field **Schmidt telescope,** an instrument that uses a correcting plate in addition to a primary mirror to further bring objects into focus across a wide area. It was used between the years 1952 and 1959 to conduct the Palomar Sky Survey, a comprehensive survey of the northern sky, as well as part of the southern sky. The survey, a joint project with the National Geographic Society, consisted of 935 photographic prints, each made in both blue and red light. Together, they formed a panorama of cosmic objects, a resource that has been widely used by astronomers all over the world.

The Oschin Telescope has been upgraded since that time and is currently involved in a second survey of the northern sky. The film being used this time is much more sensitive and can record objects one-fourth as faint as those in the original survey.

In addition, Palomar is home to a 60-inch (152-centimeter) reflector telescope. Like its much larger counterpart, the Hale Telescope, it is outfitted with a spectrograph and has infrared capabilities. It is co-owned by CalTech and the Carnegie Institution, a private Washington, D.C.-based foundation. Palomar is also home to an 18-inch (46-centimeter) Schmidt telescope.

Astronomers are at work at Palomar every clear night of the year. Their research ranges from studies of **asteroid**s and **comet**s; to stars at the far reaches of the **Milky Way**; to the extremely bright and distant objects known as **quasar**s. Other projects include research into the life cycles of stars and the formation of the planets and the sun.

The observatory is open to the public year-round for tours of the grounds and the museum. No public programs are available in the evenings, however, since the telescopes are wholly dedicated to research.

See also **Hale, George**; **Hale Telescope**; and **Mount Wilson Observatory**

Penzias, Arno (1933–)

German-born American astrophysicist

Arno Allan Penzias was born in Munich, Germany. When he was a child, his family emigrated to the United States to escape the Nazis.

Penzias later attended Columbia University, where he earned a doctorate for his research using masers (**microwave** amplification by stimulated emission of radiation) to measure radio signals coming from hydrogen gas in the space between **galaxies.** His later work in the field of **radio astronomy** inadvertently uncovered faint background radiation coming from all directions in space, very compelling evidence in support of the **big bang theory** of how the universe began.

In 1961, Penzias began working for Bell Telephone Laboratories in New Jersey. His main interest there was to continue charting cosmic sources of **radio waves**, using Bell's 20-foot (6-meter) horn-shaped antenna. For two years, however, the antenna was used to transmit signals to and from the *Echo* communications satellite, so Penzias was unable to do his research.

During this period Penzias met Robert Wilson, who had just earned his Ph.D. at the California Institute of Technology. Wilson was another new Bell employee, also interested in radio astronomy. He had already mapped the radio signals coming from the **Milky Way** galaxy.

Arno Penzias.

Detection of a Mysterious Background Noise

When Penzias and Wilson were finally able to observe the sky in 1963, they realized they had a big problem: unexplained excess noise was everywhere. Thinking that the noise might be due to ham radios and other human inventions, they aimed the antenna directly at a large concentration of humans, New York City, but the background hum remained the same.

Penzias and Wilson next looked to the **solar system** as the source. They reasoned that if the noise was coming from the sun or a planet, then the noise level would change as the Earth moved along its orbit. So they waited and observed, and still the noise was constant. For nearly a year, Penzias and Wilson attempted to identify the source of the background noise. Yet it remained the same and seemed to be coming from all directions.

Eventually the two researchers sought help from astronomers at the Massachusetts Institute of Technology, who led them to physicist Robert Dicke and his student Jim Peebles. Dicke and Peebles believed that the entire universe was filled with a faint background radiation ("noise"), left over from the "big bang," the theoretical start of the universe, fifteen to twenty billion years ago. This idea had first been proposed in 1948 by astronomer George Gamow, who estimated that the radiation, by the present time, would have cooled to just a few degrees above **absolute zero.**

Measurements made by Penzias and Wilson exactly matched those of an object radiating at about 3 degrees above absolute zero, or -465 degrees Fahrenheit (-276 degrees Celsius). Both men remained skeptical, however, and continued gathering data through the early 1970s.

For their important discovery, Penzias and Wilson shared the Nobel Prize for physics in 1978.

See also **Big bang theory**

Photometry

Photometry is the measurement of the properties of a light source. In astronomy, photometry pertains to the measurement of the brightness and colors of stars which, in turn, are indicators of surface temperature. Astronomers use sophisticated equipment for such measurements, but one can also conduct a simple form of photometry with the naked eye. Just look at the stars on a dark night and you will notice that some are brighter than others. If you study them very closely, you will also see that they are different colors. Stars may appear not only white, but blue, red, yellow, or orange.

A star's color is a function of the wavelength at which it radiates light with the greatest intensity. The light we perceive from stars is a form of **electromagnetic radiation,** which includes everything from **radio waves** (the longest wavelengths) to **gamma rays** (the shortest wavelengths). The visible range of light, which occupies only one small part of the **electromagnetic spectrum,** contains the entire rainbow of colors. Red is at one end with the longest wavelength, followed by orange, yellow, green, blue, indigo, and violet at the shortest wavelength end.

In photometry, the intensity of a star's light is measured at various wavelengths. This measurement is accomplished by using a telescope with a device at the end that captures light, such as a **charged coupling device (CCD)**—a small, computerized, high-technology version of the old, large photographic plates—along with color filters. The three most commonly used filters are blue (B), ultraviolet (U), and the yellow-green central portion of the visible spectrum, similar to that seen by the human eye (V, for "visible").

The brightness of a star is recorded three times, once with each of the three filters in place. By plotting these data points on a graph with wavelength on the horizontal axis and intensity on the vertical axis, a curve known as a star's intensity curve is produced.

A star's overall color can be determined by calculating the difference between intensities found through the three filters. For instance, when there is the greatest difference between intensities, with the light shone through V being the strongest, the star is red. On the other hand, where there is the greatest difference between intensities, with U being the strongest, the star is blue. And if light shines with about the same intensity through all three filters, the star is white.

A star's temperature is directly related to its color. Blue stars are hottest, red stars are coolest, and yellow-white stars fall somewhere in between. The color index of a given star, which is found by subtracting the value for V from the value for B, corresponds to its surface temperature.

See also **Electromagnetic waves** and **Spectroscopy**

Pioneer program

The Pioneer series of **space probe**s have been involved in four distinct space exploration programs, starting in the year 1958 and continuing right up to the present. They have been sent to destinations as close to home as the moon and Venus and as far away as Jupiter, Saturn, and even beyond the limits of our **solar system.** The success of these **probe**s has been as widely varied as their targets.

The first Pioneer launches were attempted in 1958, the year after the **Soviet Union** launched *Sputnik 1*. Late 1957 and early 1958 saw two more

March 3, 1972.
Pioneer 10 *blasts off*
toward Jupiter
while the moon
looks on.

satellite launches, *Sputnik 2* and the United States' *Explorer 1*. While the **space age** had begun, it was still in its infancy and getting a vessel into space was still a tremendous challenge. The early space programs saw more failures than successes, and Pioneer was no exception.

The Pioneer program was initiated in 1958 by the U.S. Department of Defense and the newly formed National Aeronautics and Space Administration (NASA). It called for five spacecraft to be launched to the moon. The first three of these, designed by the Air Force, were drum-shaped satellites weighing 84 pounds (38 kilograms) apiece. They were intended to go into orbit around the moon and collect scientific data, but none made it into space. In the case of *Pioneer 1,* the probe did not attain enough speed to escape the Earth's gravitational field. With the latter two *Pioneers,* the launchers failed. Each of these probes fell back to Earth and was destroyed.

Then in December 1958, the Army-designed, 13-pound (6-kilogram) *Pioneer 4* was launched with the goal of flying past the moon, as opposed to the much more difficult feat of attaining lunar orbit. This *Pioneer* was the first to the succeed in entering space. The closest it got to the moon, however, was 37,200 miles (59,855 kilometers) away, a distance too great to collect any data. After four more failed attempts to launch moon probes, the program was discontinued.

Initial Successes

The Pioneer series saw new life in 1960, when the first of five probes was launched into orbit around the sun, to collect information about interplanetary space. A solar orbit is far easier to achieve than a lunar orbit because it is a much less precise task. Any object launched beyond the Earth's gravitational field will naturally go into solar orbit—due to the sun's immense gravitational pull—unless specifically directed into orbit around another body. *Pioneer 5,* launched in March 1960, was a sphere just over 25 inches (64 centimeters) in diameter and weighing 95 pounds (43 kilograms). This mission was considered a success in that *Pioneer 5* was the first satellite to maintain communications with Earth even at the great distance of 23 million miles (37 million kilometers).

The next four Pioneer craft—*Pioneer 6* through *9*—were also successfully launched into solar orbit between 1965 and 1968. These probes had a different design than their predecessor. Each weighed about 140 pounds (64 kilograms), was covered with solar cells, and carried instruments to measure **cosmic rays**, **magnetic fields**, and the **solar wind.** *Pio-*

neers 5 through 9 arc all still in solar orbit and numbers 6 and 8 are still transmitting information.

The two most celebrated *Pioneers,* numbers *10* and *11,* left Earth in 1972 and 1973 respectively, and headed toward the outer planets. The dominant feature on each of the twin spacecraft was a 9-foot-diameter (3-meter-diameter) radio antenna dish. Scientific instruments, an energy generator, and a **rocket** motor were attached to the back of the dish.

Pioneer 10 was the first spacecraft ever to cross the **asteroid** belt, the region between Mars and Jupiter containing a large concentration of asteroids. Prior to this event, scientists had not known whether the asteroid density of the belt was too great for a ship to traverse without being smashed. The nearest *Pioneer 10* came to a known asteroid was 5.5 million miles (8.8 million kilometers).

In 1973, *Pioneer 10* reached Jupiter and took the first close-up photographs of the giant planet. It then kept traveling, crossed the orbit of Pluto, and left the solar system in 1983. It is expected to continue transmitting information about conditions in deep space at least through the end of 1996.

Pioneer 11 also headed first to Jupiter, using that planet's gravitational field to propel it toward Saturn. It arrived at Saturn in 1979 and proceeded to photograph and collect other valuable information about that planet's rings and moons. In 1990, *Pioneer 11* exited the solar system and in September 1995, after twenty-two years of operation, its power supply ran out.

Both *Pioneer 10* and *Pioneer 11* are carrying gold plaques engraved with information about Earth, in case they encounter another civilization while journeying through deep space.

The final two probes bearing the name *Pioneer* were launched in 1978 to explore Venus. The first, called *Pioneer-Venus Orbiter,* studied the planet's atmosphere and mapped about 90 percent of its surface. It also made observation of several **comet**s that passed near Venus. The *Orbiter* ran out of fuel in October 1992, at which point it descended to the planet and burned up.

The second probe in the pair, the *Pioneer-Venus Multiprobe,* was launched in August 1978, three months after the *Orbiter.* The *Multiprobe* distributed four probes around the planet, which traveled down through the atmosphere and onto the surface. They measured atmospheric temperature, pressure, density, and chemical composition at various altitudes. Only one probe survived after impact, transmitting data from the surface for sixty-seven minutes.

See also **Jupiter**; **Moon**; **Saturn**; **Space probe**; and **Venus**

Planet X

There are presently nine known planets in our **solar system.** It is possible that a tenth planet, known as Planet X, exists and is waiting to be discovered.

In 1781, William Herschel discovered Uranus, doubling the known dimensions of the solar system. Sixty years later, however, it was clear that Uranus was veering off its predicted orbit. Scientists hypothesized that there was another planet beyond the orbit of Uranus, the gravitational field of which was tugging at Uranus.

This hypothesis led to the discovery in 1841 of Neptune, independently by English astronomer John Couch Adams and French astronomer Urbain Leverrier. The existence of Neptune, however, was not able to explain the orbital eccentricities of Uranus. So the search continued for an elusive Planet X.

In 1930, American astronomer Clyde Tombaugh, after painstakingly examining thousands of photographic plates, discovered a ninth planet, Pluto. Pluto, however, contains just two-tenths of 1 percent of the Earth's **mass,** and is really too tiny to influence significantly the orbit of an object the size of Uranus.

So what is the answer? Is there a Planet X still out there? This question has intrigued astronomers for decades. If another planet does exist, there are several possible reasons it has not been detected. First, it may be too far away for telescopes to see and has an orbit that takes it close to one thousand years to complete. And perhaps its orbit is at such a steep angle compared to that of other planets, that we don't know where to look for it. It is also possible that its distance from the sun is so great that it reflects only a small amount of sunlight, making it a very dim object.

Some calculations place Planet X within the **constellation** Scorpius, which has a dense concentration of stars. Finding a planet there would be like finding a particular grain of sand on the beach. Other predictions place Planet X within the Gemini or Cancer constellations.

Some astronomers believe that the mysterious Planet X travels through the **Oort cloud,** the area on the edges of the solar system from which **comet**s originate. As the planet passes through this region, it might trigger comets to leave the cloud and begin orbiting the sun.

Other astronomers dismiss the notion of a Planet X altogether. They believe that the reason that Tombaugh's extensive search found only Pluto, was that Pluto was the only planet there. These scientists attribute the perceived irregularities in Uranus' orbit to errors made in predicting the orbit.

Other planets have been discovered since Pluto, but not in our solar system. In late 1995 and early 1996, three new planets were found, ranging from thirty-five to forty-five **light-year**s from Earth. The first planet, discovered by Swiss astronomers Michael Mayor and Didier Queloz of the Geneva Observatory, orbits a star in the constellation Pegasus. The next two planets were discovered by Americans Geoffrey Marcy and Paul Butler. One is in the constellation Virgo and the other is in the Big Dipper.

Planetary motion

Since ancient times, astronomers have been attempting to understand the patterns in which planets travel throughout the **solar system** and the forces that propel them. From Ptolemy and Copernicus to Newton and Einstein, great thinkers have corrected and built on each others' theories, leading to our present understanding of planetary motion.

In about 260 B.C., Greek astronomer Aristarchus had theorized that the solar system was **heliocentric,** meaning the sun was at the center, with the planets circling around it. However, in A.D.100, this theory was replaced by the **geocentric,** or Earth-centered, **model** of Alexandrian astronomer Ptolemy. This notion was warmly welcomed by church officials (who claimed that God placed Earth at the center of the heavens), and consequently was accepted as truth for over fourteen hundred years.

The geocentric model did not accurately describe the observed motions of the other planets relative to Earth, however. It appeared that Mars, Jupiter, and Saturn moved backwards from time to time, but Mercury and Venus did not. Ancient scientists devised elaborate models involving orbits within orbits to explain these observations.

Copernicus and Kepler Describe Planetary Motion

In 1507, Nicholas Copernicus revisited the heliocentric view of the solar system, insisting that the sun was indeed at the center. He explained that the perceived backward motion of some planets described in the geocentric model was merely an illusion that disappeared in the heliocentric model.

Copernicus sketched the planets' orbits as concentric circles, with the sun as the common center point, each one larger than the next. Since the orbits of Mars, Jupiter, and Saturn were larger than (outside of) the Earth's orbit, the Earth "overtook" those planets as it circled the sun. By the same token, Mercury and Venus, because they are closer to the sun, have smaller orbits and thus race around the sun in less than one Earth year. Despite decades of active opposition by the Roman Catholic Church, Copernicus' model eventually gained acceptance in the scientific community.

Copernicus mistakenly assumed, however, that planetary orbits were perfectly circular. It was not until a century later that Johannes Kepler determined that the orbits are elliptical (oval-shaped).

In 1595, Kepler (assistant to the Danish astronomer Tycho Brahe) set out to construct the orbit of Mars from a set of data collected by his boss. No matter how many ways he tried, he could not make Brahe's observations fit a circular path. Finally, Kepler gave up on circles and tried working with an ellipse. Brahe's observations matched perfectly.

Kepler's discovery led to the publication in 1609 of his first two laws of planetary motion. The first law states that a planet travels on an elliptical path with the sun at one focus point. The second states that a planet moves faster when closer to the sun and slower when farther away.

Ten years later, Kepler discovered a third law of planetary motion, which makes it possible to calculate a planet's relative distance from the sun. Specifically, the law states that the cube of a planet's average distance from the sun is equal to the square of the time it takes that planet to complete its orbit.

Scientists now know that Kepler's planetary laws also describe the motion of moons, stars, and human-made satellites.

Newton Explains Planetary Motion

In 1687, English mathematician Isaac Newton greatly expanded the world's body of knowledge about the forces responsible for the motion of planets. In that year he published *Philosophiae Naturalis Principia Math-*

ematica (*Mathematical Principles of Natural Philosophy*), the book containing his three laws of motion and the law of universal gravitation. This treatise proved similarities exist between the way actions occur on Earth and in the **cosmos.**

Newton was the first to apply the notion of **gravity** to orbiting bodies in space. He explained that gravity was the force that made planets remain in their orbits, instead of falling away in a straight line. Specifically he showed that planetary motion is the result of movement along a straight line combined with the gravitational pull of the sun.

Newton discovered three laws of motion, which explain interactions between objects. The first is that a moving body tends to remain in motion and a resting body tends to remain at rest unless acted on by an outside force. The second law states that any change in the acceleration of an object is proportional to, and in the same direction as, the force acting on it. In addition, the effects of that force will be inversely proportional to the mass of the object (meaning that a heavier object will move more slowly than a lighter object, when affected by the same force). Newton's third law is that for every action there is an equal and opposite reaction.

Newton used these laws to come up with the law of universal gravitation. This law states that the gravitational force between any two objects depends on the **mass** of each object and the distance between them. The greater each object's mass, the stronger the pull, but the greater the distance between them, the weaker the pull.

Using Newton's laws it became possible to chart the orbits of planets and their moons with great accuracy.

Einstein and Theories of Planetary Motion

More than two centuries later, in the early 1900s, Albert Einstein presented a revolutionary explanation for how gravity works. Whereas Newton viewed space as flat and time as constant (progressing at a constant rate—not slowing down or speeding up), Einstein proposed the theory that space is curved and time is relative (it can slow down or speed up).

According to Einstein, gravity is actually the curvature of space around the mass of an object. As a lighter object (like a planet) approaches a heavier object in space (like the sun), the lighter object follows the lines of curved space, which draws it near to the heavier object. To understand this concept, imagine space as a huge, stretched sheet. If you were to place a large heavy ball on the sheet, it would cause the sheet to sag. Now imagine a marble rolling toward the ball. Rather than traveling a straight line, the marble would follow the curves in the sheet caused by the ball's depression.

Einstein's theories have been helpful in explaining irregularities in the orbit of Mercury, which passes very near the sun. In most cases, however, Newtonian theory can still be relied on to describe accurately the motion of planets.

See also **Ancient Greek astronomy; Copernicus, Nicholas; Einstein, Albert; Gravity; Kepler, Johannes; Newton, Isaac; Newton's laws of motion;** and **Ptolemy**

Planetesimals and protoplanets

Planetesimals and **protoplanet**s are two stages in the evolution of a planet. According to the most commonly accepted theory today on the formation of the **solar system,** the planets formed by a process of accretion, or the sticking together of solid particles and gas.

Planetesimals are the first stage in the development of a planet. They are relatively small, solid bodies, generally several hundred miles across. They combine with one another, under the force of **gravity,** to form protoplanets. A protoplanet is the earliest form of a planet or one of its moons. It is also possible that some planetesimals became moons. Although a protoplanet is much larger than a planetesimal, it is still in the process of accretion of both solid particles and—in the cases of the large, outer planets—vast amounts of gas.

The theory of the solar system's formation to which most scientists now subscribe is the modified nebular hypothesis. According to that theory, the sun and planets formed from the solar **nebula** (a cloud of interstellar gas and dust) about 4.56 billion years ago. Due to the mutual gravitational attraction of the material in the nebula—and possibly triggered by shock waves from a nearby **supernova**—the nebula eventually collapsed in on itself.

As the nebula contracted, it began to spin more rapidly, leading to frequent collisions between dust grains. These grains accreted to form ever larger objects—first pebbles, then boulders, then planetesimals, and finally protoplanets.

As the nebula continued to condense, the temperature at its core rose to the point where **nuclear fusion** could begin. It then became a star (our sun) and the bodies farther from the core became the planets.

Planetesimals and protoplanets are believed to exist today within protoplanetary systems (planetary systems in formation) surrounding some stars. The Infrared Astronomical Satellite (IRAS), an international orbiting satellite that detects **infrared radiation,** has located over forty stars with cocoons of dense dust, where accretion of particles is most likely taking place. Computer simulations indicate that accretion around a typical star like our sun lasts around one hundred million years and produces about six planets.

See also **Solar system**

Plasma

Plasma is not a solid, a liquid, or a gas. It is a completely different state of matter. Plasma is made of ions (electrically charged atoms) and electrons and is found in stars and the **interstellar medium** where gas is heated to over 18 million degrees Fahrenheit (10 million degrees Celsius). The particles within plasma appear to move at random and are affected by electric and **magnetic field**s.

Plasma can also be found in **solar wind,** the flow of charged particles out of the sun's **corona.** It can also be found within planetary **magnetosphere**s, regions surrounding planets in which charged particles from the sun are controlled by a planet's magnetic field. Proponents of the **big bang theory** claim that an opaque plasma filled the early universe for the first ten thousand years after the "big bang."

Plasma is also formed by explosions in the central regions of a radio **galaxy,** such as Centaurus A. An explosion in this galaxy throws out jets of ions and electrons, which move at incredible speeds. Their motion creates magnetic fields, which restrain the area through which the particles can move. The particles pile up, forming lobes of plasma at the end of each jet. When the explosion stops sending out the jets, the lobes of plasma continue growing, forming clouds that are "visible" through **radio telescope**s.

A **neutron star** is another place to find concentrations of plasma. A neutron star creates a strong magnetic field, which traps plasma at its magnetic poles. Plasma found in these regions has a temperature as high as about 180 million degrees Fahrenheit (about 100 million degrees Celsius).

Plasma research falls into the field of magnetohydrodynamics (MHD), the study of fluids that conduct electricity in a magnetic field. In the case of plasma, charged particles spiral along the lines of a magnetic field, but cannot cross those lines. At the same time, this spiraling creates an electric current, which carries along the magnetic field, in effect combining the actions of plasma and magnetic field, or "freezing" them together.

History of Plasma Research

The first research into plasma-like materials was undertaken in the 1830s by English physicist Michael Faraday. Faraday passed electrical discharges through gases at low pressures. In the 1870s, another English physicist, William Crookes, conducted research similar to that of Faraday's. Crookes experiments led him to suggest that ionized gas constitutes a fourth state of matter.

A hot, ionized substance was first given the name "plasma" in 1920 by American chemist Irving Langmuir. Around the same time, astronomers recognized that at the temperatures present in stars, matter must exist in the state of plasma.

Swedish astrophysicist Hannes Olof Göst Alfvén conducted extensive research on plasma and founded the field of MHD. For his work on the interactions of plasma and magnetic fields, Alfvén shared in the Nobel Prize for physics in 1970.

In the 1940s, scientists recognized the tremendous energy contained in plasma and began to experiment with ways to harness that energy—through **nuclear fusion** reactions—for human use. However, nuclear fusion reactions release so much energy they are difficult to contain.

Nuclear fusion is the combination of two small nuclei to produce one larger nucleus. For this reaction to occur, temperatures must be so high (greater than 18 million degrees Fahrenheit, or 10 million degrees Celsius) that matter exists as plasma.

Scientists have looked to the use of magnetic fields to contain plasma and thereby control fusion reactions. The most practical tool for this purpose is called a tokamak. Designed by Russian physicist Lee Artsimovich in the late 1950s, the tokamak consists of a circular tube containing a strong magnetic field, which traps plasma.

The ability to generate energy for widespread use from nuclear fusion is something physicists have yet to achieve.

See also **Plasma theory**

Plasma theory

The most popular theory today as to how the universe began is the **big bang theory.** This theory states that fifteen to twenty billion years ago the universe exploded outward from a single point producing a "big bang." Another idea, called the **steady-state theory,** proposes the notion that the universe has always existed as it is now, that it is unchanging in space and time. Recent evidence has lent credibility to the big bang theory while reducing the likelihood of the steady-state theory.

A third theory, suggested by Swedish astrophysicist and Nobel Prize-winner Hannes Olof Göst Alfvén is the **plasma theory.** This theory proposes that the universe was born out of electrical and magnetic phenomena involving **plasma.** Plasma consists of ions (electrically charged atoms) and electrons, at a very high temperature.

Alfvén is the father of magnetohydrodynamics (MHD), the study of the behavior of plasma in a **magnetic field.** He has argued that 99 percent of the matter in the universe is composed of plasma. His theory states that electrical currents in plasma interact with each other to produce swirling strands, which initiate a chain reaction. The strands cause matter to clump together, which produces greater swirling, followed by more matter, and so on. According to the theory, stars, planets, and other celestial objects were formed by this process.

Plasma theorists believe that surges of electricity that are continually detected in space can be explained in the same way: that a **galaxy** spinning in a magnetic field produces electricity, which flows into the center of the galaxy and out again along the **magnetic axis.** The current then "short circuits," sending energy into the core and back out in the form of intense bursts of electrons and ions.

Alfvén's biggest criticism of the big bang theory is that the scenario was proposed first, and then scientists went looking for evidence to support it. Alfvén, in contrast, made observations first, and then crafted a theory based on those observations. He believes that the creation and evolution of the **cosmos** must be based on what we can see occurring today.

Big Bang Versus Plasma Theory

Plasma theorists also explain how recent findings that appear to support the big bang theory (such as universal expansion and cosmic background radiation) actually support their views. For instance, in 1929 Edwin Hubble proved that all matter in space is moving away from all other matter, in an expanding universe. Alfvén and his colleagues claim that this expansion is due to the interaction of matter and anti-matter. Anti-matter is composed of anti-particles, which have the same **mass** as regular particles but an opposite charge. In theory, these two substances would destroy each other on contact, producing waves of electrons and positrons (positively charged electrons) that would force plasma apart.

Another piece of evidence cited by big bang supporters is cosmic background radiation. This phenomenon was discovered in the 1960s as a faint hum picked up by a radio antenna. The noise, which came from every direction, was consistent with that of an object radiating at -465 degrees Fahrenheit (-276 degrees Celsius), the temperature to which radiation left over from the big bang was predicted to have cooled by now.

Plasma theorists attribute this radiation to **supernova**e, explosions of massive stars at the end of their lifetime. They claim that energy from these explosions is absorbed by interstellar dust, then ejected back into space.

The remarkable progress presently being made in space exploration is likely to produce new evidence that either supports or contradicts plasma, big bang, and other theories of the universe's origin.

See also **Big bang theory**; **Plasma**; and **Steady-state theory**

Pleiades star cluster

The Pleiades is a jewel-like cluster of stars, about four hundred **light-year**s from Earth. It is located in the **constellation** Taurus, near the shoulder of the bull. It contains about three thousand stars, although only six or seven are visible to the naked eye. The cluster is visible only in the evening sky in the winter. Also within this cluster is a reflection **nebula,** a cloud of gas and dust in which the dust particles are illuminated by starlight.

The Pleiades is the most famous **open cluster** of stars in our **galaxy.** An open cluster is a loose grouping of relatively hot, young stars (formed just a few million to a few billion years ago) and stars in formation. These clusters, which number over one thousand, are located in the disk of the **Milky Way** as opposed to the spiral arms.

The Pleiades, also known as the Seven Sisters for its seven brightest stars, is laden with lore and legend. The details vary from story to story, but most often the stars represent women or children who, for some reason or another, have ascended to the heavens. According to Greek mythology, the Pleiades were the daughters of Atlas (the man who had to support the heavens on his shoulders as punishment for turning against the gods) and his wife, Pleione. The Pleiades were being pursued by the hunter Orion, and Zeus helped them escape. He first turned them into doves and then lifted them to the sky, as stars.

An Australian aboriginal folktale also portrays the Pleiades as a group of pursued women. That version names the moon, at one time a man called "Kulu," as the pursuer. Two lizard men, together known as "Wati-kutjara," came to the rescue of the women. They pelted Kulu with their boomerangs and killed him. The blood drained from his face, he turned white, and rose to the sky to become the moon. The lizard men became the constellation Gemini, and the women turned into the Pleiades.

In some ancient cultures, the Pleiades has been associated with the changing of the seasons. The reason for this connection is that the star cluster becomes visible in the sky at dawn in the spring and at sunset in the fall. For that reason, it also came to symbolize the times of sowing and harvest.

The ancient Aztecs of Mexico even based their fifty-two-year **calendar** on the position of the Pleiades. They began each new cycle when the Pleiades ascended to a position directly overhead. At midnight on that day the Aztecs performed an elaborate ritual, culminating in a human sacrifice.

See also **Star cluster**

Pluto

Pluto stands at the center of a decades-long astronomical debate over its classification as a planet. Pluto, after all, is by far the smallest planet in the solar system and travels on an inclined orbit that crosses the plane of all other planetary orbits. Furthermore, it doesn't obey planetary spacing the way the other planets do. Although it's orbit is mostly outside of that of its closest neighbor, Neptune, at times it crosses over Neptune's orbit. For instance, Pluto has been closer to the sun than Neptune since 1979 and will continue that way until 1999. Pluto, however, does not quite fit the description of other bodies orbiting the sun, such as **asteroid**s or **comet**s either. So what is Pluto? While that question remains open, for practical purposes most astronomers consider it to be a planet.

Pluto was discovered in 1930 during a painstaking search of photographic plates by American astronomer Clyde Tombaugh. He and other astronomers (chief among them was Percival Lowell) were looking for a planet (then called Planet X) to explain disturbances in the orbit of Uranus. The gravitational field of Neptune accounted for some of its neighbor's orbital irregularities, but not all of them.

Pluto in the first quarter.

The search for Planet X yielded only Pluto. But at just two-tenths of 1 percent of the Earth's **mass,** that planet is too small to significantly influence the orbit of an object the size of Uranus. Thus astronomers have not given up on the idea that another Planet X is out there.

Pluto is only 1,457 miles (2,344 kilometers) across, just 18 percent of the Earth's diameter. It is so far from the sun that it takes almost 250 years to complete one revolution around the sun. A Plutonian day, however, is only 6.39 times longer than an Earth day. That is, it takes 6.39 of our days for Pluto to complete one rotation about its own axis.

In Greek mythology, Pluto is the god of the underworld. The ninth planet was given its name for several reasons. First, due to its great distance from the sun, Pluto is almost always dark. The sunlight it receives is about the intensity of moonlight on the Earth. Another reason is that Pluto is the mythological brother of Jupiter and Neptune. And finally, the planet's name begins with "PL," the initials of Percival Lowell, the astronomer who spent the final years of his life searching unsuccessfully for the elusive planet.

The Properties of Pluto

Before Pluto was located, astronomers expected it to be a large planet, about the size of Jupiter. They thought it would be able to influence the path of Uranus, a whole two planets away. At that time, the solar system appeared to fit a neat pattern: small, dense planets were closest to the sun and giant, gaseous planets were farthest away. Pluto broke this pattern, since it is a small, dense planet at the farthest reaches from the sun.

Pluto is so distant that no Earth-bound telescope has been able provide a detailed picture of its surface features. The best image we have at this point was taken by the Hubble Space Telescope (HST) in early 1996, in which the planet looks like a fuzzy soccer ball. The HST revealed only that Pluto has frozen gases, icy polar caps, and mysterious bright and dark spots.

Beyond that, astronomers can only rely on imprecise observations and what is known about the planet's density to paint a more complete picture of the planet. Pluto is probably composed mostly of rock and some ice, with a surface temperature between -350 and -380 degrees Fahrenheit (-212 and -228 degrees Celsius). The bright areas on its surface are most likely nitrogen ice, solid methane, and carbon monoxide. The dark spots may hold some form of organic material, possibly hydrocarbons from the chemical splitting and freezing of methane.

Pluto's atmosphere is probably made of nitrogen, carbon monoxide, and methane. At Pluto's **perihelion** (the point on its orbit closest to the sun) its atmosphere exists in a gaseous state. But for most of its orbit the atmosphere is frozen.

Much of what we know about Pluto was learned following the 1978 discovery of Pluto's moon, Charon (pronounced "Karen," and named for the mythological character who transported the dead to the underworld). Pluto and Charon were observed moving together into the inner solar system. As the two bodies eclipsed one another, astronomers observed brightness curves, enabling them to plot rough maps of the light and dark areas on both planet and moon.

Prior to the discovery of Charon, astronomers thought that Pluto and its moon together were one larger object. Charon has a diameter over half that of Pluto, making it the largest moon relative to its planet in the solar system. For this reason some scientists consider the two bodies to be a double-planet.

Various theories have been suggested regarding Pluto's origin. Most of these theories connect Pluto with Neptune's moon Triton. The reason is that Pluto, like Triton, rotates in a direction opposite that of most other planets and their satellites.

One theory states that Pluto, Triton, and Charon are the only remaining members of a group of similar objects, the rest of which drifted into the **Oort cloud** (the area surrounding the solar system in which comets originate). Another idea is that Pluto used to be one of Neptune's moons, and was struck by a massive object. This impact broke Pluto in two, creating its moon, and sending both Pluto and Charon into orbit around the sun. The more popular theory, however, is that both Pluto and Triton started out in independent orbits and that Triton (unlike Pluto) was captured by Neptune's gravitational field.

More questions about Pluto and Charon may be answered early next century, when the National Aeronautics and Space Administration (NASA) sends the first unpiloted mission to Pluto and its moon. The *Pluto Express* will consist of two spacecraft, each taking about twelve years to reach Pluto. They are expected to encounter Pluto near its perihelion, before its atmosphere freezes. The goals of the mission are to learn about the atmosphere, surface features, and geologic composition of Pluto and Charon.

See also **Planet X**; *Pluto Express*; and **Tombaugh, Clyde**

Pluto Express

Pluto is the only planet in the **solar system** not to have been visited by a **space probe.** In fact, Pluto is so distant—at 3.66 billion miles (5.86 billion kilometers) from the sun—that scientists do not even have a detailed picture of its surface features. In about the year 2013, all that will change. In that year the National Aeronautics and Space Administration's *Pluto Express* will arrive for a close look at Pluto and its moon, Charon.

Pluto Express will consist of two small spacecraft launched in 2001, each taking around twelve years to reach Pluto. The spacecraft are slated to arrive when Pluto is at its **perihelion** (the point along its orbit where its closest to the sun) since the planet's atmosphere freezes as it recedes from the sun. The goals of the mission are to learn about the atmosphere, surface features, and geologic composition of Pluto and Charon.

Artist's depiction of the Pluto Express *on its mission to look at Pluto and its moon, Charon.*

Each spacecraft will be a six-sided aluminum structure. Since the **probe**s are traveling too far from the sun for solar panels to be of much use, internal power will be provided by radioisotope thermal generators (RTGs). RTGs are a type of nuclear power generator that converts the heat from decaying radioactive isotopes to electricity, similar to those used on the *Voyager 1* and *2* missions. The spacecraft will also carry telescopes that can observe **electromagnetic radiation** in infrared and ultraviolet wavelengths, as well as visible light.

Discussions are presently underway with the Russian Space Agency regarding the use of a Russian probe to explore the Plutonian atmosphere. Plans are for the probe to separate from one of the *Pluto Express* vessels about thirty days before the its closest approach to Pluto, at a distance of about 9,300 miles (14,900 kilometers) from the planet. The probe would then continue to the planet, enter the atmosphere, and relay information back to the spacecraft. Also under consideration is an extended mission to explore the **Kuiper belt,** the region of space beyond Pluto that is believed to contain inactive **comet**s.

One possible trajectory for *Pluto Express,* after launching in March 2001, would be to fly first to Venus. The spacecraft could then use the **gravity assist** technique, relying on the gravitational field of Venus to swing it around like a slingshot in the direction of Jupiter. The spacecraft would reach Jupiter in July 2006 and use that planet's gravitational field to propel it towards Pluto, arriving there in May 2013. The mission would either end the following year or continue on to the Kuiper belt.

The timing of this mission to Pluto is critical. If astronomers pass up the opportunity to study this planet as it approaches its closest point to the sun, another 250 years will pass before it returns to that position.

See also **Kuiper belt** and **Pluto**

Ptolemy (c. A.D. 100–170)
Alexandrian astronomer

Ptolemais Hermii was born in Alexandria, Egypt. He later adopted the Latin version of his name, Claudius Ptolemaeus, and finally shortened it to Ptolemy.

Very little information about Ptolemy's early life has survived the years. Historians are not even sure whether he was Greek or Egyptian. Most of what we know about Ptolemy's adult life has been pieced together by examining his surviving written works. All said, Ptolemy is considered the most influential astronomer of ancient times.

Ptolemy is perhaps best known for his articulation of the flawed **geocentric** (Earth-centered) **model** of the **solar system,** also known as the **Ptolemaic model.** His greatest contribution to science, however, is a series of books in which he compiled the knowledge of the ancient Greeks. Ptolemy titled this thirteen-volume catalogue *Megale mathematike systaxis* (*Great Mathematical Compilation*). When the Arabs translated the work, they called it *Almagest* (*The Greatest*), the title by which it is known today.

The primary scholar mentioned in Ptolemy's writings was Hipparchus, perhaps the greatest ancient Greek astronomer. In addition to being the original architect of the geocentric model, Hipparchus also made a catalogue of the stars. He grouped them into forty-eight **constellation**s. He also established some of the basic principles of trigonometry; studied the **lunar** and **solar eclipse**s to create a **calendar** based on a year containing 365.2467 days; estimated the relative sizes of the sun and the moon; and calculated that the moon is 29.5 Earth radii (a distance using the radius of the Earth as a unit of measurement) from the Earth.

Ptolemy.

Because most of Hipparchus' own writings have been lost over the years, many of his accomplishments, such as the so-called Ptolemaic system, have been wrongly attributed to Ptolemy. Ptolemy has even been accused of copying and taking credit for the writings of Hipparchus.

Ptolemy's Writings About the Physical World

The Ptolemaic model of the solar system placed the Earth at the center, with the sun, moon, and planets all traveling around it. The most serious problem with this theory was that it was not consistent with the observed movements of the planets. To account for this inconsistency, Ptolemy added small secondary orbits to the planetary paths that he called **epicycles.** These secondary orbits turned the planets' nice, neat circular paths into elaborate figure-eight patterns, to account for the periods in which the planets appeared to move backwards with respect to the Earth. Despite the flaws inherent in this system, it was held as truth until Nicholas Copernicus came along with a new theory in 1543, placing the sun at the center of the planets. One reason the theory lasted so long is that the church encouraged and upheld the belief that the Earth was the center of the heavens.

Ptolemy was also known for his work in **astrology.** In Ptolemy's time, this field was considered a science as legitimate as any other. In his four-volume book *Tetrabiblios,* he attempted to show how patterns of stars could influence human events. Ptolemy charted the stars using primitive observational instruments such as a plinth (a stone block with an engraved arc used to measure the height of the sun) and a triquetrum (a triangular rule).

Optics and geography were two other sciences advanced by Ptolemy. In a book called *Optics,* he wrote about the reflection and refraction of light and composed tables for the refraction of light as it passes into water at different angles. His maps and tables of **latitude** and **longitude** (although based on a much-too-small estimate of the size of the Earth) appeared in his book entitled *Geography.* In one of Ptolemy's later writings, *The Planetary Hypothesis,* he attempted to calculate the distances of the planets and the moon from the sun. Unfortunately, only part of this work has survived the centuries.

See also **Ancient Egyptian astronomy**; **Ancient Greek astronomy**; and **Copernicus, Nicholas**

Pulsar

When the first **pulsar** was discovered, it was almost mistaken for communication attempts by an alien civilization. The pulsar was given the name LGM (for "Little Green Men") by its half-serious discoverers. After all, no one had ever witnessed a space object that would emit radio signals in rapid-fire form (at a rate of up to one thousand times per second), with unfailing regularity. The discoverers eventually realized that the signal was not the work of little green men, but the flash of a **neutron star** spinning about its axis, ejecting radiation from its poles like a lighthouse beacon.

In August 1967, Jocelyn Bell Burnell was a graduate student at Cambridge University. She and her supervisor, Antony Hewish, built a giant **radio telescope** designed to track **quasar**s, powerful sources of energy extremely far from Earth. The telescope was able to detect even very faint energy signals and record them on long rolls of paper.

One day, while looking over the paper, Bell Burnell noticed some strange markings. They came and went regularly, at a period of just over one second. Soon she found three other pulsating sources. Once Bell Burnell and Hewish gave up on the idea that they had found extraterrestrial intelligent life, they named these objects pulsars, short for "pulsating radio sources."

Hewish hypothesized that the pulsars might be **white dwarf** stars or neutron stars. By the end of the following year, two pulsars were located within **supernova** remnants. This discovery led astronomers Thomas Gold and Franco Pacini to the conclusion that neutron stars were indeed the source of the pulses.

Neutron stars, the debris left after the implosion of a massive star, are incredibly dense and they spin extremely fast. For example, a neutron star in the Crab **nebula** rotates about thirty times per second. The spinning generates a **magnetic field** causing the star to act as a giant magnet. The star spews radiation out of its magnetic poles and if the **magnetic axis** is tilted in a certain way, the rotating star's on-and-off signal is visible from Earth.

Hundreds of pulsars have now been catalogued, including many in spots where a supernova is known to have occurred. Scientists believe that more than one hundred thousand active pulsars may exist in our **galaxy.**

See also **Bell Burnell, Jocelyn**; **Neutron star**; **Nova and supernova**; and **Stellar evolution**

Purcell, Edward (1912–)

American physicist

Edward Purcell was an atomic physicist, meaning that he studied the structure and behavior of atoms, the smallest particles of matter. Purcell is most famous for his development of nuclear resonance absorption—a method

*Edward Mills
Purcell thanks the
Swedish Royal
family after
receiving his Nobel
Prize for physics on
December 12, 1952.
Purcell shared the
award with Felix
Bloch.*

of measuring the frequencies of rotation of atomic nuclei in a **magnetic field,** and learning about their structures. He applied this practice to the field of **radio astronomy** by detecting the frequency of **radio wave**s coming from hydrogen clouds in space.

Edward Mills Purcell was born in 1912 in Taylorville, Illinois. Both of his parents were teachers when Purcell was in his childhood; his father later became the general manager of a telephone company. Purcell discovered his father's Bell System technical magazines and found them to be interesting reading. They were partly responsible for his decision to go into electrical engineering.

Purcell attended public schools near his hometown before entering Purdue University in 1929. There he studied electrical engineering, receiving his bachelor's degree in 1933. Purcell then spent a year as an exchange student in Germany. Upon returning, he began his graduate studies at Harvard University and completed his Ph.D. in 1938. He then remained at Harvard teaching physics for the next three years.

During World War II, Purcell joined other scientists conducting research to assist the U.S. war effort. He worked on a **microwave**-based radar system, for use in night fighting. The project was headed by physicist Isidor Isaac Rabi at the Massachusetts Institute of Technology's Radiation Laboratory. Rabi, several years earlier, had developed a method of observing the magnetic properties of atoms.

In 1946, after the war, Purcell accepted a teaching position at Harvard, where he remained until his retirement in 1980. There he began designing a new process for determining the magnetic strength of atomic nuclei, ultimately advancing Rabi's work several steps.

Rabi's process required that a substance first be vaporized (converted to a gaseous state) in order to measure the spin of its nucleus. Then one could learn about the nature of the atom by placing the sample in a magnetic field. Purcell's method, in contrast, did not require that a substance be vaporized. He placed it in the field of a strong electromagnet and then introduced the field of a second magnet that was powered by radio waves. He changed the frequency of the radio waves until he found one that caused the atoms in his sample to vibrate. That frequency was then noted as the sample's "signature frequency."

At the same time, American physicist Felix Bloch was also applying radar theory to atomic magnetic fields. For their independent achievements, the two physicists shared the Nobel Prize for physics in 1952.

Several practical applications have been found for this technology (known as "nuclear magnetic resonance" or NMR), particularly in the areas of chemistry and medicine. Chemists use the process to identify the elements contained in samples, as well as to learn about the structure of atoms. In medicine, NMR has been used as an alternative to **X-ray**s to "see" inside the body, and has proven to be a valuable tool in cancer research.

Discovery of the Radio Telescope

In 1951, Purcell found that NMR also has applications in astronomy. He and astronomy graduate student Harold Ewen built a **radio telescope** that used NMR to measure radio waves coming from space. They swept the skies looking for the signature frequency of hydrogen—by far the most plentiful element in the universe. In this way they were the first to detect dark clouds of interstellar hydrogen invisible to optical telescopes.

Toward the end of his career, Purcell conducted research in biophysics. He studied the behavior and movement of bacteria; in particular, the physics of swimming microscopic organisms.

In addition to the Nobel Prize, he won several other awards and honors over the span of his long career. Purcell was elected to the National Academy of Science in 1951 and appointed to the President's Scientific Advisory Committee under Presidents Eisenhower and Johnson. He was awarded the National Medal of Science by the National Science Foundation in 1978.

See also **Radio astronomy**

Sources

Books

Abbott, David, ed. "Seyfert, Carl Keenan," *The Biographical Dictionary of Scientists: Astronomers,* New York: P. Bedrick Books, 1984.

Abell, George O. *Realm of the Universe,* 3rd edition, Philadelphia: Saunders College Publishing, 1984.

Anderson, Julie. "Edward Mills Purcell," *Notable Twentieth-Century Scientists,* Volume 3, Ed. Emily J. Mc-Murray, Detroit: Gale Research, 1995.

Apfel, Necia H. *Astronomy Projects for Young Scientists,* New York: Prentice Hall Press, 1984.

Asimov, Isaac. *Isaac Asimov's Library of the Universe: Ancient Astronomy,* Milwaukee: Gareth Stevens Publishing, 1989.

Asimov, Isaac. *Isaac Asimov's Library of the Universe: Projects in Astronomy,* Milwaukee: Gareth Stevens Publishing, 1990.

Bali, Mrinal. *Contemporary World Issues: Space Exploration,* Santa Barbara, CA: ABC-CLIO, Inc., 1990.

Barone, Michael and Grant Ujifusa. *The Almanac of American Politics 1996,* Washington, D.C.: National Journal Inc., 1995, pp. 1032-36.

Beck, R. L. and Daryl Schrader. *America's Planetariums & Observatories,* St. Petersburg, FL: Sunwest Space Systems, Inc., 1991.

Bernstein, Joanne E. and Rose Blue. *Judith Resnik: Challenger Astronaut,* New York: Lodestar Books, 1990.

Blaauw, Adriaan. *ESO's Early History,* Garching bei München, Germany: European Southern Observatory, 1991.

Blaauw, Adriaan. "Sitter, Willem de," *Dictionary of Scientific Biography,* Volume XII, Ed. Charles Coulston Gillispie, New York: Charles Scribner's Sons, 1973.

Bonnet, Robert L. and G. Daniel Keen. *Space and Astronomy: 49 Science Fair Projects,* Blue Ridge Summit, PA: Tab Books, 1992.

Booth, Nicholas. *Encyclopedia of Space,* London: Brian Trodd Publishing House Limited, 1990.

Brecher, Kenneth and Michael Feirtag, eds. *Astronomy of the Ancients,* Cambridge, MA: The MIT Press, 1979.

Carroll, Peter N. *Famous in America: The Passion to Succeed,* New York: Dutton. 1985.

Cassut, Michael. *Who's Who in Space: The First 25 Years,* Boston: G. K. Hall & Co., 1987.

Cornell, James. *The First Stargazers: An Introduction to the Origins of Astronomy,* New York: Charles Scribner's Sons, 1981.

Couper, Heather and Nigel Henbest. *How the Universe Works,* Pleasantville, NY: Reader's Digest Association, Inc., 1994.

Davies, J. K. *Space Exploration,* Edinburgh: W & R Chambers Ltd., 1992.

Davies, Kay and Wendy Oldfield. *The Super Science Book of Time,* New York: Thomson Learning, 1992.

D'Occhieppo, Konradin Ferrari. "Oppolzer, Theodor Ritter Von," *Dictionary of Scientific Biography,* Volume X, Ed. Charles Coulston Gillispie, New York: Charles Scribner's Sons, 1973.

Drake, Frank D. *Is Anyone Out There?: The Scientific Search for Extraterrestrial Intelligence,* New York: Delacorte Press, 1992.

"Drake, Frank Donald," *American Men and Women of Science,* 18th edition, Vol. 2, New Providence, New Jersey: R. R. Bowker, 1972.

Eastwood, Bruce S. "Grimaldi, Francesco Maria," *Dictionary of Scientific Biography,* Volume V, Ed. Charles Coulston Gillispie, New York: Charles Scribner's Sons, 1973.

Friedman, Herbert. *The Astronomer's Universe,* New York: W.W. Norton & Company, 1990.

Gatland, Kenneth. *The Illustrated Encyclopedia of Space Technology,* New York: Crown Publishers, Inc., 1981.

Goldsmith, Donald. *The Astronomers,* New York: St. Martin's Press, 1991.

Graham, Judith, ed. "Jemison, Mae C.," *Current Biography Yearbook 1993,* New York: H.W. Wilson, 1993.

Gray, Chris Hables. "Carl Sagan," *Notable Twentieth-Century Scientists,* Volume 3, Ed. Emily J. McMurray, Detroit: Gale Research, 1995.

Gump, David P. *Space Enterprise: Beyond NASA,* New York: Praeger, 1990.

Hadingham, Evan. *Early Man and the Cosmos,* New York: Walker and Company, 1984.

Haskins, Jim and Kathleen Benson. *Space Challenger: The Story of Guion Bluford,* Minneapolis: Carolrhoda Books, Inc., 1984.

Hathaway, Nancy. *The Friendly Guide to the Universe,* New York: Penguin Books, 1994.

Hawking, Stephen W. *A Brief History of Time: From the Big Bang to Black Holes,* Toronto: Bantam Books, 1988.

Heidman, Jean. *Extraterrestrial Intelligence,* Cambridge, England: Cambridge University Press, 1995.

Hoffleit, Dorrit. "Mitchell, Maria," *Dictionary of Scientific Biography,* Volume IX, Ed. Charles Coulston Gillispie, New York: Charles Scribner's Sons, 1973.

Hunley, J. D. "Hermann Oberth," *Notable Twentieth-Century Scientists,* Volume 3, Ed. Emily J. McMurray, Detroit: Gale Research, 1995.

Ilingworth, Valerie, ed. *The Facts on File Dictionary of Astronomy,* 3rd edition, New York: Facts on File, Inc., 1994.

Itard, Jean. "Legendre, Adrien-Marie," *Dictionary of Scientific Biography,* Volume VIII, Ed. Charles Coulston Gillispie, New York: Charles Scribner's Sons, 1973.

Kaufmann, William J., III. *Discovering the Universe,* 3rd edition, New York: W. H. Freeman and Company, 1993.

Kippenhahn, Rudolf. *Bound to the Sun: The Story of Planets, Moons, and Comets,* New York: W. H. Freeman and Company, 1990.

Kirby-Smith, H.T. *U.S. Observatories: A Directory and Travel Guide,* New York: Van Nostrand Reinhold Company, 1976.

Kopal, Zdenek. "Römer, Ole Christensen (or Roemer, Olaus)," *Dictionary of Scientific Biography,* Volume XI, Ed. Charles Coulston Gillispie, New York: Charles Scribner's Sons, 1973.

Kragh, Helge. "Lemaitre, Georges," *Dictionary of Scientific Biography,* Volume 18-Supplement II, Ed. Charles Coulston Gillispie, New York: Charles Scribner's Sons, 1990.

Krauss, Lawrence M. *The Physics of Star Trek,* New York: BasicBooks, 1995.

Lerner, Eric. *The Big Bang Never Happened,* New York: Times Books, 1991.

Lévy, Jacques R. "Le Verrier, Urbain Jean Joseph," *Dictionary of Scientific Biography,* Volume VIII, Ed. Charles Coulston Gillispie, New York: Charles Scribner's Sons, 1973.

Lohne, J. A. "Harriot (or Hariot), Thomas," *Dictionary of Scientific Biography,* Volume VI, Ed. Charles Coulston Gillispie, New York: Charles Scribner's Sons, 1973.

MacDonald, D.K.C. *Faraday, Maxwell, and Kelvin,* Garden City, NY: Doubleday & Company, Inc., 1964.

Mallas, John H. and Evered Kreimer. *The Messier Album: An Observer's Handbook,* Cambridge, MA: Sky Publishing Corp, 1978.

Marsden, Brian G. "Newcomb, Simon," *Dictionary of Scientific Biography,* Volume X, Ed. Charles Coulston Gillispie, New York: Charles Scribner's Sons, 1973.

Marx, Siegfried and Werner Pfau. *Observatories of the World,* New York: Van Nostrand Reinhold Company, 1982.

McDonald, Avril. "Grote Reber," *Notable Twentieth-Century Scientists,* Volume 3, Ed. Emily J. McMurray, Detroit: Gale Research, 1995.

Moore, Patrick. *Fireside Astronomy: An Anecdotal Tour through the History and Lore of Astronomy,* Chichester, England: John Wiley & Sons, 1992.

Moore, Patrick. *The Guinness Book of Astronomy,* Middlesex, England: Guinness Publishing Ltd., 1988.

Moore, Patrick. *The International Encyclopedia of Astronomy,* New York: Orion Books, 1987.

Moore, Patrick. *Patrick Moore's History of Astronomy,* 6th edition, London: MacDonald & Co. Ltd., 1983.

Moyer, Don F. "Langley, Samuel Pierpont," *Dictionary of Scientific Biography,* Volume VIII, Ed. Charles Coulston Gillispie, New York: Charles Scribner's Sons, 1973.

Multhauf, Lettie S. "Olbers, Heinrich Wilhelm Matthias," *Dictionary of Scientific Biography,* Volume X, Ed. Charles Coulston Gillispie, New York: Charles Scribner's Sons, 1973.

Munitz, Milton K., ed. *Theories of the Universe,* Glencoe, IL: The Free Press, 1957.

Neal, Valerie, Cathleen S. Lewis and Frank H. Winter. *Spaceflight: A Smithsonian Guide,* New York: Macmillan • USA, 1995.

Newton, David E. "Martin Ryle," *Notable Twentieth-Century Scientists,* Volume 3, Ed. Emily J. McMurray, Detroit: Gale Research, 1995.

North, John. *The Norton History of Astronomy and Cosmology,* New York: W. W. Norton & Company, Inc., 1995.

O'Connor, Karen. *Sally Ride and the New Astronauts: Scientists in Space,* New York: Franklin Watts, 1983.

Office of Technology Assessment. *Civilian Space Policy and Applications,* Washington, D.C.: U.S. Government Printing Office, 1982.

O'Neil, W. M. *Early Astronomy from Babylonia to Copernicus,* Sydney, Australia: Sydney University Press, 1986.

Parker, Barry. *Stairway to the Stars: The Story of the World's Largest Observatory,* New York: Plenum Press, 1994.

Pasachoff, Jay M. *Contemporary Astronomy,* 4th edition, Philadelphia: Saunders College Publishing, 1989.

Pasachoff, Jay M. *Journey Through the Universe,* Fort Worth, TX: Saunders College Publishing, 1992.

Pendick, Daniel. "Clyde W. Tombaugh," *Notable Twentieth-Century Scientists,* Volume 4, Ed. Emily J. McMurray, Detroit: Gale Research, 1995.

Riabchikov, Evgeny. *Russians in Space,* Garden City, New York: Doubleday & Company, Inc., 1971.

"Rocket and Rocket Engine," *Science and Technology Illustrated: The World Around Us,* Volume 22, Chicago: Encyclopedia Britannica, Inc., 1984.

Ronan, Colin A. *The Natural History of the Universe,* New York: MacMillan Publishing Company, 1991.

Sagan, Carl. *Cosmos,* New York: Random House, 1980.

Schmittroth, Linda, Mary Reilly McCall, and Bridget Travers, eds. *Eureka!* 6 Volumes, Detroit: U•X•L, 1995.

Smith, Julian A. "Valentina Tereshkova," *Notable Twentieth-Century Scientists,* Volume 4, Ed. Emily J. McMurray, Detroit: Gale Research, 1995.

Smith, Julian A. "Vera Cooper Rubin," *Notable Twentieth-Century Scientists,* Volume 3, Ed. Emily J. McMurray, Detroit: Gale Research, 1995.

Smith, Robert W. *The Space Telescope: A Study of NASA, Science, Technology and Politics,* Cambridge, MA: Cambridge University Press, 1993.

Stuewer, Roger H. "Gamow, George," *Dictionary of Scientific Biography,* Volume V, Ed. Charles Coulston Gillispie, New York: Charles Scribner's Sons, 1973.

Swenson, Loyd S. Jr. "Michelson, Albert Abraham," *Dictionary of Scientific Biography,* Volume IX, Ed. Charles Coulston Gillispie, New York: Charles Scribner's Sons, 1973.

Swift, David W. *SETI Pioneers: Scientists Talk About Their Search for Extraterrestrial Intelligence,* Tucson, AZ: The University of Arizona Press, 1990.

Thurston, Hugh. *Early Astronomy,* New York: Springer-Verlag, 1994.

Travers, Bridget, ed. *The Gale Encyclopedia of Science,* 6 Volumes. Detroit: Gale Research, 1996.

Travers, Bridget, ed. *World of Invention,* Detroit: Gale Research, 1994.

Travers, Bridget, ed. *World of Scientific Discovery,* Detroit: Gale Research, 1994.

Tucker, Wallace H. *The Star Splitters: The High Energy Astronomy Observatories,* Washington, D.C.: National Aeronautics and Space Administration, 1984.

Walter, William J. *Space Age,* New York: Random House, 1992.

Wilson, Colin. *Starseekers,* New York: Doubleday & Company, Inc., 1980.

Wilson, Philip K. "Allan R. Sandage," *Notable Twentieth-Century Scientists,* Volume 4, Ed. Emily J. McMurray, Detroit: Gale Research, 1995.

Zeilik, Michael and John Gaustad. *Astronomy: The Cosmic Perspective,* 2nd edition, New York: John Wiley & Sons, Inc., 1990.

Articles

Acton, Scott. "Untwinkling Our Own Star," *Sky & Telescope,* June 1994: 26-27.

"Allan Sandage Receives 1991 Crafoord Prize," *Physics Today,* December 1991: 91.

Allen, Jane E. "Probe Finds Jupiter Surprisingly Windy, Drier Than Expected," *Detroit Free Press,* 23 January 1996: A1.

Allen, Jane E. and Russell Grantham. "By Jupiter! Probe's Findings Surprise Scientists," *The Ann Arbor News,* 23 January 1996: A3.

"Americans Get the Mir Experience," *Astronomy,* April 1995: 28.

"Astronaut at Home on Mir," *The Ann Arbor News,* 26 March 1996: A4.

"Astronomers Are Closer to Agreeing on the Age of the Universe," *Chronicle of Higher Education,* 17 May 1996: A10.

Banke, Jim. "The Story of Apollo 13: The Movie," *Ad Astra,* March/April 1995: 50.

Bartusiak, Marcia. "Head in the Stars," *The New York Times Book Review,* 10 December 1995: 22.

Bond, Bruce. "100 Years on Mars Hill," *Astronomy,* June 1994: 28-39.

Boyd, Robert S. "Astronomers See Potential for Life on Newly Found Planets," *Detroit Free Press,* 18 January 1996: A3+.

Boyd, Robert S. "Exploring the Big Bang and Beyond," *Detroit Free Press,* 7 January 1996: H1+.

Boyd, Robert S. "Origin of Life on Earth Eludes Scientists," *Detroit Free Press,* 7 January 1996: H4.

Boyd, Robert S. "Somewhere, Some Other Planet Must Sustain Life," *Detroit Free Press,* 7 January 1996: H4.

Broad, William J. "Could Life on Loose Bit of Mars Survive a Short Cut to Earth?" *The New York Times,* 12 March 1996: C1.

Broad, William J. "Russian Space Momentos Show Gagarin's Ride Was a Rough One," *The New York Times,* 5 March 1996: B12.

Browne, Malcolm W. "'Neutrino Bomb' Idea Expands Debate on Human Extinction," *The New York Times,* 23 January 1996: D4.

Brunier, Serge. "Temples in the Sky," *Sky and Telescope,* February 1993: 18-24.

Bruning, David. "Hubble: Better Than New," *Astronomy,* April 1994: 44-49.

Chang, Kenneth. "Two More Planets Found Near Stars Similar to the Sun," *The Los Angeles Times,* 18 January 1996: A3.

Chartrand, Mark. "A Measure of Space," *Ad Astra,* November/December 1993: 52.

Clary, Mike. "U.S. Woman Will Spend Months in Mir," *The Los Angeles Times,* 21 March 1996: A18.

"COBE Mission Launched," *Astronomy,* February 1990: 16+.

Cole, Richard. "NASA Mission May Unlock a Few Cosmic Secrets," *The Detroit News,* 3 December 1995: A2.

Cowley, Anne. "The Catherine Wolfe Bruce Medal to Maarten Schmidt," *Mercury,* November-December 1992: 197-98.

"Dr. Mae Jemison Becomes First Black Woman in Space," *Jet,* 14 September 1992: 34-38.

Drago, Mike. "Shuttle Retrieves NASA Probe," *The Ann Arbor News,* 16 January 1996.

Dunn, Marcia. "Female Astronaut Settles In on Mir," *USA Today,* 25 March 1996: A3.

Dunn, Marcia. "Shuttle, Mir Are Linked After Tricky Docking," *The Boston Globe,* 16 November 1995: A3.

Dyson, Freeman. "Hidden Worlds: Hunting for Distant Comets and Rogue Planets," *Sky & Telescope,* January 1994: 26-30.

Eicher, David J. "Descent Into Darkness," *Astronomy,* April 1995: 66-69.

Friedlander, Blaine P. Jr. "The Comet With Two Tails," *The Washington Post,* 6 March 1996: B5.

"Gamma-Ray Telescope Takes Shape," *Astronomy,* July 1995: 26.

Gauthier, Daniel James. "One Hundred Stars of Space," *Ad Astra,* July/August 1991: 8+.

Goldman, Stuart J. "Astronomy On the Internet," *Sky & Telescope,* August 1995: 21-27.

Grantham, Russell. "By Jupiter! Instruments From U-M to Explore It," *The Ann Arbor News,* 6 December 1995: B1+.

Grantham, Russell. "Expert Shares Jupiter Surprises," *The Ann Arbor News,* 8 February 1996: B3.

Grantham, Russell. "Hyakutake Brightest Comet in Sky Since 1976," *The Ann Arbor News,* 20 March 1996: B1+.

Grantham, Russell. "New Technology Has Accelerated Advances In Field of Astronomy," *The Ann Arbor News,* 11 April 1996: D1+.

Grantham, Russell. "Star Potential," *The Ann Arbor News,* 11 April 1996: D1+.

Gurshtein, Alexander. "When the Zodiac Climbed into the Sky," *Sky & Telescope,* October 1995: 28-33.

Hathaway, David H. "Journey to the Heart of the Sun," *Astronomy* January 1995: 38-43.

Horgan, John. "Beyond Neptune: Hubble Telescope Spots a Vast Ring of Ice Protoplanets," *Scientific American,* October 1995: 24+.

Hotz, Robert Lee. "Quest for Ice: Polar Prospecting." *The Los Angeles Times,* 14 January 1996: A1.

Hoversten, Paul. "Hubble's Time Travel Finds Galaxies," *USA Today,* 16 January 1996: A1.

"Hubble Observes the Violent Birth of Stars," *Astronomy* October 1995: 22.

Jaroff, Leon. "Listening for Aliens," *Time*, 5 February 1996: 55+.

"Jemison, Endeavour Crew Return To Earth After Successful Science Mission," *Jet*, 5 October 1992: 9.

Johnson, George. "Dark Matter Lights the Void," *The New York Times*, 21 January 1996: E1+.

Knight, Tony. "To Explore Strange New Worlds—Galileo Streaks Toward Jupiter," *Daily News of Los Angeles*, 27 November 1995.

Lemonick, Michael D. "Astronomers Have Detected Water-Bearing Planets Around Nearby Stars. Now They're Focused on a Deeper Mystery: Where Are the Friendly, Earthlike Worlds?" *Time*, 5 February 1996: 53+.

Lemonick, Michael D. "Beyond Pluto," *Time*, 28 September 1992: 59.

Luxner, Larry. "Southern Space: Down South Looks To The Stars," *Ad Astra*, November/December 1992: 46-47.

Mallon, Thomas. "Galileo, Phone Home," *The New York Times Magazine*, 3 December 1995: 57+.

Mann, Paul. "Spacelab's Demise?" *Aviation Week & Space Technology*, 1 August 1994: 23.

McDonald, Kim A. "A Great Comet," *The Chronicle of Higher Education*, 5 April 1996: A10.

Nash, Nathaniel C. "Starry-Eyed But Resolute: Astronomers in Race," *The New York Times*, 6 January 1994: A4.

"New Life for McMath Solar Telescope," *Sky & Telescope*, October 1990: 346.

Nicholson, Thomas D. "Observatory Hill," *Natural History*, April 1991: 78+.

"100-Inch Mount Wilson Telescope to Reopen," *Astronomy*, January 1988: 86-87.

O'Toole, Thomas. "The Man Who Didn't Walk On the Moon," *The New York Times Magazine*, 17 July 1994: 26+.

Owen, Tobias. "Ice in the Solar System: How the Earth Got its Atmosphere," *Ad Astra*, November/December 1995: 26-29.

Powell, Andrew. "Spaced Out," *Harper's Bazaar*, September 1994: 332-36.

Preston, Richard. "Beacons in Time: Maarten Schmidt and the Discovery of Quasars," *Mercury*, January-February 1988: 2-11.

Recer, Paul. "And It's Colder Than Michigan in March: Hubble Telescope Captures First Surface Images of Remote, Frozen Pluto," *The Ann Arbor News*, 8 March 1996: A6.

"Rendezvous in Space," *Astronomy*, October 1995: 23.

"Report: Insulation Puncture Caused Tether Failure," *The Ann Arbor News*, 5 June 1996: A4.

Ressmeyer, Roger H. "Tradition & Technology at Yerkes Observatory," *Sky & Telescope*, September 1995: 32-34.

Robinson, Cordula. "Magellan Reveals Venus," *Astronomy*, February 1995: 32-41.

Roylance, Frank D. "'Right Stuff' Old Stuff to Him; 'I Love Space': A 29-Year Astronaut, Dr. Storey Musgrave at 61 Will be the Oldest Human to Fly in Space When Columbia Takes Off in November," *The Baltimore Sun*, 26 April 1996: 1A.

Rudich, Joe. "The Electronic Frontier," *Ad Astra*, September/October 1995: 32-36.

Sawyer, Kathy. "Space Fleet Stares Deep Into Sun," *The Washington Post*, 20 May 1996: A3.

Sawyer, Kathy. "'Tadpoles' In Nebula Suggest Presence of Rogue Planets," *The Washington Post*, 20 April 1996: A3.

Shibley, John. "Glow Bands & Curtains," *Astronomy*, April 1995: 76-81.

"Space Flight: Endeavor Is a Symbol of Dreams," *The Ann Arbor News*, 14 January 1996.

Stephens, Sally. "The End of Hubble's Troubles," *Ad Astra*, March/April 1994: 50-52.

Stephens, Sally. "Telescopes that Fly," *Astronomy*, November 1994: 46-53.

Stern, Alan. "Chiron: Interloper From the Kuiper Disk?" *Astronomy*, August 94: 26-33.

Stevens, William K. "One Hundred Nations Move To Save Ozone Shield," *The New York Times*, 10 December 1995: A6.

"Subrahmanyan Chandrasekhar (1910-1995)," *Astronomy*, December 1995: 32.

"Taking the Long View: Hubble Images Shed Light On the Unknown, the Unseen," *Detroit Free Press*, 18 January 1996: F8.

Tyson, Neil de Grasse. "Romancing the Mountaintop," *Natural History*, January 1995: 70-73.

Watson, Traci and William J. Cook. "A New Solar System?" *U.S. News & World Report*, 30 October 1995: 69-72.

Weissman, Paul R. "Comets At the Solar System's Edge," *Sky & Telescope*, January 1993: 26-29.

Wilford, John Noble. "Ear to Universe Is Plugged by

Budget Cutters," *The New York Times,* 7 October
1993: B12.

Wilford, John Noble. "Found: Most of Missing Matter
Lost Around Edges of Universe," *The New York
Times,* 17 January 1996: A1+.

Wilford, John Noble. "Gifts Keep Alive Search for Other
Life In Universe," *The New York Times,* 25 January
1994: C5.

Wilford, John Noble. "Life in Space? Two New Planets
Raise Thoughts," *The New York Times,* 18 January
1996: A1+.

Wohleber, Curt. "The Rocket Man," *Invention & Technology,* Summer 1996: 36-45.

Websites

About La Silla. [Online] Available
http://lw10.ls.eso.org/lasilla/generalinfo/html/
aboutls.html, April 7, 1996.

Allen, Jesse S. The Uhuru Satellite: December 1970-
March 1973. [Online] Available
http://heasarc.gsfc.nasa.gov/docs/heasarc/missions/
uhuru.html, June 5, 1996.

Altschuler, Daniel. General Information on Arecibo Observatory. [Online] Available http://www.naic.edu/,
April 4, 1996.

Arnett, Bill. Pluto. [Online} Available http://seds.lpl.arizona.edu/billa/tnp/pluto.html, March 14, 1996.

Astronaut Alan B. Shepard, Jr. News & Photo Archives,
NASA Ames Public Affairs Home Page. [Online]
Available http://ccf.arc.nasa.gov/dx/basket/storiesetc/Shepa.html, May 9, 1996.

Bartlett, Don. A Practical Guide to GPS. [Online] Available
http://www.fys.uio.no/~kjetikj/fjellet/GPS1.html,
June 25, 1996.

Beatty, J. Kelly. Life from Ancient Mars? *Sky & Telescope's Weekly News Bulletin: Special Edition.* [Online] Available
http://www.skypub.com/news/marslife.html, August
8, 1996.

Behr, Bradford. Big Bear Solar Observatory. [Online]
Available
http://astro.caltech.edu.observatories/bbso/bluebook.html, July 26, 1996.

Behr, Bradford. Palomar Observatory. [Online] Available
http://astro.caltech.edu.observatories/palomar/, May
27, 1996.

Bell, Edwin V. Cassini. [Online] Available
http://nssdc.gsfc.nasa.gov/planetary/cassini.html,
March 18, 1996.

Bell, Edwin V. Pluto Express. *NSSDC Master Catalog
Display Spacecraft.* [Online] Available
http://nssdc.gsfc.nasa.gov/cgi-bin/database/www-
nmc?PFF, July 22, 1996.

Biography of Dr. Buzz Aldrin. [Online] Available
http://www.nss.org/askastro/biography.html, April 3,
1996.

Capt. Charles 'Pete' Conrad, Jr. (Ret.). [Online] Available
http://www.nauts.com/astro/conrad/conrad.html,
May 8, 1996.

Columbia Lands in Florida. [Online] Available http://shuttle.nasa.gov/sts-75, May 8, 1996.

Dettling, J. Ray. Beyond Hubble. [Online] Available
http://ori.careerexpo.com/pub/docs/hubble.html, July
22, 1996.

Donahue, Bob. Mount Wilson Observatory. [Online]
Available http://www.mtwilson.edu/, April 7, 1996.

Double Nucleus of the Andromeda Galaxy M31. [Online]
Available
http://galaxy.einet.net/images/galaxy/m31c.html,
May 1, 1996.

Dr. Buzz Aldrin. *The National Space Society and the
Space, Planetary, and Astronomical Cyber-Experience Present...Ask An Astronaut.* [Online] Available
http://www.nss.org/askastro/#question, April 3,
1996.

Duarte, Luis Sánchez. SOHO-Solar and Heliospheric Observatory Home Page. [Online] Available http://sohowww.nascom.nasa.gov/, July 17, 1996.

Dumoulin, Jim. Space Shuttle Orbiter Atlantis. [Online]
Available http://www.ksc.nasa.gov/shuttle/resources/orbiters/atlantis.html, April 6, 1996.

Dumoulin, Jim. Space Shuttle Orbiter Challenger. [Online] Available http://www.ksc.nasa.gov/shuttle/resources/orbiters/challenger.html, April 6, 1996.

Dumoulin, Jim. Space Shuttle Orbiter Columbia. [Online]
Available http://www.ksc.nasa.gov/shuttle/resources/orbiters/columbia.html, April 6, 1996.

Dumoulin, Jim. Space Shuttle Orbiter Discovery. [Online]
Available http://www.ksc.nasa.gov/shuttle/resources/orbiters/discovery.html, April 6, 1996.

Dumoulin, Jim. Space Shuttle Orbiter Endeavour. [Online] Available http://www.ksc.nasa.gov/shuttle/resources/orbiters/endeavour.html, April 6, 1996.

Educator's Guide to Convection. [Online] Available
http://bang.lanl.gov/solarsys/edu/convect.html, April
22, 1996.

Educator's Guide to Eclipses. [Online] Available
http://bang.lanl.gov/solarsys/edu/eclipses.html, April
22, 1996.

Frommert, Hartmut. M31: The Andromeda Galaxy. [Online] Available http://ftp.seds.org/messier/m/m031.html, April 30, 1996.

George Ellery Hale. *The Bruce Medalists-Brief Biographies.* [Online] Available http://yorty.sonoma.edu/people/faculty/tenn/BM2H-L.html#13, June 5, 1996.

Goldstein, Bruce E. Welcome to the Ulysses Mission Home Page! [Online] Available http://ulysses.jpl.nasa.gov/ULSHOME.html, May 30, 1996.

Grote Reber. *The Bruce Medalists-Brief Biographies.* [Online] Available http://yorty.sonoma.edu/people/faculty/tenn/BM2Q-R.html#55, June 5, 1996.

Haizen's Astrology FAQ. [Online] Available http://www.sedona.net/nen/haizen/faq.html, April 12, 1996.

Hamilton, Calvin J. Chronology of Space Exploration. [Online] Available http://bang.lanl.gov/solarsys/craft2.html, April 22, 1996.

Hamilton, Calvin J. Magellan Mission to Venus. [Online] Available http://bang.lanl.gov/solarsys/magellan.html, April 22, 1996.

Hamilton, Calvin J. Neptune. [Online] Available http://bang.lanl.gov/solarsys/neptune.html, July 11, 1996.

Hamilton, Calvin J. Saturn. [Online] Available http://bang.lanl.gov/solarsys/saturn.htm#stats, March 26, 1996.

Hamilton, Calvin J. Sun. [Online] Available http://bang.lanl.gov/solarsys/sun.html, April 22, 1996.

Hamilton, Calvin J. Uranus. [Online] Available http://bang.lanl.gov/solarsys/uranus.html, April 22, 1996.

Hamilton, Calvin J. Venus Introduction. [Online] Available http://bang.lanl.gov/solarsys/venus.html, April 22, 1996.

Hamilton, Calvin J. Venusian Impact Craters.[Online] Available http://bang.lanl.gov/solarsys/vencrate.html, April 22, 1996.

Hamilton, Calvin J. Venusian Volcanic Features. [Online] Available http://bang.lanl.gov/solarsys/venvolc.html, April 22, 1996.

Hamilton, Calvin J. Voyager Uranus Science Summary: December 21, 1988. [Online] Available http://bang.lanl.gov/solarsys/vgrur.html, April 22, 1996.

Harris, Pete. Star Facts: The Andromeda Galaxy—The Most Distant Thing Human Eyes Can See. [Online] Available http://ccnet4.ccnet.com/odyssey/sfa995.html, April 30, 1996.

Harvard-Smithsonian Center for Astrophysics (CfA). [Online] Available http://sao~www.harvard.edu/hco~home.html, July 17, 1996.

Hathaway, David H. Skylab. [Online] Available http://ally.ios.com/~skylab19/skylab19.html, March 22, 1996.

Hill, Frank. The National Solar Observatory at Kitt Peak. [Online] Available http://www.nso.noao.edu/nsokp/nsokp.html, July 17, 1996.

Hoffman, Kay. Shuttle/Mir. [Online] Available http://shuttle-mir.nass.gov/, May 8, 1996.

The Infrared Space Observatory (ISO). [Online] Available http://isowww.estec.esa.nl/ISO/ISO.html, March 27, 1996.

Intelsat. [Online] Available http://www.intelsat.int:8080/info/html/intelsat.html, May 21, 1996.

International Space Station: Frequently Asked Questions. [Online] Available http://issa-www.jsc.nasa.gov/ss/sshpt.html, March 28, 1996.

International Ultraviolet Explorer Satellite. [Online] Available http://inewwww.gsfc.nasa.gov/iue/iue_homepage.html, March 27, 1996.

Introduction to SOHO. [Online] Available http://vulcan.sp.ph.ic.ac.uk/SOHO/soho/html, July 22, 1996.

Irving, Don. Mt. Hamilton and Lick Observatory. *XPLORE Tours*. [Online] Available http://www.ucol-ick.org/, June 5, 1996.

James Clerk Maxwell. [Online] Available http://www~groups.dcs.st~and.ac.uk/~history/Mathematicians/, June 5, 1996.

Jenkins, Dawn. Maya Astronomy Page. [Online] Available http://www.astro.uv.nl/michielb/maya/astro.html, July 25, 1996.

Johannesson, Anders. Big Bear Solar Observatory www page. [Online] Available http://sundog.caltech.edu/, July 26, 1996.

JPL Space Very Long Baseline Interferometry Project. [Online] Available http://sgra.jpl.nasa.gov/mosaic_v0.0/svlbi.html, June 3, 1996.

Judith Resnik. *STS 51-L (Challenger) Crew Biography.* [Online] Available http://flight.osc.on.ca/documentation/judy.html, May 9, 1996.

Judith A. Resnik: Biography. *The Challenger Accident: January 28, 1986.* [Online] Available http://www.dartmouth.edu/~wsk/challenger/resnik.html, May 9, 1996.

King, J. H. Pioneer 10. *NSSDC Master Catalog Display Spacecraft.* [Online] Available http:nssdc.gsfc.nasa.gov/cgi-bin/database/www-nmc?72-012A, June 18, 1996.

King, J. H. Pioneer 11. *NSSDC Master Catalog Display Spacecraft.* [Online] Available http:nssdc.gsfc.nasa.gov/cgi-bin/database/www-nmc?73-019A, June 18, 1996.

King, J. H. Voyager Project Information. [Online] Available http:nssdc.gsfc.nasa.gov/planetary/voyager.html, June 18, 1996.

Kitt Peak. [Online] Available http://www.noao.edu/kpno/pubpamph/pub.html, April 7, 1996.

Launius, Roger D. Chronology of Selected Highlights in the First 100 American Spaceflights, 1961-1995. [Online] Available http://www.hq.nasa.gov/office/pao/History/Timeline/100flt.html, April 4, 1996.

Levine, Deborah A. Brief Introduction to IRAS. [Online] Available http://www.gsfc.nasa.gov/astro/iras/iras_home.html, March 27, 1996.

Liebacher, John. Global Oscillation Network Group. [Online] Available http://www.gong.noao.edu/, July 17, 1996.

Lyndon B. Johnson Space Center. Biographical Data: Shannon W. Lucid. [Online] Available http://www.jsc.nasa.gov/Bios/htmlbios/lucid.html, May 9, 1996.

Maarten Schmidt. *The Bruce Medalists-Brief Biographies.* [Online] Available http://yorty.sonoma.edu/people/faculty/tenn/BM2S.html#85, June 5, 1996.

MacRobert, Alan. When, Where, and How to See Comet Hyakutake. [Online] Available http://www.skypub.com, March 23, 1996.

Malin, David. General Information About the AAO. [Online] Available http://www.aao.gov.au/general.html, April 4, 1996.

Mariner Space Probes. [Online] Available http://www.hq.nasa.gov/office/pao/History/mariner.html, May 30, 1996.

Mars 96. [Online] Available http://www.iki.rssi.ru/mars96/mars96hp.html, July 2, 1996.

Mauna Kea Observatories. [Online] Available http://www.ifa.hawaii.edu/mko/mko.html, April 7, 1996.

McClaughlin, Siobhan. Anglo-Australian Observatory. [Online] Available http://www.aao.gov.au/aaohome-page.html, April 4, 1996.

McCurdy, Andrea and Mark Stokes. Jim Lovell: An Astronaut's Story. [Online] Available http://www.mcn.org/Apollo 13/Home.html, May 9, 1996.

McDonald Observatory Visitors Center Home Page. [Online] Available http://vulcan.as.utexas.edu//vc/vc_home.html, June 5, 1996.

McDonnell Douglas Spacelab Homepage. [Online] Available http://hvsun21.mdc.com:8000/~mosaic/main.html, July 15, 1996.

Napier, Beth. Activity: Precession of the Equinoxes. [Online] Available http://cea-ftp.cea.berkeley.edu/Education/beth/precess.html, April 12, 1996.

NASA Headquarters. International Space Station. [Online] Available http://www.dfrc.nasa.gov/PAIS/HQ/HTML/FS-004-HQ.html, May 8, 1996.

NASA Headquarters. An Overview of NASA. [Online] Available http://www.dfrc.nasa.gov/PAIS/HQ/HTML/FS-001-HQ.html, May 8, 1996.

National Solar Observatory. [Online] Available http://argo.tuc.noao.edu/, March 22, 1996.

Naumann, Michael. ESO Telescopes, Instrumentation & Detectors. [Online] Available http://www.hq.eso.org/telescopes-instruments.html, April 7, 1996.

Nemiroff, Robert and Jerry Bonnell. Astronomy Picture of the Day. M31: The Andromeda Galaxy. [Online] Available http://antwrp.gsfc.nasa.gov/apod/ap950724.html, May 1, 1996.

Neufeld, Christopher. The Physics of Solar Sailing. [Online] Available http://caliban.physics.utoronto.ca/neufeld/sailing.txt, March 21, 1996.

Pluto Express Home Page. [Online] Available http://www.jpl.nasa.gov/pluto/, July 22, 1996.

Project Mercury. [Online] Available http://www.osf.hq.nasa.gov/mercury/, May 8, 1996.

Rapp, Michael. Dr. Carl Sagan Honorary Page. [Online] Available http://wwwvms.utexas.edu/~mrapp/sagan/sagan.html, March 18, 1996.

Reflection. [Online] Available http://covis.atmos.uiuc.edu/guide/optics/html/reflection.html, June 14, 1996.

Refraction. [Online] Available http://covis.atmos.uiuc.edu/guide/optics/html/refraction.html, June 14, 1996.

Rudd, Richard. Voyager Project Home Page. [Online] Available http://vraptor.jpl.nasa.gov/voyager/voyager.html, July 2, 1996.

Sally Kristen Ride. Juanita Kreps Award. [Online] Available http:www.jcpenney.com/nrelease/jkreps/content/sride.html, May 9, 1996.

Sargent, Wallace W. Caltech Astronomy: Keck Observatory. [Online] Available http://astro.caltech.edu/observatories/keck/bluebook.html, April 7, 1996.

Satellite Tracking of Threatened Species. [Online] Available http://sdcd.gsfc.nasa.gov/ISTO/satellite_tracking/satelliteDRO.html, June 25, 1996.

Search for Extraterrestrial Radio Emissions from Nearby Developed Intelligent Populations (SERENDIP). [Online] Available http://albert.ssl.berkeley.edu/serendip/, April 12, 1996.

Simmons, Michael. The History of Mount Wilson Observatory. [Online] Available http:www.mtwilson.edu/history/history.html, June 5, 1996.

Simon Newcomb. *The Bruce Medalists-Brief Biographies*. [Online] Available http://yorty.sonoma.edu/people/faculty/tenn/BM2MN.html#1, June 5, 1996.

Smith, Woody. The Flights of Project Gemini. [Online] Available http://www.osf.hq.nasa.gov/gemini/, May 8, 1996.

Smith, Woody. STS-71 Press Kit: The Space Station Mir. [Online] Available http://www.osf.hq.nasa.gov/shuttle/sts71/mir.html, May 8, 1996.

Smithsonian Astrophysical Observatory. [Online] Available http://cfa~www.harvard.edu/sao~home.html, May 27, 1996.

SOHO Ultraviolet Coronograph Spectrometer-UVCS. [Online] Available http://sao~www.harvard.edu/uvcs/, July 17, 1996.

SOHO-CDS at Imperial College. [Online] Available http://www.sp.ph.ic.ac.uk/SOHO/, July 22, 1996.

Solar and Heliospheric Observatory (SOHO). [Online] Available http://www.hq.nasa.gov/office/oss/enterprise/II/ii-soh82.html, July 22, 1996.

Space Shuttle Launches. [Online] Available http://www.ksc.nasa.gov/shuttle/missions/missions.html, July 15, 1996).

Space Telescopes. [Online] Available http://meteor.anu.edu.au/anton/astro_space.html, March 27, 1996.

Spacecraft: SOHO Brief Description. [Online] Available http://www~istp.gsfc.nasa.gov/ISTP/soho.html, July 22, 1996.

Spacelab. [Online] Available http://www.ksc.nasa.gov/shuttle/technology/sts-newsref/spacelab.html, July 15, 1996.

Spend an Out-of-this-World Evening at McDonald Observatory. [Online] Available http://numedia.tddc.net/hot/bigbend/mdo, June 5, 1996.

Stanton, Ed. Six Reasons Why America Needs the Space Station. [Online] Available http://issa-www.jsc.nasa.gov/ss/prgview/prgview.html, March 28, 1996.

STS-75 Payloads: TSS-1R, USMP-3 & MGBX. [Online] Available http://liftoff.msfc.nasa.gov/sts-75/welcome.html, May 8, 1996.

Tethered Satellite System (TSS-1R). [Online] Available http://liftoff.msfc.nasa.gov/sts-75/tss-1r/tss-1r.html, May 8, 1996.

Tribute to Carl Sagan. [Online] Available http://wea.mankato.mn.us:80/tps/sagan.html, March 18, 1996.

Urbain Jean Joseph Le Verrier. [Online] Available http://www~groups.dcs.st~and.ac.uk/~history/Mathematicians/, June 5, 1996.

Weisstein, Eric. Janksy, Karl (1905-1950). *Eric's Home Page.* [Online] Available http://www.gps.caltech.edu/~eww/bios/jnode2.html#SECTIONO, June 5, 1996.

Welcome to CTIO! [Online] Available http://www.ctio.noao.edu/ctio.html#visitors, April 7, 1996.

Welcome to Lowell Observatory.[Online] Available http://www.lowell.edu/, May 27, 1996.

Welcome to the Yerkes Observatory Virtual Tour! [Online] Available http://astro.uchicago.edu/vtour/, June 5, 1996.

What is the VLA? [Online] Available
http://www.nrao.edu/doc/vla/html/VLAintro.html,
June 5, 1996.

Wirth, Fred. Pioneer Project Home Page. [Online] Available
http://pyroeis.arc.nasa.gov/pioneer/PNhome.html,
July 2, 1996.

Wyoming Infrared Observatory. [Online] Available
http://faraday.uwyo.edu/physics.astronomy/
brochures/wiro.html, July 17, 1996.

Yerkes Observatory, University of Chicago. [Online]
Available http://astro.uchicago.edu/Yerkes.html,
June 5, 1996.

Index

Italic type indicates volume numbers;
boldface type indicates entries and their page numbers;
(ill.) indicates illustrations.

A

Aberration of light *1:* 70; *3:* 514, 612
Absolute magnitude *1:* 86, 219; *2:* 318; *3:* 631
Absolute zero *1:* 192; *2:* 267, 439; *3:* 494
Absorption lines *2:* 298; *3:* 610
Accretion *2:* 448
Achromatic lens *2:* 432
Adams, John Couch *1:* **1-2,** 1 (ill.), 119-20; *2:* 325, 407, 444
Adaptive optics *1:* 204; *2:* 250, 393, 401
Adel, Arthur *2:* 335
Adenosine triphosphate (ATP) *3:* 522
Adilade *1:* 39
"Adoration of the Magi" *1:* 183
Advanced X-ray Astrophysics Facility *1:* **2-4,** 3 (ill.); *3:* 591, 696
Aerobee rocket *3:* 662, 695, 697
Aerodrome *2:* 309
Agassiz station *1:* 212
Agena rocket *1:* 35, 107, 180; *2:* 400
Agrippa, Marcus Vipsanius *1:* 207
Airy, George *1:* 2
Akiyama, Toyohiro *2:* 383
Al-Sufi *1:* 19
Albrecht, Andreas *2:* 268
Aldrin, Buzz *1:* **4-7,** 5 (ill.), 23, 35, 182; *2:* 302, 330, 345, 391; *3:* 582, 596
Alexander the Great *1:* 32-33
Alfvén, Hannes Olof Göst *2:* 450-52
ALH 84001 *2:* 356
Almagest *2:* 459
Alnilan *1:* 11
American Academy of Arts and Sciences *2:* 385
American Astronomical Society *3:* 536
American Ephemeris *2:* 414-15

American Ephemeris and Nautical Almanac *2:* 386
Ames, Joseph *2:* 399
Ames Research Center (ARC) *2:* 399
Ampere, André *1:* 29
Analytical Mechanics *2:* 308
Anaxagoras *1:* 12
Anaximander *1:* 12
Ancient Chinese astronomy *1:* **7-9**
Ancient Egyptian astronomy *1:* **9-11**
Ancient Greek astronomy *1:* **11-14**
Ancient Mayan astronomy *1:* **16-17**
Anderson, Carl *1:* 22
Andromeda galaxy *1:* **17-20,** 18 (ill.), 49, 168-69; *2:* 254, 256, 312, 373, 382, 404, 436; *3:* 504, 551, 614, 704
Anglo-Australian Observatory *1:* **20-21**
Anglo-Australian Telescope (AAT) *1:* 20-21
Anti-matter *1:* **21-22,** 106; *2:* 268
Apache Point Observatory *3:* 701
Apogee *2:* 324
Apollo objects *1:* 38
Apollo program *1:* 7, **22-24,** 35, 100, 107, 161-62, 179, 182; *2:* 343, 369, 372, 399; *3:* 532, 534, 548, 565, 582, 589, 596, 600, 604-05, 689
***Apollo-Soyuz* Test Project** *1:* **24-25,** 24 (ill.); *2:* 324, 370; *3:* 578, 583, 634
Apollo Telescope Mount *3:* 548, 587
Apollo 1 *1:* 23; *3:* 682, 689
Apollo 7 *1:* 23; *2:* 345
Apollo 8 *1:* 6, 23, 76; *2:* 331, 345; *3:* 512, 532
Apollo 9 *1:* 23
Apollo 10 *1:* 23; *3:* 592
Apollo 11 *1:* 6, 23, 35, 182; *2:* 353, 391, 426; *3:* 532, 582, 595 (ill.), 596, 605
Apollo 12 *1:* 108; *2:* 345

Apollo 13 *1:* 23, **25-28,** 27 (ill.), 182; *2:* 329, 331, 345
Apollo 14 *2:* 331, 345; *3:* 544-45
Apollo 15 *2:* 345, 347
Apollo 16 *2:* 345, 347
Apollo 17 *1:* 24; *2:* 345, 347; *3:* 583
Apollo 18 *1:* 6, 27; *2:* 324; *3:* 583
Apparent solar time *3:* 642
Arabsat *2:* 337
Arachnoids *3:* 673
Arago, Dominique-Francois-Jean *1:* **28-29,** 28 (ill.)
Arecibo Observatory *1:* **29-31,** 30 (ill.), 130; *3:* 494, 498, 675
Argos *2:* 403
Ariane rocket *1:* 154 (ill.), 155, 183; *2:* 247, 316
Ariel *1:* 51; *3:* 656
Aristarchus *1:* 14, 112, 118; *2:* 445
Aristotle *1:* 13, **32-33,** 32 (ill.), 71, 98, 131, 171, 193; *2:* 260
Armagh Observatory *1:* 50
Armillary sphere *1:* 72
Armstrong, Neil *1:* 6, 23, **33-36,** 34 (ill.), 180, 184; *2:* 302, 331, 345, 391; *3:* 582, 596
Artsimovich, Lee *2:* 450
Association for the Advancement of Women *2:* 385
Association of Universities for Research in Astronomy (AURA) *2:* 299, 400
Asteroid belt *2:* 443
Asteroid Gaspra *1:* 37 (ill.)
Asteroids *1:* **36-39,** 99, 119, 174, 204, 211-12, 218; *2:* 271, 300, 308, 335, 356, 374, 376, 389, 406-07, 414, 427, 437, 443, 454; *3:* 506, 562, 565-66, 602, 646-47, 656, 659
Astrolabe *1:* **39-40,** 39 (ill.), 72; *2:* 265, 402
Astrology *1:* 14, **40-42,** 71; *2:* 294, 460

Astrometric binary star *1:* 53, 63; *3:* 623

Astrometry *3:* 658

Astronomer Royal *1:* 69, 207, 216

Astronomical Almanac 3: 659

Astronomical Society of the Pacific *3:* 536

Astronomical unit (AU) *1:* 85; *2:* 305

Astronomy 3: 557

Astronomy websites *1:* 15

Astrophysical Journal 3: 501

Astrophysics *1:* 94, 200

AT&T *1:* 104

Attila the Hun *1:* 98

Atlantis 1: **42-44,** 43 (ill.), 90, 96, 106, 127, 149, 172, 176; *2:* 336-37, 349, 385, 395; *3:* 580, 586, 591, 607, 636

Atlas rocket *2:* 316, 369

Atmospheric Compensation Experiment *2:* 394

Atomic bomb *1:* 55, 145

Aurora australis *1:* 44, 117

Aurora borealis *1:* 44, 45 (ill.), 117

Aurorae *1:* 9, **44-45;** *3:* 573, 630, 638, 662

Autumnal equinox *1:* 152

B

Baade, Walter *1:* 19, **47-50,** 48 (ill.); *2:* 256, 421, 436; *3:* 704

Ballistic missile. *See* Intercontinental ballistic missile (ICBM)

Barnard, Edward E. *3:* 701

Barnard Observatory *3:* 539

Barred spiral galaxy *1:* 168; *3:* 615

Barringer meteor crater *2:* 375 (ill.)

Bassett, Charles A. *1:* 180

Baum, L. Frank *1:* 129

Bean, Alan *1:* 108

Bell Burnell, Jocelyn *1:* 47, **50-52,** 192; *2:* 244-45, 412, 461; *3:* 494, 520

Bell Telephone Laboratories *1:* 104

Belyayev, Pavel *2:* 323; *3:* 680

Bennett, David *1:* 124

Benzenberg, Johann *2:* 376

Beregovoy, Georgi *3:* 576

Berlin Observatory *1:* 2; *2:* 325

Bessel, Friedrich *1:* **52-53,** 52 (ill.), 62, 70; *2:* 428

Bethe, Hans *1:* **53-56,** 54 (ill.), 140

Big bang theory *1:* 31, **56-59,** 57 (ill.), 61, 113, 117, 120, 176-77, 191-92; *2:* 250, 256, 262, 267, 320, 410, 438-39, 449, 451-52; *3:* 489, 494, 498, 515, 546, 619

Big Bear Solar Observatory *1:* **59-60;** *2:* 402

Big bore theory *1:* 60

Big crunch theory *1:* **60-61,** 125

Big dipper *1:* 159; *2:* 445; *3:* 570

Billion-channel Extra-Terrestrial Assay *1:* 159

Binary star *1:* **62-63,** 66; *2:* 328, 387, 419; *3:* 541, 621-22, 651, 676, 694, 696

Binary star system *1:* 62 (ill.)

Biot, Jean-Baptiste *2:* 376

Black dwarf star *1:* 61, 123; *2:* 394, 398-400; *3:* 506, 513, 532, 580, 586, 593, 596-97, 599, 605, 636-38, 653, 691, 705

Black hole *1:* 3, 18, 22, 61, **63-66,** 64 (ill.), 93, 106, 123, 140, 167, 169, 175-76, 195, 214, 220; *2:* 274, 311, 314, 328, 380, 411, 417, 420-21; *3:* 488, 503, 589, 614, 622, 631, 651, 676, 691, 695, 697, 701, 705

Bloch, Felix *2:* 463

Blue-shift *3:* 504, 552

Bluford, Guion *1:* **66-68,** 90

Bode, Johann Elert *1:* 37, **68-69,** 68 (ill.), 111

Bode's Law *1:* 37, 68-69

Bohr, Neils *1:* 176

Bolometer *1:* 147; *2:* 309

Bolshevik Revolution *3:* 648

Bonaparte, Napoleon *2:* 308

Bondi, Hermann *1:* 121; *2:* 250

Bondone, Giotto Ambrogio di *1:* 183

Borman, Frank *3:* 545

The Boston Herald 1: 188

Bradley, James *1:* **69-70,** 69 (ill.); *3:* 514, 612

Brahe, Tycho *1:* **70-73,** 71 (ill.), 85, 119; *2:* 294, 390, 420, 446; *3:* 553

Brand, Vance *1:* 27

Brandes, Heinrich *2:* 376

Braun, Wernher von *1:* **73-76,** 74 (ill.), 156; *2:* 425; *3:* 513, 532, 665

Brezhnev, Leonid *1:* 27; *2:* 323

A Brief History of Time 1: 215

Brown dwarfs *1:* 61, **76-77,** 77 (ill.), 123; *2:* 300, 406-07; *3:* 624, 659, 705

Brownian movement *1:* 143

Brunhes, Bernard *1:* 138

Bunsen, Robert *2:* 297

Bureau of Longitudes *1:* 28

Burke, Bernard *3:* 494

Burney, Venetia *3:* 646

Burrell-Schmidt telescope *2:* 299

Butler, Paul *1:* 159; *2:* 445; *3:* 569

Bykovsky, Valery *3:* 635

C

C. Donald Shane Telescope *2:* 328

C-141 Starlifter *2:* 302

Caesar, Julius *1:* 79, 98

Calendar *1:* 8, 10-11, 14, **79-81,** 80 (ill.); *2:* 453, 459; *3:* 514, 625

Calendar of Works and Days, 1281 1: 9

Callipus *1:* 13

Caloris Basin *2:* 368

CalTech Submillimeter Observatory *2:* 362

Cambridge Observatory *1:* 2, 140; *2:* 325; *3:* 517

Cannon, Annie Jump *1:* **81-83,** 82 (ill.)

Cape Canaveral *1:* 24; *2:* 293, 337, 398; *3:* 505

Capture trajectory *3:* 604

Carnegie, Andrew *1:* 200; *3:* 516

Carnegie Institution *1:* 152; *2:* 391, 437; *3:* 515-16, 661

Carpenter, Scott *2:* 369, 371

Carter, Jimmy *3:* 658, 686

Cassini, Gian Domenico *1:* **83-85,** 84 (ill.); *3:* 513, 530

Cassini 3: 531, 581

Cassini Division *1:* 85; *3:* 530

Catherine Wolfe Bruce Medal *3:* 536

Cavendish, Henry *1:* 193

Cavendish Laboratory *1:* 54

Celestial mechanics *2:* 319

Celestial Mechanics 2: 311, 413

Celestial Police *1:* 69

Celestial sphere *1:* 42, 108

Centaur rocket *1:* 174; *2:* 317, 400; *3:* 510 (ill.)

Centaurus A *2:* 449

Cepheid variables *1:* 19, 49, **85-87,** 220; *2:* 248, 254, 318, 404, 436; *3:* 541-42, 618, 632, 666

Ceres *1:* 36-37, 119, 178; *2:* 427; *3:* 566

Cernan, Eugene *1:* 182

Cerro Tololo Interamerican Observatory *1:* **87-89,** 88 (ill.), 130, 152; *2:* 298, 313, 400, 402

Cesarsky, Catherine *2:* 274

CGRO. *See* Compton Gamma Ray Observatory

Chaffee, Roger *1:* 23; *3:* 596, 689

Challenger 1: 36, 44, 66, **90-92,** 91 (ill.), 94, 96, 114, 125, 127, 134, 149, 161-63, 173; *2:* 257, 316, 395; *3:* 505-07, 513, 585 (ill.), 586, 592, 653, 685

Chandrasekhar, Subrahmanyan *1:* **92-94,** 93 (ill.), 140; *2:* 417, 421; *3:* 701

Chandrasekhar's limit *1:* 93; *2:* 421

Chang-Diaz, Franklin *1:* 96

Charged coupling device (CCD) *1:* 20; *2:* 440

Charon *2:* 305, 388, 456-57; *3:* 659

Chiron *1:* 38

Chladni, E. F. F. *2:* 375

Christian constellations *1:* 111

Christian IV *1:* 73

Christy, James *3:* 659

Chromatic aberration *2:* 432

Chromosphere *2:* 394; *3:* 555-56

Chronometer *2:* 402

Goddard, Robert *1:* 6, **188-91,** 189 (ill.); *2:* 423; *3:* 511

Goddard Space Flight Center (GSFC) *2:* 280, 399; *3:* 554

Gold, Thomas *1:* 51, 121, **191-93,** 191 (ill.); *2:* 245, 250, 412, 461; *3:* 619

Goldin, Daniel *1:* 160; *2:* 357

Gordon, Richard *1:* 107

Goryacheva, Valentina Ivanovna *1:* 167

Göttingen Observatory *1:* 178

Grand Unified Theory *1:* 215

Grant, Ulysses S. *2:* 377

Granules *1:* 561, *3:* 627

Gravity *1:* 56, 61-62, 107, 120, 131, 139-40, 142, 145, 172, 182, **193-95,** 206, 208, 214-15; *2:* 320, 340, 412, 418; *3:* 546, 598, 600, 602, 609, 622, 631, 639, 666, 690

Gravity assist *1:* 172; *3:* 604

Grazing incidence telescope *2:* 246

Great Debate *3:* 542

Great Galaxy *1:* 19

Great Mathematical Compilation *1:* 12; *2:* 459

Great Pyramid *1:* 10-11

The Greatest *2:* 459

Green Bank Telescope *3:* 675

Greenhouse effect *1:* **195-97,** 196 (ill.); *3:* 673

Greenstein, Jesse *3:* 536

Greenwich Observatory *1:* 207

Gregorian calendar *1:* 81; *3:* 514

Gregory X *3:* *1:* 80

Grimaldi, Francesco *1:* 83, **197-98**

Grissom, Virgil "Gus" *1:* 23, 76, 179; *2:* 369; *3:* 594, 596, 689

Group for the Study of Jet Propulsion (GIRD) *2:* 300

Gurman, Joseph *3:* 555

Guth, Alan *1:* 58; *2:* 267-68

Gyroscope *1:* 164; *2:* 259

H

H-K Project *2:* 394

Haise, Fred *1:* 24

Hale, George *1:* **199-203;** *2:* 249-50, 253, 261, 391, 435; *3:* 571, 700

Hale Observatories *3:* 527, 534, 536

Hale Telescope *1:* 202 (ill.), **203-04;** *2:* 250, 256, 314, 435, 436 (ill.); *3:* 488, 535

Hall, Asaph *3:* 657

Halley, Edmond *1:* 98, **204-07,** 205 (ill.), 208; *2:* 296, 307, 375, 417-18

Halley's comet *1:* 52, 96-97, 99, 155, 182, 184, **207-09,** 208 (ill.), 210; *2:* 304, 306, 372, 428; *3:* 564, 667-68, 694

Halo *1:* 18, 168; *2:* 381; *3:* 614

Halo orbit *3:* 554

Hard X-rays *1:* 3; *3:* 695, 697

Hariot, Thomas. *See* Harriot, Thomas

Harlan Smith Telescope *2:* 366

Harper, William Rainey *1:* 200; *3:* 701

Harriot, Thomas *1:* **209-10**

Harvard College Observatory *1:* 81, 199; *2:* 318, 414; *3:* 542-43, 687

Harvard-Smithsonian Center for Astrophysics *1:* **210-13;** *3:* 687

Hawking, Stephen *1:* 65, **213-15,** 213 (ill.)

Hawking radiation *1:* 65, 214

HEAO-1 *2:* 246

HEAO-3 *2:* 246

Heavenly Spheres *1:* 112

Helen B. Warner Prize *3:* 536

Heliacal rising *1:* 17

Heliocentric model *1:* 72, 112, 118, 131, 138, 172; *2:* 445; *3:* 567

Helios 1 *3:* 629

Helios 2 *3:* 629

Helioseismograph *1:* 60

Heliosphere *3:* 553

Heliostat *2:* 401; *3:* 571-72

Heliotrope *1:* 178

Hellas *2:* 355

Henry, Joseph *2:* 413

Henry Draper Catalogue of Stars *1:* 82

Heraclitus *1:* 12

Hercules *1:* 111

Hermes *1:* 38

Hero of Alexandria *3:* 509

Herschel, Caroline *1:* **215-16,** 215 (ill.)

Herschel, John *1:* 2, 62, 216

Herschel, William *1:* 1, 37, 62, 119, 215, **216-18,** 217 (ill.); *2:* 444; *3:* 654, 656

Hertz, Rudolf Heinrich *1:* 147

Hertzsprung, Ejnar *1:* **218-20;** *3:* 518

Hertzsprung-Russell diagram *1:* 219 (ill.), 220; *3:* 518, 631

Hess, Victor *1:* 115; *2:* **243,** 243 (ill.)

Hevelius, Johannes *1:* 98, 208; *2:* 390

Hewish, Antony *1:* 47, 50, 192; *2:* **244-45,** 244 (ill.), 412, 461; *3:* 494, 520

High Energy Astrophysical Observatories *2:* 4, 106; *2:* **246;** *3:* 590, 696

High Precision Parallax Collecting Satellite *2:* 247

Hipparchus *1:* 13, 14; *2:* 247, 459

Hipparcos *2:* 247

Hitler, Adolf *1:* 54, 73, 145; *3:* 543

Hobby-Eberly Telescope (HET) *2:* 364

Hogg, Frank *2:* 248

Hogg, Helen Sawyer *2:* **247;** *3:* 667

Homogeneity *1:* 58; *2:* 268

Hooker, John D. *1:* 201; *2:* 249, 393

Hooker Telescope *1:* 201; *2:* **248-50,** 254, 256, 380, 404, 435

Horoscope *1:* 42

Horowitz, Paul *1:* 160

Hourglass *3:* 642

House Un-American Activities Committee *3:* 543

Hoyle, Fred *2:* **250-53,** 251 (ill.); *3:* 619

Hubble, Edwin *1:* 19, 49, 58, 86, 114, 120, 169, 192; *2:* 249, 252, **253-57,** 255 (ill.), 261, 267, 320, 382, 391, 404, 430; *3:* 504, 526-27, 542, 548, 552, 619

Hubble constant *2:* 259

Hubble Space Telescope *1:* 2, 19, 87, 97, 118, 121, 127, 151, 155, 160, 169; *2:* 256, **257-59,** 258 (ill.), 280, 305, 314, 318, 395, 434, 455; *3:* 531, 589-90, 592

Hubble's Law *2:* 256, 261; *3:* 527

Huggins, William *2:* **259-60,** 260 (ill.)

Humason, Milton *1:* 58; *2:* 254, 256, **261-62;** *3:* 504, 527

Hummel, Mathilde *2:* 424

Huxley, Aldous *2:* 417

Huygens, Christiaan *1:* 83; *2:* **262-64,** 262 (ill.), 364; *3:* 530-31, 553

Huygens *3:* 531, 581

Hyakutake, Yuji *1:* 96

Hyakutake. *See* Comet Hyakutake

Hydrometer *2:* 265

Hydroscope *2:* 265

Hypatia of Alexandria *2:* **264-66,** 265 (ill.)

I

Icarus *3:* 523

Ida *1:* 174

Inertia *1:* 131

Inflationary period *2:* 267

Inflationary theory *1:* 58; *2:* **267-68**

Infrared Astronomical Satellite *2:* **268-71,** 269 (ill.), 273, 305, 449; *3:* 590

Infrared astronomy *1:* 52, 77; *2:* **271-73,** 302, 335; *3:* 494, 518, 605, 692

Infrared galaxy *2:* 268, 363

Infrared radiation *1:* 20; *2:* 270-73, 302, 363, 393, 406, 449; *3:* 487, 491, 518, 539, 652

Infrared Space Observatory *2:* 271, **273-74;** *3:* 590

Infrared Spatial Interferometer *2:* 393

Infrared telescope *2:* 271, 273, 382, 406, 431; *3:* 701

Intelligent Life in Space *1:* 130

Intelsat *1:* 104, 151; *2:* **274-77,** 275 (ill.)

Intensity curve *2:* 440

Intercontinental ballistic missile (ICBM) *2:* 301, 317; *3:* 512

Intercontinental VLBI *3:* 496

Interferential refractometer *2:* 379

Interferometer *1:* 160; *2:* 379, 393

Rockoon technique *3:* 662
Roemer, Olaus *1:* 83; *3:* **513-14,** 514 (ill.), 612
Roosevelt, Franklin D. *1:* 55
ROSAT satellite *1:* 4
Royal Astronomical Society *1:* 2, 216
Royal Irish Academy *1:* 216
Royal Observatory *1:* 21, 51
Royal Radar Establishment *3:* 519
Royal Society of Edinburgh *2:* 364
Royal Society of London *2:* 364
RR Lyrae stars *3:* 666-67
Rubin, Vera *1:* 125; *3:* **515-17**
Rudolph II *1:* 73
The Rudolphine Tables 2: 296
Russell, Henry *1:* 219; *3:* **517-18,** 517 (ill.), 541
Russian Space Agency *2:* 458
Rutherford, Ernest *1:* 176
Ryle, Martin *1:* 51; *2:* 244-45; *3:* 493, **518-20,** 519 (ill.)

S

Sacramento Peak Observatory *2:* 400-01
Sagan, Carl *1:* 130, 159; *2:* 357; *3:* **521-23,** 522 (ill.), 685
Sagittarius *2:* 282, 285; *3:* 500
Salyut program *2:* 324, 340; *3:* **523-26,** 578, 583
Salyut 1 2: 383; *3:* 523, 525, 576, 587
Salyut 2 3: 524
Salyut 3 3: 524
Salyut 4 3: 525
Salyut 5 3: 524
Salyut 6 3: 525, 587
Salyut 7 3: 525, 587
Sandage, Allan *3:* 487, **526-28,** 534
Saturn *1:* 2, 9, 13, 38, 45, 68, 112, 119, 134, 171, 218; *2:* 262, 310, 333, 335, 364, 366, 386, 409, 440, 443, 445; *3:* **528-31,** 529 (ill.), 565, 567-68, 580, 604, 655, 683-85
Saturn I rocket *3:* 532
Saturn IB rocket *3:* 532
Saturn V rocket *1:* 23, 76, 190; *3:* 513, **532-34,** 533 (ill.)
Schiaparelli, Giovanni *2:* 333, 357, 377
Schiller, Julius *1:* 111
Schirra, Walter *2:* 371
Schmidt, Maarten *3:* 488, **534-36**
Schmidt telescope *2:* 433
Scientific American 2: 306
Search for Extraterrestrial Intelligence (SETI) *1:* 158 (ill.), 159-60
Seasat 1: 134
Seasons *3:* **536-38,** 537 (ill.)
See, Elliot M. *1:* 180
Service module *1:* 22
SETI. *See* Search for Extraterrestrial Intelligence (SETI)

Seven Sisters *2:* 453
Sextant *1:* 40
Seyfert, Carl *3:* **539-40**
Seyfert galaxies *3:* 539-40
Shapley, Harlow *1:* 86, 220; *2:* 254; *3:* **540-43,** 540 (ill.)
Sharpe, Mitchell *3:* 636
Shepard, Alan *2:* 331, 370; *3:* **543-46,** 544 (ill.)
Shooting stars *2:* 376
Shuttle Autonomous Research Tool for Astronomy (SPARTAN) *2:* 337
Sidereus Nuncius 1: 171
Sigma 2: 371
Sitter, Willem de *1:* 56, 120; *3:* **546-48,** 547 (ill.)
61 Cygni *1:* 52
Sky & Telescope 3: 705
Skylab space station *1:* 108; *2:* 394, 399; *3:* 534, **548-51,** 549 (ill.), 583-84, 587, 589, 601, 629
Slayton, Donald "Deke" *1:* 27
Slipher, Vesto Melvin *3:* 548, **551-53,** 551 (ill.)
Small Astronomical Satellite 1 *3:* 651
Small Magellanic Cloud (SMC) *1:* 4, 86, 89, 168, 220; *2:* 312, 318; *3:* 542
Smithsonian Astrophysical Observatory (SAO) *3:* 687
Smithsonian Submillimeter Array *2:* 362
Snell, Willebrord *3:* **552-53**
Snell's law *3:* 553
Snow, Helen *1:* 201
Snow Solar Telescope *1:* 201; *2:* 391, 393-94
Society for Space Travel *1:* 73
Society of Jesuits *1:* 197
Soft X-rays *1:* 3; *3:* 695, 697
Sokolov, Andrei *2:* 324
Solar and Heliospheric Observatory *3:* **553-55,** 629
Solar atmosphere *3:* **555-57**
Solar chromosphere *1:* 29
Solar eclipse *1:* 12, 13, 45; *2:* 243, 246, 340, 374; *3:* 556, **557-60,** 559 (ill.), 570
Solar energy transport *3:* **560-62**
Solar flare *1:* 45, 59, 106, 137; *2:* 246; *3:* 550, 556, 571, 573, 588, 627, 629-30
Solar Maximum Mission 3: 592, 629
Solar rotation *3:* **562-63**
Solar sail *3:* **563-65,** 564 (ill.)
Solar system *1:* 9, 13-14, 24, 37, 56, 99, 111, 118-19, 131, 134, 138, 140, 167, 171, 174, 193, 207, 217; *2:* 253, 273, 290, 295, 305-06, 308, 310-11, 334, 342, 354, 366, 368, 376, 381, 397, 399, 406-09, 411, 417, 429-30, 438, 440, 443-45, 448, 454, 456-57, 459; *3:* 488, 494, 513, 527, 535, 551,

553, 557, 562, 564, **565-70,** 567 (ill.), 572, 579, 583, 591, 596, 598, 602, 604, 626, 652, 655, 683, 685
Solar telescope *1:* 199; *2:* 298, 391-92, 394, 400; *3:* 525, **570-72**
Solar wind *1:* 44, 98, 116, 137, 158, 183; *2:* 347, 352, 442, 449, 553; *3:* 557, 566, **572-73,** 627, 629, 654
Solstice *1:* 9, 14, 151; *3:* **573-75,** 625
Sommerfeld, Arnold *1:* 53
Sosigenes *1:* 79
South magnetic pole *1:* 137
South pole *3:* 574
Southern lights *1:* 117; *3:* 573, 630, 638
Soyuz program *1:* 167; *2:* 278; *3:* **575-79,** 605, 679-80
Soyuz T series *3:* 578
Soyuz TM series *3:* 578
Soyuz TM-11 3: 577 (ill.)
Soyuz 1 2: 323; *3:* 575-76
Soyuz 2–9 3: 576
Soyuz 10 3: 524, 576
Soyuz 11 3: 524, 576
Soyuz 12 3: 578
Soyuz 17 3: 578
Soyuz 19 1: 6, 27; *2:* 324; *3:* 578, 583
Space age *2:* 442
Space Infrared Telescope Facility *3:* 591
Space probe *1:* 24, 172; *2:* 301, 354, 368, 390; *3:* **579-81,** 586, 653-54, 673-74
Space race *1:* 26, 179; *2:* 302, 321, 343, 351, 369; *3:* 513, 523, 543, **582-84,** 586, 593, 616, 665, 679, 681
Space shuttle *1:* 6, 24, 42, 66-67, 90, 94, 96, 114, 125, 127, 134, 149, 161, 172-73, 176; *2:* 257-58, 276, 278, 287, 291, 294, 316, 331, 336-37, 349, 384; *3:* 505, 507, 564, 583, **584-86,** 592, 601, 604, 606, 685
Space Shuttle Orbiter *1:* 162
Space sickness *2:* 288; *3:* 682
Space station *1:* 127, 156; *2:* 247, 278, 317, 324, 336, 338, 340, 359, 382, 394, 425; *3:* 511, 523-24, 534, 548, 551, 575-76, 578, 583-84, **586-89,** 591-92, 596, 602, 605, 629
Space telescope *3:* **589-91**
Space-time continuum *1:* 144
Space trash *3:* **591-93**
Spacecraft, piloted *3:* **593-96**
Spacecraft design *3:* **596-99**
Spacecraft equipment *3:* **601-02**
Spacecraft voyage *3:* **602-05**
Spacelab *1:* 67, 90, 96, 155; *2:* 288, 399; *3:* 586, **605-07**
Spacelab 1 *3:* 606
Spacelab 2 *2:* 395; *3:* 606
Spacelab 3 *3:* 606
Spacesuits *1:* 101; *2:* 394; *3:* 598, 601, 605, 680

Spacetime *1:* 117; *3:* **607-09**

Spark gap *1:* 147

SPARTAN. *See* Shuttle Autonomous Research Tool for Astronomy (SPARTAN)

Spatial interferometry *2:* 277

Special theory of relativity *1:* 143; *3:* 608

Specific gravity *2:* 265

Spectrograph *1:* 21, 204; *2:* 328, 335, 401, 436-37; *3:* 610

Spectroheliograph *1:* 199; *3:* 571

Spectroheliometer *3:* 610 (ill.)

Spectrohelioscope *1:* 199; *3:* 571

Spectrometer *1:* 19; *3:* 554

Spectroscope *1:* 63, 199; *2:* 259, 261, 297; *3:* 571, 609, 623

Spectroscopic binary stars *1:* 63; *3:* 623

Spectroscopy *1:* 81, 119; *2:* 259, 297, 365; *3:* **609-11**

Speed of light *1:* 58, 64, 69, 83, 115, 120, 147, 164; *2:* 243, 363, 378, 415; *3:* 504, 513-14, 535, 607, **611-14,** 613 (ill.)

Speed of sound *1:* 161

Spicules *3:* 556

Spiral galaxy *1:* 18, 148-49, 168; *2:* 254, 273, 429; *3:* 516, 539, **614-16,** 615 (ill.)

SPOT (Satellite Pour l'Observation de la Terre) *1:* 155

Spring tides *3:* 640

Sputnik 1 *1:* 76, 104, 156, 187; *2:* 301, 316-17, 343, 440; *3:* 512, 543, 575, 582, 593, **616,** 617 (ill.), 649, 663, 665

Sputnik 2 *1:* 442; *3:* 593

Sputnik 4 *3:* 682

Sputnik 10 *3:* 682

Stafford, Thomas *1:* 27

Star cluster *1:* 106; *2:* 328, 372, 387; *3:* **617-19,** 617 (ill.), 621

Star Trek *3:* 586

Star Trek: The Next Generation *1:* 117

Star Wars *3:* 670

Starburst galaxy *2:* 271

The Starry Messenger *1:* 171

Steady-state theory *1:* 61, 120, 191-92; *2:* 250, 253, 451; *3:* **619-20**

Steinhardt, Paul J. *2:* 268

Stellar evolution *3:* **621-22,** 621 (ill.)

Stellar masses *3:* **622-24**

Stellar nurseries *1:* 21; *2:* 270, 272, 313, 335; *3:* 693

Stellar spectrophotometry *2:* 248

Stern, F. Alan *2:* 306

Stonehenge *3:* **624-26,** 625 (ill.)

Stratosphere *1:* 136; *3:* 662

Stratospheric Observatory for Infrared Astronomy (SOFIA) *2:* 304

Struve, Otto *3:* 501

Subaru-Japan National Large Telescope *2:* 362

Sullivan, Kathryn *3:* 507

Summer solstice *3:* 573-74

Sun *1:* 11-13, 59, 99, 116, 118, 129, 159, 199-200, 204, 218; *2:* 244, 285, 305, 326, 335, 340, 347, 352, 391, 393, 399, 401, 413, 431, 437, 449, 457; *3:* 498-99, 550, 555, 557, 561-62, 565-66, 568, 570-73, 570 (ill.), 588, 602, 612, 622, **626-29,** 628 (ill.), 631, 636, 640, 653, 658, 683, 698

Sundial *1:* 10; *3:* 642

Sun's atmosphere *3:* 627-28

Sunspot *1:* 8, 45, 59, 171, 210; *2:* 373, 392; *3:* 556, 562, 571, 573, 627, **629-31,** 630 (ill.)

Supercluster *1:* 168; *2:* 382

Supergiant *1:* 85, 169, 220; *2:* 248, 254; *3:* 541, **631-32,** 666

Supernova *1:* 47, 65, 71, 106, 116, 124, 176, 192, 211; *2:* 243, 245-46, 280, 295, 313, 404-05, 411-12, 419-20, 436, 448, 452, 461; *3:* 503, 568, 590, 631, 651, 653, 676, 703-04

Supernova Cassiopeia A *2:* 420 (ill.)

Surveyor probes *1:* 108; *2:* 344, 399; *3:* 579

Swigert, Jack *1:* 24

Swiss Polytechnique Institute *1:* 143

Symmetry *1:* 22

Syncom *1:* 104

Synesius of Cyrene *2:* 265

A Synopsis of the Astronomy of Comets *1:* 206, 209

The System of the World *2:* 311

T

Taft, William H. *2:* 415

Tarter, Jill *1:* 77

Tau Ceti *1:* 129

Taurus *2:* 306, 373, 405, 452

Telecommunications Research Establishment *3:* 519

Telescopes in Education Project *2:* 393

Teller, Edward *1:* 53

Telstar *1:* 104; *2:* 337

Tereshkova, Valentina *2:* 301; *3:* 507, **633-36,** 634 (ill.), 682

Tethered Satellite System *3:* **636-38,** 637 (ill.)

Tetrabiblios *1:* 42

Thagard, Norm *2:* 383

Thales *1:* 12

Theology *2:* 295

Theon of Alexandria *2:* 265

Thermochemistry *2:* 310

Thermosphere *1:* 136

Third quarter moon *2:* 348

Three-stage rocket *1:* 76

Thuban *1:* 11

Tides *3:* **639-40,** 640-41 (ills.)

Time *3:* **640-44**

Titan rocket *2:* 294, 316-17; *3:* 531, 581, 685

Titania *3:* 656

Titius, Johann *1:* 37, 68

Titov, German *1:* 185; *3:* 682

Tombaugh, Clyde *2:* 334-35, 444-45, 454; *3:* **644-47,** 645 (ill.)

TOMS-Meteor 3 *1:* 134

Total Ozone Mapping Spectrometer (TOMS) *1:* 134

Totality *3:* 557-58

Tower telescope *3:* 571

Tracking and Data Relay Satellite *2:* 338

Traité de Méchanique Céleste *2:* 311, 413

Transactions of the Royal Society of Edinburgh *2:* 363

Transit *2:* 373

Transit *2:* 402

Transit circle *2:* 414

Travel to the Moon *2:* 423

Triquetrum *1:* 14; *2:* 460

Triton *2:* 409

Trojan asteroids *1:* 38

Tropic of Cancer *3:* 574

Tropic of Capricorn *3:* 574

Tropical year *1:* 10

Troposphere *1:* 136

Tsiolkovsky, Konstantin *2:* 423; *3:* 511, **647-49,** 648 (ill.)

Tunnel effect *1:* 176

U

Udaipur Solar Observatory *2:* 402

Uhuru *1:* 4, 66; *3:* **651-52,** 696

UK Infrared Telescope *2:* 360 (ill.), 362

UK Schmidt Telescope (UKST) *1:* 20-21

Ultraviolet astronomy *3:* 605, **652-53**

Ultraviolet radiation *1:* 158; *2:* 279, 363, 431; *3:* 487, 491, 518, 695-96

Ultraviolet telescope *2:* 280; *3:* 652

Ultraviolet waves *1:* 147

Ulysses *2:* 349; *3:* 586, 629, **653-54**

Umbra *3:* 558, 629

Umbriel *3:* 656

Unbarred spiral galaxy *1:* 168; *3:* 615

United Nations *2:* 385

University of Tübingen *1:* 54

Uraniborg *1:* 72

Uranus *1:* 1, 37-38, 69, 119, 196, 216-17; *2:* 304, 325, 366, 407, 409, 444-45, 454-55; *3:* 530, 565, 604, **654-57,** 655 (ill.), 673, 685, 701

Ursa Major *1:* 111

U.S. Department of the Interior *1:* 133

U.S. National Oceanic and Atmospheric Administration *2:* 403

U.S. Naval Observatory *2:* 413-15; *3:* **657-60,** 658 (ill.)

V

V-2 rockets *1:* 190; *2:* 425; *3:* 512, 662
Vacuum Solar Telescope *2:* 401
Vacuum tower *3:* 572
Valle Marineris *2:* 355
Van Allen, James *1:* 116, 156; *3:* **661-63,** 662 (ill.)
Van Allen belts *1:* 44, 116, 129, 137, 156; *3:* 661, **663-64,** 664 (ill.)
Van de Hulst, Hendrik *2:* 429
Vanguard program *1:* 156; *3:* **665-66**
Variable stars *1:* 85-86; *2:* 248, 318; *3:* **666-67**
Vega program *3:* 580, **667-68**
Vega 1 *1:* 183; *3:* 667
Vega 2 *1:* 183; *3:* 668
Velas *1:* 106, 175
Venera program *3:* 580, **668-71**
Venera 1 *3:* 670
Venera 2 *3:* 670
Venera 3 *2:* 301; *3:* 669 (ill.)
Venera 4 *3:* 670
Venera 5–14 *3:* 671
Venera 15 *3:* 670-71
Venera 16 *3:* 670-71
Vengeance Weapon 2 *1:* 75
Venus *1:* 13, 31, 68, 135, 172, 174, 196, 218; *2:* 290, 296, 301, 333, 340, 349, 351, 368, 440, 443, 445, 458; *3:* 498, 506, 521, 564-65, 567-68, 579-80, 592, 667-68, **672-74,** 672 (ill.)
Venus Orbiting Imaging Radar *2:* 349
Venus Radar Mapper (VRM) *2:* 349
Vernal equinox *1:* 80, 152
Verne, Jules *2:* 423
Very Large Array *1:* 130; *2:* 278; *3:* 493, 495, **674-76,** 675 (ill.)
Very Long Baseline Array (VLB) *2:* 361; *3:* 496
Very Long Baseline Interferometry (VLBI) *1:* 212; *3:* 495
Vesta *1:* 38; *2:* 356, 428
Viking program *2:* 317; *3:* 523, **676-79**
Viking 1 *2:* 356; *3:* 579, 677-79, 677 (ill.)
Viking 2 *2:* 356; *3:* 579, 677-78
Virtual particles *1:* 65
Visible light *1:* 147; *2:* 412

Visual binary star *1:* 53, 62; *3:* 623
VLBI Space Observatory Program (VSOP) *3:* 496
Volkov, Vladislav *3:* 578
Voskhod program *3:* **679-80**
Voskhod 1 *3:* 680
Voskhod 2 *2:* 321; *3:* 680
Vostok program *1:* 165, 167; *2:* 317; *3:* 633, 679, **680-83**
Vostok 1 *1:* 165; *2:* 301; *3:* 543, 594, 633, 680, 682
Vostok 2 *3:* 682
Vostok 3 *3:* 635, 682
Vostok 4 *3:* 682
Vostok 5 *3:* 635, 682
Vostok 6 *3:* 633, 635, 681 (ill.), 682
Voyager program *1:* 85; *2:* 317, 366, 399; *3:* 523, **683-86**
Voyager 1 *1:* 45, 173; *2:* 291, 349, 458; *3:* 528, 530-31, 580, 598, 604, 683-85, 684 (ill.)
Voyager 2 *1:* 173; *2:* 291, 349, 407, 458, 528; *3:* 530, 573, 580, 598, 604, 655-56, 683-85
Vulcan *2:* 326; *3:* 566

W

Wakata, Koichi *1:* 151
Waldheim, Kurt *3:* 686
Waning crescent phase *2:* 348
Waning gibbous phase *2:* 348
Washington Monument *2:* 415
The Washington Post *3:* 555
Waxing crescent phase *2:* 348
Waxing gibbous phase *2:* 348
Ways to Spaceflight *2:* 425
Weber, Wilhelm *1:* 178
Weightlessness *1:* 194 (ill.)
Weiler, Edward *2:* 259
Westar *1:* 105
Wheeler, John A. *1:* 65
Whipple, Fred L. *3:* 687
Whipple Observatory *1:* 210, 213; *3:* **687-89**
Whirlpool galaxy *2:* 273
White, Edward *1:* 23, 180; *3:* 596, **689-90,** 689 (ill.)
White dwarf star *1:* 47, 51, 53, 61, 65, 93-94, 123, 140, 192, 220; *2:* 245,

335, 411, 419, 461; *3:* 503, 518, 622, 628, 631, **690-91,** 691 (ill.), 694, 701, 705
William III *1:* 52
Wilson, Robert *1:* 58, 114, 177, 192; *2:* 438-39; *3:* 494, 620
WIMPs *1:* 123
Winter solstice *3:* 573, 575
Woodward, Charles *3:* 694
World Ocean Circulation Experiment *1:* 134
World War I *1:* 201; *2:* 249, 254, 320, 379, 393, 423
World War II *1:* 26, 166, 185, 190, 203-04; *2:* 293, 301, 335, 337, 399, 424-25, 429, 463; *3:* 493, 495, 498, 501, 512, 519, 532, 535, 543, 545, 633, 661-62, 703
World Wide Web. *See* Astronomy websites
Wyoming Infrared Observatory *3:* **692-94,** 693 (ill.)

X

X-ray astronomy *2:* 246, 337; *3:* 494, 605, 651, **695-96**
X-ray stars *2:* 363; *3:* **696-98,** 697 (ill.)
X-ray telescope *1:* 4; *3:* 695, 697

Y

Yeager, Chuck *2:* 371
Yegorov, Boris *3:* 680
Yeliseyev, Aleksei *3:* 576
Yerkes, Charles *1:* 200; *3:* 701
Yerkes Observatory *1:* 94, 200; *2:* 249, 432; *3:* **699-701,** 700 (ill.)
Yohkoh *3:* 629
Young, John *1:* 179
Young, Judy *3:* 516
Young, Thomas *2:* 264

Z

Zodiac *1:* 42 (ill.)
Zwicky, Fritz *1:* 47, 124; *2:* 421, 436; *3:* 516, **703-05,** 704 (ill.)